Faces, People and Places
The Cameras of Ilford Ltd.
1899 - 2005

Andrew J. Holliman

First published September 2006

British Library Cataloguing in Publication Data
A catalogue record for this book is available from the British Library

ISBN Number: 0-9545342-1-2

Disclaimer:
Some statements and views given by some of those who have been kind enough to help me are reproduced but may be a matter of their opinions or conjecture. No offence is intended against any person or company.

Editing, design and layout
Andy Holliman

Published by:
Andrew J. Holliman
20 Brewers Wharf
Newark
Nottinghamshire
U.K.

Email: a.j.holliman@netmatters.co.uk

Printed by:
TJ International Ltd
Trecerus Industrial Estate, Padstow, Cornwall, PL28 8RW

Contents:

Acknowledgements and Sources

Acknowledgements

I wish to thank the following organisations and individuals for their help in supplying me with information for this book:

Between 1981 to 1985:

- Ilford Ltd Employees - Past and Present
- Arthur Holliman, My late father, 1918-1997
- James Mitchell, Director of the Camera and Equipment Division
- Len Ryan, Engineer at Ilford
- Philip Jenkins, Colleague of my father
- Alan Mitchell, Sam Welford F.R.P.S., Sid Woodland, and others

Science Museum,

- Mr. J.P. Ward, Photography & cinematography collections
- Ms. J. Ffyfe, Archivist

- Old Timer Cameras Ltd, Write ups, articles and test reports, http://www.oldtimercameras.com/

- Ilford Ltd., Extracts from 'Silver by the Ton' reprinted with permission. Logos used with permission.

Between 2004 to date:

- Maurice Fisher, PCCGB member and Ilford collector, http://website.lineone.net/~mauricefisher/index.html
- David Gardner, PCCGB 'Tailboard' editor and UK Camera collector.
- Mike Moore, Ilford Imaging UK Limited, UK Sales - Technical Support.
- Michel Beaumont, Retired employee of CIBA-Lumiere.
- J.W. Fokkelman, Retired camera retailer in Holland. Many thanks for his input regarding Ilford's activities in Europe.
- Camera Shopper, USA web site and magazine articles: http://www.camera-shopper.com/
- Jacques Charrat, French collector web site: http://clicclac.free.fr/
- London Borough of Redbridge, Library Department.
- Colin Harding, National Museum of Photography, Film and TV.
- Doug McKee, PCCGB member and UK Camera collector.
- Dave Todd, PCCGB member and Witness researcher. Many thanks to Dave for his contributions and help with the Witness camera chapter.
- Mrs. Hawarden, Former employee of Northern Scientific Equipment Ltd.
- James Kennedy, Director of David Kennedy (Engineers) Ltd.
- Arthur Marshall, Machine shop supervisor at David Kennedy (Engineers) Ltd.
- Jim Edwards, Ilford's camera inspection manager.
- Christie's, London, for permission to reproduce their catalogue text and illustrations. www.christies.com/cameras
- Michael Pritchard for his support, encouragement, design and content suggestions and post production assistance.

Sources:

- European Patents Agency http://gb.espacenet.com/espacenet/gb/en/

  Free search facility by Applicant, Inventor, Title, Number. Provides scanned images of patent applications with full text and any associated drawings.
- Companies House http://wck2.companieshouse.gov.uk/

  Free search facility of all UK registered companies. Some basic details can be displayed. For older companies that have been dissolved they have archived information on microfiche that you can purchase.

Images

This book contains many images that I have collected over a period of more than 20 years. Some are digital scans of black and white photographs, some have been sent to me by various people, others I have taken myself. In several cases I no longer have the original camera or indeed the original photograph should I have wished to obtain a better image.

This means that the image quality within this book is not consistent and in some case not at a very high standard. Additionally this has been my first serious excursion into digital photography and the software required to manipulate the images. When I started I am not sure that the digital camera had even been invented!

For these reasons I apologise if the pictures are not as good as you might have hoped or expected.

Where required, I have credited any individuals who have been kind enough to supply information and/or photographs. I apologise if I have missed any credits.

PREFACE
Collecting Ilford Cameras

My collection and documentation of Ilford cameras started very subtly. My father Albert Holliman (but known as Arthur within the company, for some unknown reason) was employed by Ilford all his working life. His grandfather, father and younger brother, like many residents in Brentwood, also worked for the company at the SELO factory, which was just up the road from where we lived.

In September 1964 he was presented with a gold Rolex watch for, '30 years loyal service'. This would indicate that he joined Ilford in 1934 when he was 16 or 17 years old. He had worked for them for 9 years when on 21st December 1943 he received his call up papers and joined the Royal Air Force.

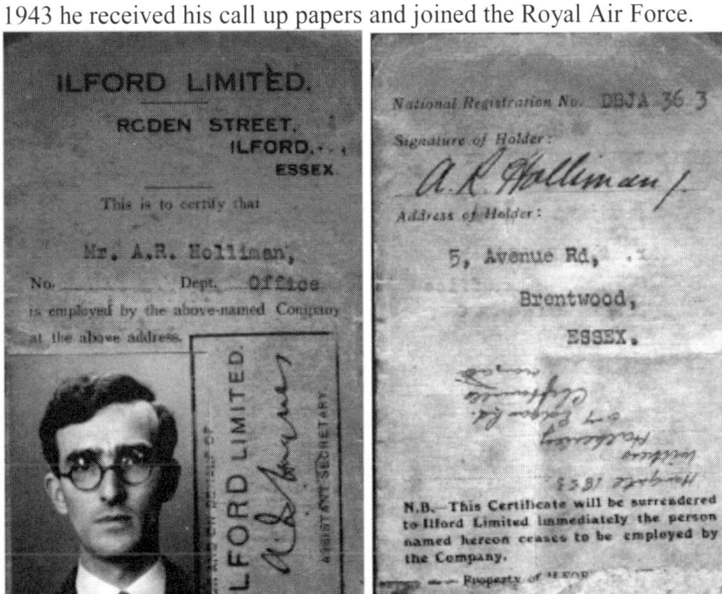
ILFORD LIMITED.
RODEN STREET,
ILFORD.
ESSEX.
This is to certify that
Mr. A.R. Holliman,
No. Dept. Office
is employed by the above-named Company at the above address.
ILFORD LIMITED.
ASSISTANT SECRETARY

National Registration No. DBJA 36 3
Signature of Holder:
Address of Holder:
5, Avenue Rd,
Brentwood,
ESSEX.
N.B.—This Certificate will be surrendered to Ilford Limited immediately the person named hereon ceases to be employed by the Company.

This is the Ilford pass my father was issued with by the company.

During World War 2 he held the rank of LAC - Leading Aircraftsman. He was a model maker. His knowledge of photography and his practical skills put him in a group that was provided with aerial reconnaissance photographs and they turned them into three-dimensional models of attack locations. Trees and hedges were made from painted foam rubber, hills from papier-mache and all painted and textured to be incredibly realistic. It was here that he further developed his skills to make things and turn his hand to just about anything. He had a keen eye for detail and a dedication to follow every job through to the best of his ability and usually to a very high standard.

When he left the Air Force he rejoined Ilford Limited. His Royal Air Force Service and Release book states that he was released from service on 30th April 1946 to take up employment as an Assistant Manager with Messrs. Ilford Ltd.

I know little of his early years at Ilford but by 1948 he was Works Manager of the equipment factory at Leytonstone and later at Basildon, until 1965. From 1965 to 1969 he was first Marketing Manager (Cameras) and then Product Group Manager (Equipment).

All of these activities passed me by, partly due to my youth and partly due to my father's reticence to discuss work matters at home. So how was it that I was within 'Vintage Cameras' shop in 1981 buying an Ilford Advocate? Perhaps it was the recollection of a camera so distinctive to have remained with in my memory for the last 30 years. Perhaps it was the 'Roots' syndrome - tracing the activities and results of my father's work for 47 years. Whatever the cause was, the effect was a relentless pursuit of the activities of Ilford, clouded in people's memory and time with few clues and little documented history.

One source of information I had high hopes in was the book, 'Silver By The Ton' by Hercock and Jones. The history of Ilford Limited 1879-1979. I had hoped to find a definitive list of all the cameras made. However as this book is predominately concerned with their film making business it did not reveal many clues; it even had one red herring. On page 78 it mentions an Ilford Penguin - this should have been the Ilford Prentice. I have also discovered that the book had an error regarding one of Ilford's most significant cameras, the Witness. In the same paragraph as the Penguin/Prentice error it also records that the designer of the Witness was D.A. Rothschild. His name was in fact Werner Julius Rothschild and the main designer of the Witness was Robert Sternberg. These details are explained in detail in the Witness section of this book.

My next potential source of information was the Science Museum. In their photographic collection are several Ilford cameras. These formed an adjunct to my father's own memories. When Ilford ceased their camera business a lot of files of company information were given to the Science Museum's library. None of these items had been collated and documented then. So when I visited the library I had to wade through boxes of paperwork extracting what details I could find. These records have recently (October 2004) been moved to the National Museum of Photography and Cinematography at Bradford. Here I found out a few more Ilford camera model names and variants that were produced.

Having 'got the bug' I advertised in *Amateur Photographer* for 'Ilford Cameras - All Models Considered'. Each week that the advertisement appeared I receive about 10 replies. During this period I suffered from constant indigestion as most people telephoned during the time of my evening meal. Gradually however, I increased my collection. As my collection grew my questions of people contacting me got more and more obscure,

'Has it got a chrome wind on lever on the top and the Ilford Logo on the right, is the lettering on the lens mount black on metal or white on plastic?'

Many of my callers must have thought me a bit odd, but I continued building up the collection. I even received one letter from Australia. The writer had just received an issue of Amateur Photographer 2 months after it had been published in the U.K. The amazing thing about most of the replies, which I received, was that most of the writers had used their Ilford camera for many years and it was still in good working order. Most held them in some affection being the camera they started photography with.

After advertising in *Amateur Photographer* between 1981 and 1983 and also in local papers I was left with scouring the junk shops, antique centres and car boot sales. This revealed one or two more cameras. The Photographic Collectors Club of Great Britain also supplied some more models from their club sales tables.

When I first started collecting the cameras my father drew up a list of all the marques and models that he could remember and put them into a chronological order. Each time I purchased a new camera or discovered the name of a new model I would discuss it with him and he would recall details about the camera, the personalities, the problems and the successes. My notes soon turned into chapters and then had to be managed on my computer.

In the late 1980's I discovered that some of the Ilford records had been deposited at the Chelmsford records office. There they hold several prints and negatives of a small number of Ilford cameras, which were possibly used in brochures and publications. Once again I came across some new and initially confusing information. It was here that I discovered the three models in the Instacora range of 'Instamatic' cartridge loading cameras which were previously unknown to me, and are still somewhat of a mystery.

I started my book in 1981 and by 1997 I believed I had 'completed' my book and exhausted most avenues of research. I thought that I had discovered all of the Ilford camera variants.

Every collection has a beginning and for this one I have related how I started in my pursuit of Ilford's cameras. Every collection also has an end. (or so I thought!)

Having exhausted every attempt at finding any more cameras I decided that the collection was as complete as it would ever be. I have photographs of all the cameras and my research produced about 50% of this book.

For several years I was able to display the collection in my house and to enjoy them but eventually, after several house moves and more pressing activities, the collection was confined to a large box out of the way.

I decided, slightly reluctantly to present the collection for auction at Christies in London. The money raised would finance my return to being a student when I enrolled on the three-year diploma course of Violin Making and Repair at the Newark School of Violin Making.

So it was, on Thursday 28th August 1997, lot 366, The Holliman Collection of Ilford Cameras was auctioned.

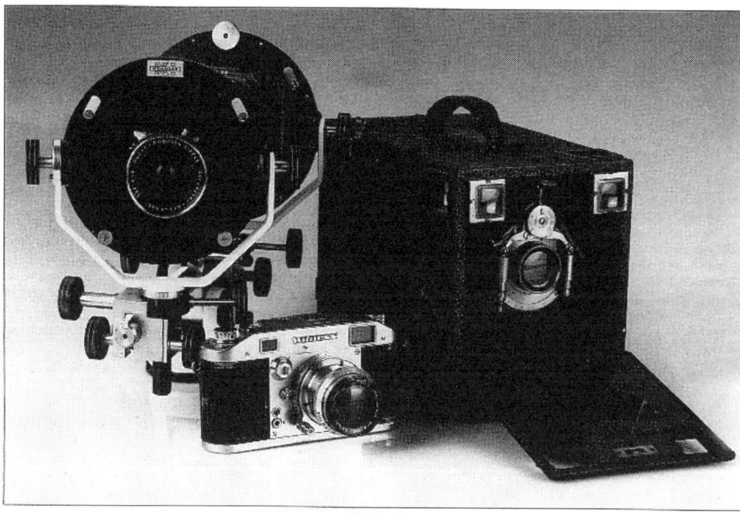

366 (part)

THE HOLLIMAN COLLECTION

366

Ilford cameras and equipment

A comprehensive collection of Ilford cameras and some associated material including a Scott's patent exposure; *Ilford Manual of Photography* (first thousand edition c.1891) and *Ilford* Elmo equipment

(a lot)

PROVENANCE:
Andy Holliman

LITERATURE:
A copy of Andy Holliman's history of Ilford cameras *(un-published)* is included with this lot.

The collection features examples of the major models (some boxed) made for or sold by Ilford Ltd from 1902 to 1968 together with some duplicates and variants. The collection includes the well-known Witness camera no. 5175 with a *Dallmeyer* Super-Six Anastigmat lens no. 381692, in maker's box (c.1946); KI Monobar technical camera outfit (c.1958) comprising a 35mm. Monorail camera with bellows, a *Schneider* Super-Angulon f/8 65mm. lens no. 5443010 in a Synchro-Compur shutter, two magazine backs and spare panels, in maker's fitted leather case; the Ilford magazine hand camera (1902).

The main pieces included are:

Advocate (series 1 and 2, plus coloured and other variants)
Craftsman
Envoy box
Envoy wide angle
Ilfoflex
Ilfomatic
Imp
KI Monobar
Magazine hand camera
Monarch
Pixie
Prentice
Sporti
Sporti 4
Sporti 6
Sportina Ilfomatic
Sportsman
Sportsmaster
Sprite
Sprite 127
Sprite 35
Witness
Ilford exposure meter (Scott's patent)
Ilford Photoelectric meter
Ilford accessories
Ilford Manual of Photography (three editions c.1891-1960)

£3,000-5,000

The auctioneer called out: "Lot number 366, 366, Ilford Cameras and equipment and I have a bid for £2000…400…600…2600…3000…on my left 3200…3500…3800…4000…200…400…4600…4800…5000…5500…Against you in the room now, at £5500…£5500…. All done now at £5500…any more…£5500. Sold".

The End! However…

Several years later I started using the Internet and in particular, Ebay. Here I found you could not only sell things that you no longer had a need for but you could seek out things that you did want. Ebay has a very active camera auction 'room' and additionally you can get it to tell you whenever anything of interest comes up for auction. I soon found that Ilford cameras were being moved from parents attics and cupboards and put up for sale. Not only that but also people in Europe and America and all over the world were selling old cameras. Not surprising then that I soon came across Ilford cameras that were new to me. The quest started again and the book needed further revision.

I have also been in contact with a few collectors of Ilford cameras who share the same enthusiasm and persistence in attempting to resolve the mysteries of camera model design, development and evolution. Of note are Maurice Fisher, David Muggleton and David Gardner who I have met on the Internet and corresponded with via Email.

The Internet also led me to camera collections around the world, which the owners have published for all to see. Here I came across a retired Dutch camera retailer, F.W. Fokkelman, who had a lot of information, camera examples and details of Ilford's marketing activities in Holland. Again, new models and variations were discovered.

It is now 2005, some 23 years after I first started this project and I am still updating the book.

My book is single-mindedly concerned with Ilford's still cameras. I have not researched the development of Ilford's entry into the motion camera business via the liaison between Ilford and the Japanese company Elmo. (Another project that my father was closely involved with). However this period of Ilford's history was not without its problems and developments and one that my father along with James Mitchell and others set up and managed.

Looking through the collection I can see the results of my fathers work, an English company's struggle in the world market and also my own attempts in the Sunday markets.

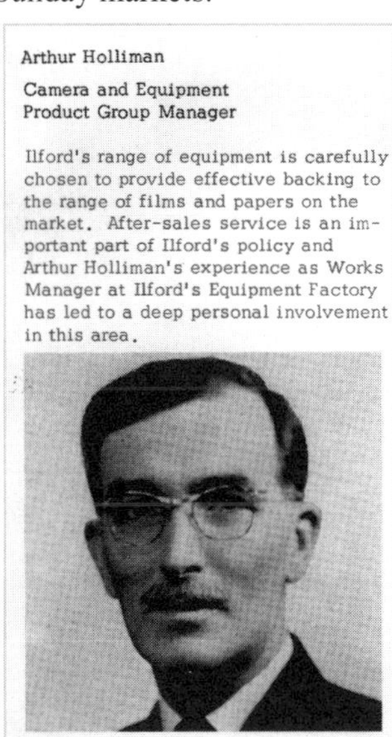
Arthur Holliman

Camera and Equipment
Product Group Manager

Ilford's range of equipment is carefully chosen to provide effective backing to the range of films and papers on the market. After-sales service is an important part of Ilford's policy and Arthur Holliman's experience as Works Manager at Ilford's Equipment Factory has led to a deep personal involvement in this area.

This picture of my father appeared in an Ilford Marketing brochure that was produced in 1966.

Camera Variations

Throughout this book I mention several camera variations that are separate to the acknowledged and documented variations of a particular model. These include badges on opposite sides, bezels rotated, different shutters used and the like. When I see a variation I will then wonder if it is a one-off or an example of an unknown 'official' style change.

Here is a list of the reasons that I will often consider.

- By Design. A few trial pieces (or maybe just one) were put together to see what it looked like, to test market reaction or to seek manufacturing approval. Ilford would test market its cameras in selected parts of the country from a limited production run and would make changes to the model if the retailers and their customers made significant comment about some aspect of the camera. The original cameras would then appear to be unusual.
- By Accident. 100% inspection was not always carried out and inevitably a few 'incorrectly' assembled cameras were released. Some of the camera parts were supplied to Ilford or their sub-contractors in large numbers. For example the Shutters supplied by AGC for the Sportsman range were ordered in their 10's of thousands. These deliveries could include an odd box or individual item not at the usual specification. For example a rogue 10 speed shutter could find its way into a box of 9 speed shutters and go un-noticed.
- End of Run. When the life of a particular model came to an end a company would want to use up all of its spare components and may have fitted 'odd/different' parts to a camera. When Ilford ended its UK Marketing activities many of their servicing and repair engineers were given the opportunity to take with them, at a favourable price, spare parts, tools and equipment so that they could set-up on their own as independent repairers. They may have assembled 'odd' cameras from the stock that they had access to.
- Repair shop assembly. Over a period of time a camera repair shop will accumulate a variety of parts. Sometimes several of these parts can then be assembled into a complete and working camera. This may result for example in a lens/shutter assembly being fitted to an earlier body style.
- Owner repair. Owners often repair their own camera especially to correct minor faults. Consequently a logo or a bezel that has come adrift may be re-fitted incorrectly positioned to the original camera.

Collectors will deliberate over these variations and wonder why they might have come about. We may probably never know the true reasons for all of them.

And so the story begins…

CHAPTER 1
Ilford Ltd 1863-1890

A fully detailed history of the company's photographic business can be found in the book, 'Silver By The Ton - A history of Ilford Limited. The following section is a précis of the early years from this book.

"The founder of Ilford Limited was Alfred Hugh Harman who was born in 1848. Very little is known of his early life. He first came to the public attention when, in 1863, an advertisement appeared in the 'British Journal Photographic Almanac' for Dages and Harman, photographic printers of 3 Albert Cottages, Hill Street, Peckham, London. He also lived at this address.

His association with Dages ceased in 1864 when he set up in business on his own at Gunnersbury Villas, Albert Road, later called Harders Road, Peckham, London. An advertisement in the 'Almanac' for that year claimed that his enlargements "are acknowledged the best" and offered a service of printing and copying and the production of slides or large transparencies for decorative purposes from photographers' own negatives. It is not known how he obtained his experience in photography or how he financed his business, but he met with early success and his business expanded from local to national level.

In 1868 he moved his business to larger premises at 79 High Street, Peckham and also opened another studio at 110, Ewell Road, Surbiton, Surrey. During these early years Harman was both a competent photographer and by the nature of the work was an experienced 'chemist' experimenting with the new dry plate emulsions. In 1879 he decided to give up his photographic business and to concentrate on the manufacture of dry gelatine plates.

Harman made his plates in the basement of his house, helped by his wife. He later employed two men and three boys. Harman's determination and dedication had much to do with his success but those attributes were commonplace in that time. Obviously he had something else that was better than the rest and that something was probably the recipe for his emulsion, which he kept a great secret. He made his plates by pouring the emulsion from a teapot onto a glass plate, which was held on fingertips and tilted until it was covered.

Having made this decision, Harman sought a site close to London, with a clean dust-free atmosphere. He settled on the then small village of Ilford in Essex and acquired a house called 'Elmhurst' on the corner of Park Avenue and Cranbrook Road. There he set up Britannia Works. Strictly speaking Ilford Limited dates from this time.

By 1883 the business had expanded so much that a special factory was built on the Clyde Estate in Ilford for plate manufacture. By 1891 he employed about 50 people and claimed to be the largest manufacturer of photographic plates in the world.

Prior to 1886 his photographic plates were sold under the name of Britannia but he changed the name from Britannia to Ilford and the name of the company to the Britannia Works Company. In 1891 when he was 43, Harman converted the Britannia Works Company into a private limited company and introduced a profit sharing scheme for his employees.

In 1897 George Eastman was looking for a manufacturing base for his company in England. He approached Harman with a proposal that the two companies should amalgamate (the first of two attempts by Kodak to take over the company). This idea was rejected as Harman's company was performing exceedingly well. In fact, that year the company had a 40 per cent return from invested capital. During 1897 and 1898 negotiations were put in hand to change the Britannia Works Company into a public company. This business was completed on 14th September 1898, when the old company ceased to exist and the new company, the Britannia Works Company (1898) Limited came into being. Harman retired at this time when he was 50 years old but continued to serve the company in a consultative capacity for a number of years.

He died in 1913 after several years of ill health.

After formation of the new company an early decision was made to change its name again and to drop the '1898', thus reverting back to 'The Britannia Works Company Limited'.

Since 1886 'Ilford' had been the brand name of the products whilst the company was called Britannia. In 1900 it was suggested that the company should take the name Ilford Limited. The Ilford Urban District Council at first objected to the proposal, but finally agreed, provided that 'limited' was spelt in full with a comma between Ilford and Limited. The new name was adopted in 1901 and the comma removed in 1951, and so Ilford Limited was born."

Ilford Limited was and still is predominately a sensitised materials manufacturing company. Whilst George Eastman was establishing a world-wide amateur business with his roll films, Ilford decided to continue their efforts with glass plates and concentrate upon the professional, commercial and graphic arts, markets, although they later entered the flat film and then the roll film market.

CHAPTER 2
Entry into the camera market 1902

The Ilford Falling Plate Magazine Camera

The first known Ilford camera was the Ilford Falling Plate Magazine Camera which was marketed between 1899 and 1907. At the time it was variously described; The Ilford Camera and The Ilford Hand Camera.

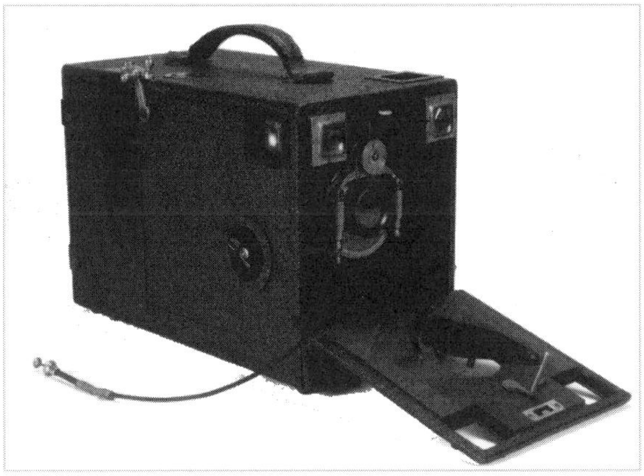

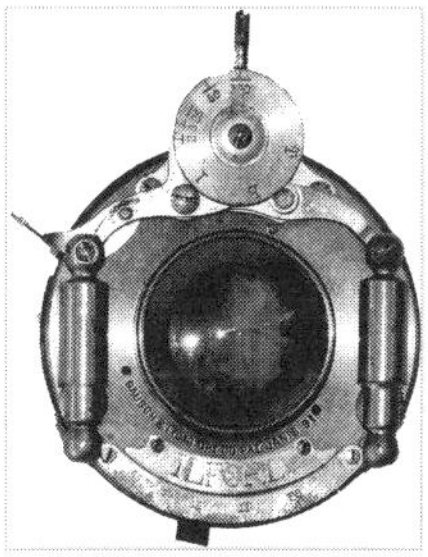

Above, the Baush and Lomb lens with Unicum shutter that was fitted to the standard camera.

One of the companies, which Ilford took over, was a film manufacturing company owned by Austin Edwards in Willoughby Lane, Tottenham, London. His son B.J. Edwards was manager of the factory, which made films for the Beck Frena magazine camera.

This camera took up to forty flat films with notched edges, exposed successively by operating a lever at the side of the camera. Frena was an acronym for "For Rapidly Exposing Negatives Automatically".

The Beck Frena camera was introduced in the early 1890's by R and J Beck.

For a time Ilford did in fact offer flat films for this camera and Harman took out a patent covering improvements to the Frena camera but never exploited it.

In 1899 the company accepted the offer of a not dissimilar flat-film camera from Arthur Charles Smith and Albert Arthur Smith, the patentees, who received a royalty of 4s. 6d per camera.

It was made in Germany and marketed as THE ILFORD CAMERA. It was strongly made in mahogany covered with leatherette and it sold for £5 with the Baush and Lomb lens and Unicum shutter or for 8 guineas with a superior Ross anastigmat lens and covered in solid morocco leather. The films were sold in boxes of twenty at 3s 4d.

It is unusual to note that whilst there are references to the camera in 1899, the British Journal Photographic Almanac reviewed the camera in 1903 and carried advertisements for it in 1903 through to 1907. In 1907 however, the Almanac had an advert for a "THE ILFORD CAMERA - New Model". I am not sure what the 'New' refers to but maybe it related to the optional Lopa Patent shutter, which was also available.

The Amateur Photographer reviewed the camera in 1902 and called it the Ilford Hand Camera.

This was the first of many cameras, which were made for Ilford by other companies and marketed by them under their own name.

The *Photographic News* reviewed the camera in July 1902 as follows:

The Ilford Camera and Films

This new camera, about which we have heard so much, is to hand from Ilford Limited. The great feature of it is the very simple and efficient manner in which it carries forty cut films, which are changed one by one as exposures are made by a very simple movement. The block here shown gives a very good idea of this beautifully made instrument and the other block shows the method of changing the film. Apart from this changing mechanism the Ilford camera is good in other ways, especially in the arrangement for focusing, which is set in a moment, and is so arranged that it is next to impossible to get an indistinct image.

The camera is perfectly simple to use, is light, compact and reliable. It can only be loaded in the dark room and white light must never be admitted to the films until they have been developed and fixed. The films are specially manufactured for the camera by Ilford Limited, and are of the company's well known special rapid quality.

They are separated each from each by cardboard backings, and films with backings are supplied in boxes of twenty films each. The camera holds any number of the films and backings up to two boxes or forty films, this being a full load. One great advantage possessed by films made for this camera, which distinguishes them from others in the market, is the fact that in case of accident to the camera, the films (of course without the special backings) can be used for an ordinary camera in case another Ilford camera should not be procurable in the place where the user happens to be.

So that, although Ilford films are necessary for the camera, the films themselves can be used in any plate or cut-film camera, care being taken to omit the backings. The camera is supplied in ¼ plate size only.

It is fitted with a Bausch and Lomb rapid rectilinear lens of a superior quality. The shutter is the well-known Unicum.

The diaphragms or stops are of the iris pattern, and are regulated by a lever working at the base of the shutter. The camera has a small light case made of solid mahogany covered with a special quality of black leatherette. The front of this is entirely closed except for the finders, so that the dust is excluded.

The camera is provided with two brilliant finders, which show the picture exactly as it will appear in the negative, one for horizontal pictures, the other for vertical. We have had the camera in use for a short time, and like it immensely.

The camera is of the box form, made of mahogany, covered in a good black leatherette, and the outside metal fittings are nickel-plated. The lens works at f/8 and the shutter gives exposures ranging from one second to one-hundredth of a second, and with which time exposures of any duration may also be given, either by the pneumatic or trigger release. Focusing is performed by partially rotating a handle at the right hand side of the camera, and to this a pointer is attached with a scale of distances. The dimensions of the camera are 9 x 5 by 6 ¼ inches. and it weighs in at 5 ½ lbs with plates.

The general principle of the camera is based on the film packs that it takes. Two of the film packs could be inserted into the back of the camera. After each exposure was made one of the two levers on the top side of the camera could be pressed. This would raise an internal trap door exposing the plate-receiving box. The other lever could then be moved which would allow the exposed plate to fall into a bottom box. The two levers would then be returned, in sequence, to their original positions and the next plate would then be ready to be exposed. As the top lever was moved the next film number would also appear on a rotating disc through the top plate. The exposed films are removed by opening a door at the bottom of the camera.

The size of the pictures exposed was 4 ¼ x 3 ¼ inches.

It is believed that the camera was made for Ilford's by the Wunsche company in Germany. Emil Wunsche produced a similar camera but the Ilford version incorporated Smith's patents. The patent application is reproduced on page 237..

Another publication, *Photography*, reviewed the camera on August 28th, 1902 and concluded their piece with the following:

"The appearance of this camera, we presume, may be taken as an indication that the Ilford Co. do not intend to limit their sphere of operations to photographic materials so strictly as they have done in the past – we do not overlook certain excellent little pieces of apparatus we owe to them. But they hardly affect the case. This stepping down into the arena of apparatus supply of one of the largest photographic businesses may be taken as a sign of the times in more ways than one. To the purchasing public it will be a welcome one, since with a lofty reputation to maintain the Ilford Co. will be bound to keep their goods at a very high level of excellence and reliability. We have no doubt whatever that the Ilford camera will be known wherever the Ilford plate is used, and we have still to discover what part of the civilised world that popular product has not reached."

CHAPTER 3
The Years Between (1902-1946)

Limited by the time and facilities available to me I have been able to find only two references to Ilford Cameras in the years 1902 to 1946. Considering that this period saw the progressive amalgamation of the small British sensitised manufactures that made up Ilford Limited, it is strange that Ilford did not acquire from them, the camera equipment and accessories know-how that certainly existed. Thus told are references to say Rajar cameras with its works at Mobberley and Soho Ltd, consisting primarily of Kershaw of Leeds. Kershaw was apparently hived off from APEM (Amalgamated Photographic Equipment Manufacturers) before its merger to Ilford in circa 1932.

In 1921 a number of companies had formed a grouping called Amalgamated Photographic Manufacturers Ltd. (APM 1921). The companies in this group were: Kershaw Optical Co. Ltd, A Kershaw and Son Ltd, Marion and Foulgar Ltd, Rotary Photographic and Rajar Ltd (including Brooks-Watson Daylight Camera Co. Ltd.), Paget Prize Plate Co. Ltd and Marion and Co. Ltd.

Later, in 1928 the groupings of these companies changed with, Kershaw Optical Co. Ltd., A Kershaw and Son Ltd. and Marion and Foulgar Ltd. forming Soho Ltd. and, Rajar Ltd, Paget Prize Plate Co. Ltd. and Marion and Co. Ltd. forming Apem Ltd.

It was these 3 companies that made sensitised materials, which joined with Ilford, leaving out the suppliers of equipment.

Possibly, it was in this period that Ilford's attitude of anti-cameras was built up. (This comment is explained further as the history is revealed)

On May 15th 1903 the Pall Mall Gazette ran a story about the possible takeover of Ilford by the Eastman Kodak Company. The story was reprinted in the Amateur Photographer on May 21st. 1903. Here is an extract:

"Yesterday the shares in Ilford (Limited) dropped smartly from 35s. to 30s., following upon an informal meeting called by a section of the board to consider a proposal for the sale of the concern to the Eastman Kodak Company on even terms. The proposal strikes us as an extraordinary one...."

One week later the Amateur Photographer reviewed the situation and stated that, "the aim of the Kodak takeover was to control the roll film business. This is considered this to be the thin end of the wedge towards getting the entire photographic plates and papers trade into their hands, despite Kodak's assurance that this was not their aim." A.P. commented that this was "difficult to reconcile with Eastman's simultaneous attempt to remove "Ilford" competition and the introduction into this country at popular or Ilford prices of the American "Seed" plate." It was reported that a section of Ilford Limited which desires to surrender to the American proposals represents only about $1/6^{th}$ of the capital interest".

The full story of the "Ilford-Kodak Raid" (a headline from the Investors Guardian) is documented in 'Silver by the Ton'. Several senior employees including the chairman of the company, Major General Blake stepped down or left the company as a result of the proposed takeover and the matter was finally closed on the 25th September following full consideration of proposals at an AGM.

The 2nd world war curtailed all research in colour films in the U.K. to allow research to be directed toward the war effort. During this time, Ilford made significant discoveries, particularly in aerial reconnaissance and X-ray films.

After the war Ilford poured a lot of effort into colour film and by 1948 had a film that rivalled its competitors. Ilford colour "D" was a transparency (slide) film and, by offering an entirely new print making service, they were able to make up much of the lost ground in the colour field.

Right through the period 1948-1969 when Ilford again marketed cameras there was apparently a body of opinion within the company that their main purpose was in the field of sensitised goods manufacture although this was interpreted to include chemicals and filters, which by their very nature, their emulsion chemists could understand.

The three exceptions I have found were the Ilford X-Ray Reduction camera, which was used for copying radiographs and making lanternslides. This was made by W. Watson and Sons of Holborn and was a glorified adaptation of one of their half plate studio cameras (brass bound mahogany of course) it was marketed in the period 1930-1940, but because it was not a positive taking camera I do not elaborate. (A Watson camera was marketed by Ilford in 1953, and is shown on page 121.)

A Twin lens test camera, which is described on page 30 and a whole plate copying camera, which is shown overleaf.

Ilford Whole Plate Copying Camera

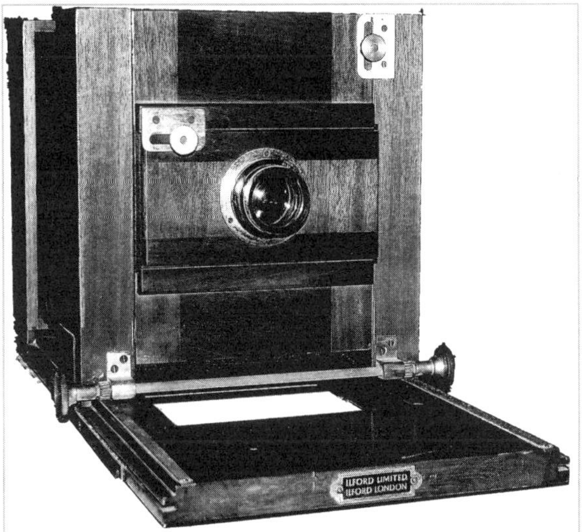

This camera was brought to my attention very late in the production of this book. It was spotted on its way to a rubbish skip. Being a mahogany and brass camera it was an interesting find and well worth saving.

The find was reported to my friend David Gardner and then, only as an afterthought, was the fact that it bore an Ilford Limited badge mentioned.

We believe it was made sometime in the 1920//30's. It is a whole plate copying camera, which runs on a wooden track 90 inches long. The camera body dimensions are 10 inches by 10 ¾ inches. It was used, so I have been told, in hospitals for copying plates and negatives. It could reduce a whole plate, approximately 8.5 inches x 6.5 inches to lantern slide size, 3.25 inches square.

It has a No. 9, Aldis Brothers Lens, 11 inch focus, f/7.7, Serial number 155393.

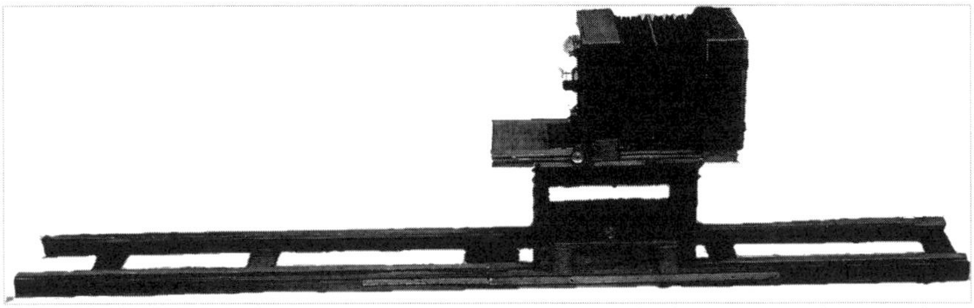

The rails are 7 foot 6 inches long and are 9 ½ inches apart. They are in 2 sections being coupled together by a hinge.

A raised box structure fits onto the rails with a pair of metal edge pieces fixed to the side of the box. These act as a guide to the camera to keep it parallel with the track and hence at right angles to the film plane.

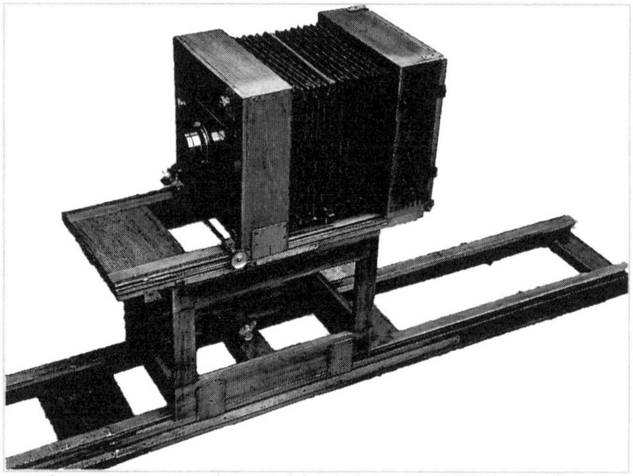

A large butterfly wing nut at the bottom of the box holds the structure in place on the rails at any desired position.

The camera can be positioned at pre-defined points along the length of the track for fixed amounts of reduction from a certain size of original. To aid the correct positioning a chart is provided as an ivorine plaque on the camera box structure.

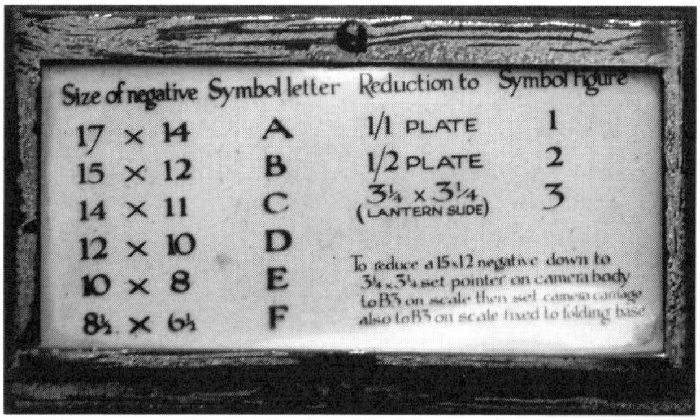

The camera is attached and held onto the top of the box structure by a single, metal edge plate, on each side of the camera. This has a line engraved so that a measured position can be made against the brass index on the top edge of the box structure.

Having positioned the camera, on the box structure, in roughly the correct position, the focusing could then be finalised using the brass knobs rack and pinion, which move the front plate of the camera forwards or backwards.

The front edge of the camera bed has the 'Ilford Limited / Ilford London' name plate

Two brass knobs lock the lens panel, holding the lens, vertically and horizontally. Either screw can be loosened to allow the lens panel to slide up and down or across to align the image with the item (or part of it) to be copied. The lens can be screwed out of the circular brass flange attached to the lens panel. The lens panel cannot be removed without removing the brass plates onto which the brass locking nuts tighten. This would not be something you would do in normal use.

The back of the camera has a rotating back, which can be removed and rotated. This allows both vertical and horizontal formats. The focusing screen is swung out of the way to allow the dark slide, holding the film, to be inserted.

The camera would be focused on the object to be copied by first setting the position of the camera according to the scale on the side of the rack for the required original and copy size. This would then be fine tuned using the camera's rack and pinion movement whilst observing the image on the ground glass screen in the film plane.

Once in focus, the screen would be flipped out of the way and replaced by the wooden boxed dark slide.

The camera does not have a shutter. The lens cap would be removed and then an external light source applied for the time necessary to expose the film.

Ilford Twin Lens Test Camera

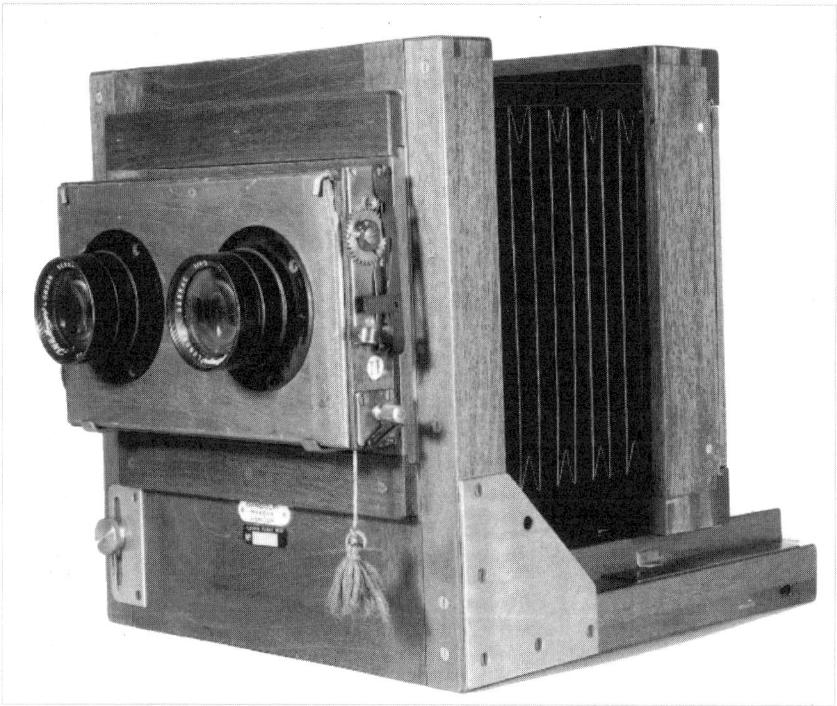

The Twin lens test camera was used within the company for comparing the quality of a sample plates over a 'standard'. I believe that these 'cameras' were adaptations of craftsman made Gandolfi models in mahogany and brass. Three of these cameras were presented to the Kodak museum, the Science Museum and the Birmingham Science museum respectively.

Ilford at War

During the second world war there was little manufacture of amateur type cameras in the U.K. although some expertise was built up in the field of gun cameras, recording cameras and the like.

On the outbreak of war in 1939 the company's activities came wholly under the control of the Ministry of Aircraft Production.

At the close of the war in Europe, Ilford personnel (notably Dr. S.O. Rawling) took part in several commissions that un-armed German industry. Many Ilford scientists had been seconded to the services in view of their special qualifications to work in fields related to photography.

They also had many opportunities to keep abreast of developments in the area of cameras and apparatus. However nothing seemed to have come of this and to be fair no great impact was made on the U.K. photographic makers generally.

From Germany came the views of the relatively primitive equipment and methods used to produce such cameras as the Leica and Zeiss Ikonta.

It was felt that England could learn little from them. After all we had won the war and we didn't need to take lessons from any Germans! and yet by 1956 (in 10 years) German cameras were the envy of the world when they in turn suffered at the hand of their own national characteristics. German cameras e.g. Leica, Contax, Rollieflex were of extremely high repute and quality before the war in the late twenties and thirties.

This ostrich like attitude gave Ilford and other U.K. manufacturers some troubles. For instance although Germany had a DIN standard for co-axial flash connectors, Ilford was intent on pioneering its own 2 pin plug, making difficult the availability of off the shelf flash guns for their cameras. However market demands would cause the company to fall into line with their competition and produce the 'standard' co-axial attachment.

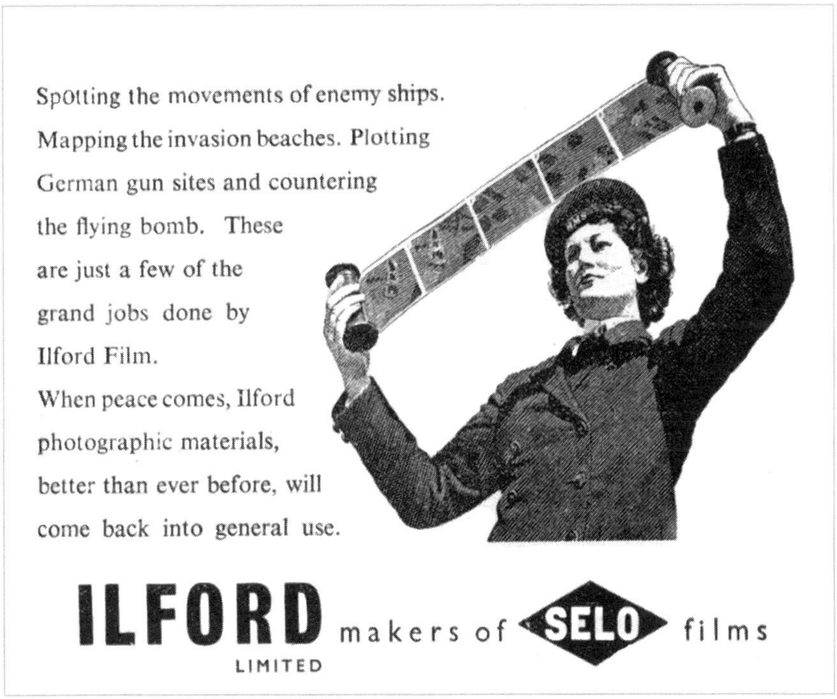

CHAPTER 4
Re-entry into the Camera Market

Phase 1 (1946-1949)

During the war period some fresh thinking was going on and James Mitchell, who had been works manager at the film factory in the war, was raised to the board and given the task (for which he had probably asked) of developing a camera and equipment division. In fact from the year 1930, Ilford had already established a vigorous X-Ray accessory business based on having equipment of its own design made by outside firms. This may have been an indicator to the board that a sizeable activity could be supported in this way with the minimum of research, development and manufacturing costs, also I believe that Ilford feared the might of the stickers in the Kodak cameras which ensured that at least 50% of amateur film used was Kodak film. They wanted their own, 'silent salesman' and came round to the realisation that they must meet like with like.

And so their plans developed with the following aims:

The cameras marketed must be:

1 Made for Ilford but not by them.

2 Ilford design ideas to be incorporated.

3 A range of cameras in film sizes 127, 126 and 35 mm.

4 To cover the requirements of beginners up to advanced amateurs and professionals.

5 Under the Ilford logo.

6 To carry Ilford film stickers.

These criteria would appear to have been the ideal and it became clear that if the first and last were met that in default of better opportunities a project could proceed. It meant that in the limit Ilford was prepared to factor other UK makers branded cameras providing a film sticker could be inserted. In the event that the full range of conditions were met suitable acknowledgement could be made to the actual manufacturers.

Through this facility of making friends and influencing people James Mitchell started his task in conjunction with Messrs. Rothschild and Kennedy and I start the story with their products.

During this phase and right up to the end of phase 4 all of Ilford's cameras were 100% inspected and returned to the maker or dealt with by the maker on Ilford's premises if they were unacceptable. My father established this department in 1948 with Jim Edwards being the initial camera inspector, when the Witness production started. By the time Ilford moved to Basildon quite a large inspection department was in operation inspecting cameras, lenses and accessories.

I must at this point make a note as to the 'phasing' I have applied. It is intended that the phases should be sensible in relation to the effect of market forces from outside and Ilford's reaction to them. However effort initiated in one phase would not automatically be abandoned at the outset of another because there might be stocks still left to sell, newer variations to exploit, particular market segments to exploit and so on.

Ilford Witness 1951 - 1953

The Witness is significant among Ilford's cameras for many reasons including its advanced specification, its original high retail price, its very limited production run and therefore the high value that the camera receives today. The history of its production involves several significant individuals, several manufacturing companies and many production, financial and outsourcing problems. It does not have a simple background story and so I have told it, as far as I am able, in great detail in an attempt to explain its production together with the personalities that were involved at the time.

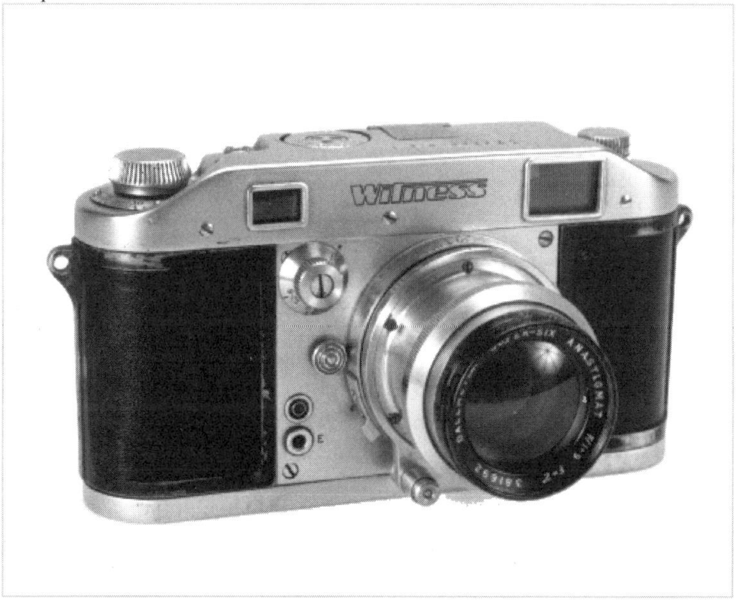

Background and Personalities

The Witness camera was originally designed by Robert Siegmund Sternberg and later with the collaboration and financial assistance of Werner Julius Rothschild.

Both were German Jews who emigrated to England before the outbreak of World War II in the 1930's. (The book, Silver by the Ton, A History of Ilford Limited, incorrectly documented Rothschild's name as D.A. Rothschild)

Robert Sternberg, at the age of 18, was a protégé of Ernst Leitz, training in optical design at the Leitz HQ in Wetzlar.

He was involved with the design of the classic pre-war Leica cameras. His enlightened and sympathetic employer, concerned that the talents of his Jewish staff should be safeguarded from the perils of Nazi Germany, secured a job for him in 1936 with Ensign Ltd. in London, with whom they had connections. Ernst Leitz III provided Robert with a letter headed, 'To whom it may concern'. In it he praised Robert's technical abilities and provided a character reference for any future employer.

At Ensign he worked on lens design with Walter Weinstein. This was not an easy time for him as he was considered an enemy alien and found himself under night time curfew during the War.

It was during this time that he started work on what would become the Witness design incorporating many features of Leica and Contax together with many of his own unique innovations.

Immediately after the war he joined up with Rothschild and took lodgings in Bolton. At this time Rothschild was running an optical business making spectacle lenses.

Sternberg's name appears on the original Witness camera blueprints.

It is reported that Rothschild worked in the German optical industry and at some time worked for Zeiss and fled Nazi Germany before the outbreak of World War II.

In the late 1940's, based on their previous experience, they set to work refining Robert's initial design with a view to producing it themselves using Rothschild's optical company.

Werner Rothschild lodged with Bill and Kathleen Freeman at 40, Mackenzie Street, Astley Bridge, Bolton and at a later time he married their niece Margaret. Margaret's father was George Freeman.

Northern Scientific Equipment Ltd.

On the 24th November 1943, George Freeman, Werner Rothschild and others registered a company called Northern Scientific Equipment Ltd. with premises in Bark Street, Bolton, Lancashire. (This company was, I believe, where Werner had his spectacle lens business)

Rothschild, like many German émigrés anglicised his name. He first changed his forename from Werner Rothschild to Vernon Rothschild. Later still he changed his surname to Ryden to avoid being confused with the wealthy Rothschild dynasty of which he was not part.

The original directors of Northern Scientific Equipment Ltd. were listed as:

Name	*Occupation*
George Freeman	None
Oscar Luis Spedding	Engineer
Henry Sidebottom Gould	Provision Merchant
Werner Julius Rothschild	Engineer

By March 1965 the directors were listed as Werner Julius Rothschild and his wife, Margaret Rothschild. Between 1965 and 1978 several directors came and went. In October 1978 they held an Extraordinary General Meeting and agreed to increase the share capital to £100,000. However by November 1978, Margaret resigned as Director and Secretary and then Werner Ryden resigned in February 1979. Various new directors are appointed and leave until December 1992 when liquidation of the company started.

Northern Scientific Equipment Ltd. was a small engineering company. In my research I have not been able to find out what specific engineering activities they performed over the life of the company apart from their early camera making activities, which included both the Witness and the Craftsman cameras.

Daroth Ltd.

In August 1945 (2 years after he had formed Northern Scientific Equipment Ltd), Rothschild registered a new company called, Daroth Ltd.

The registration documents for Daroth Ltd. held at Companies House name Harold **Da**vis and Werner Julius **Roth**schild as the directors and I believe that the name of the company was derived from the initial letters of both men's names.

Davis states that he is an engineer and Rothschild says he is an engineer and an inventor. The registered address of the company is given as, 40, Mackenzie Street, where Rothschild lodged with Bill Freeman. Davis gives his address as, 14 St Austell Road, Chorlton-Cum-Hardy, Manchester. Rothschild is recorded as being Stateless and of German origin and Davis is British.

In the registration documents they also have to declare any other directorships or occupations. Here Rothschild declares that he is also a director of Northern Scientific Equipment Limited. Davis is a director of Starco Precision Engineers Ltd.

The records held at Companies House are predominately concerned with the legal ownership of companies and the proportions of shares that may be involved. For this reason, you can determine when a company was created and by whom. You can see when Directors were changed and finally you can see when a company was eventually dissolved. Because of this there is no information about the day-to-day running of a company or any accounts in the years between when a company is created and when it is closed down.

However, the Daroth records of December 1972 do hold their final Statement of Accounts and make several references to 'Camera Development'.

I believe that Daroth Ltd. was created to 'own' the Witness project (and presumably any other camera development) and keep it separate for financial reasons from Northern Scientific Equipment Limited, even though the staff at Northern Scientific Equipment were handling the construction of the original prototype camera along with the Craftsman camera between 1948 and 1952.

Interesting to note that Robert Sternberg was not a director of the Daroth company. Maybe, like many designers and innovators he was happy that others would finance his creation and deal with the business side of the venture allowing him to concentrate on the design and innovation aspects.

Daroth did not have any specific premises and Rothschild and Robert Sternberg worked from the Northern Scientific Equipment Ltd. premises in Bark Street, Bolton.

In December 1972, Daroth Ltd. is recorded as being owned by Vernon Ryden (75%) and his wife, Margaret Ryden (25%). The company address is now; Bridge Road, Lymington and they live at, The Granary, Pickett Hill, Ringwood, Hampshire. Julius Vernon Ryden (his new name) is now a British subject. He states that he is a director of 5 other companies.

Daroth Ltd. was dissolved in December 1979.

Ilford's Initial Involvement

The original specification for the Witness was for a 35 mm format of 24 x 30 mm. This would have been ideal for enlargements of 4 x 5, 8 x 10 and 12 x 15 inches without the usual picture cropping which occurs with standard 35mm format negative enlargements. Early cameras from Nikon, Minolta and Wrayflex also tried similar formats unsuccessfully.

The overall design of the camera was very exciting but Rothschild could not finance its production.

(From a taped interview between Robert Sternberg and (the late) John Podmore (Leica Historical Society), Robert said that Rothschild asked Salford Electrical Instruments Ltd. if they would make six prototypes of the camera. This they apparently did and then they were offered a contract to make the production cameras, which they declined. This may have been around 1946. At this time Salford Electrical Instruments were making a 16mm sound projector (war model) for the Victor Cinematography Corporation. They also supplied the S.E.I. Exposure Photometer which Ilford would market in the 1950's) I have been unable to follow this lead to any further conclusion.

Two years after Daroth Ltd. had been created in 1947, Rothschild approached Ilford to see if they would finance and market the camera. After some consideration Ilford agreed to back the project. In view of their background Ilford were eager to make use of their techniques and skills.

It was widely believed in England, before the war, that the Germans must employ many sophisticated pieces of production equipment to be able to make their high quality cameras.

However, it turned out that instead of sophistication, the Germans simply had total commitment and personal investment in their companies, which spurred them on to produce high quality goods with the aid of what was simplified or even simple equipment. Rothschild and Sternberg were no exceptions to this view.

Ilford agreed to finance Rothschild with lens grinding and centrering equipment, which was purchased from Taylor Hobson.

The original camera was to have had a lens designed by Rothschild and Sternberg, which was made from optical glass rather than moulded glass blanks. This was a complicated process; making glass in a crucible, pouring it out, breaking it up, selecting pieces of the correct size and finally grinding them into shape. It was this complicated process that precluded them from getting into high volume mass production.

Ilford also requested the change of the negative format into the conventional 24mm x 36mm. The necessary redesigning caused much delay.

Ilford also looked around for alternative lenses and Galileo lenses from Italy were considered as were Dallmeyer. At this time Ilford had a Russian lens, which was available for testing. It performed quite well however on ordering a small batch the quality was found to be below standard and they were never used.

There were many delays in the project with Rothschild unable to fulfil his obligations to Ilford and to be fair, he was unable to find suitable subcontractors within the U.K. (a similar situation that both Ilford and Peto Scott would find themselves in).

At some time a part of the British Aircraft Corporation were involved in making some small components for the camera. The camera also has several chrome-plated screws, which I have been told had to be imported from Switzerland as none could be obtained to the required standard in the U.K.

I have been told that in 1949 one of the first prototypes made at Northern Scientific Equipment was being put together for a large exhibition in London. As previously stated, some prototype cameras were made by Salford Electrical Instruments Ltd. and it may have been these that were used for this exhibition. However many of the manufacturing problems were still un-resolved. This may have been the reason why Salford Electrical Instruments Ltd. declined to make the production cameras.

Transfer to Peto Scott

Frustrated by the lack of progress and the lack of resolution to the manufacturing problems, Ilford decided to transfer the manufacturing of the camera to Peto Scott (Electrical Instruments) Ltd. of Weybridge.

Peto Scott had made aircraft instruments during the war but were predominately known as makers of radios and early television sets. They were an ‘interesting’ choice of manufacturer for the camera. Ilford partially financed the project as before.

When the camera had been transferred over to Peto Scott they too set about redesigning parts of the camera so that it could be manufactured and eventually marketed by Ilford. Additionally they also set about sourcing all of the parts from the U.K. to satisfy the requirements of the Ilford Board and to be able to proclaim that it was the ‘British Made’.

Prototypes

First a word about prototypes. What is a prototype? Most cameras are not labelled as such or identified in any way to indicate that they are a prototype. A prototype could be a camera that does not have a serial number but this is not always an accurate factor, as some production cameras escaped the numbering process. Typically a prototype will show a part of the design that is refined before production starts. It is only when one camera is compared with another that is definitely a production model, that a prototype can be determined. In the case of the Witness, I believe that some 6 prototypes were made by Salford Electrical Instruments Ltd. These may have also been further modified at Northern Scientific. Later still, when Peto Scott took over the production process they too created some prototypes for final approval.

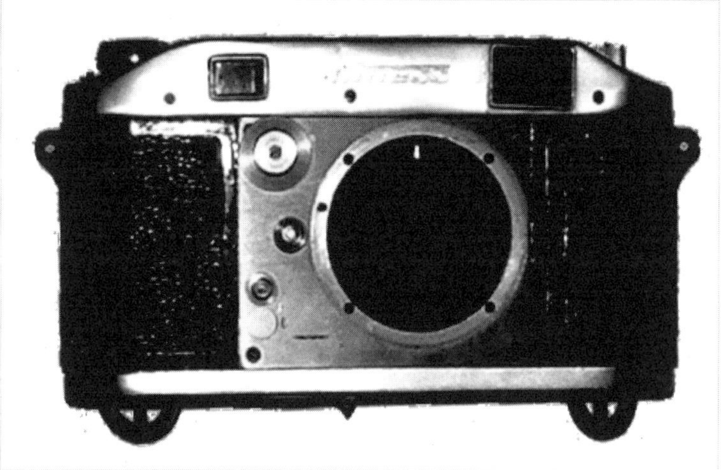

This picture shows a 'prototype' Witness. It does not have flash synchronisation, the metal top plate is very thin and has a weakly engraved logo and various other small parts are as yet unfinished.

DARON Lens

The lens that Sternberg designed for the camera was given the name DARON. It was a fully corrected, hard-coated 5 cm f/2.9 anastigmat lens. It was a collapsible lens similar to an Elmar.

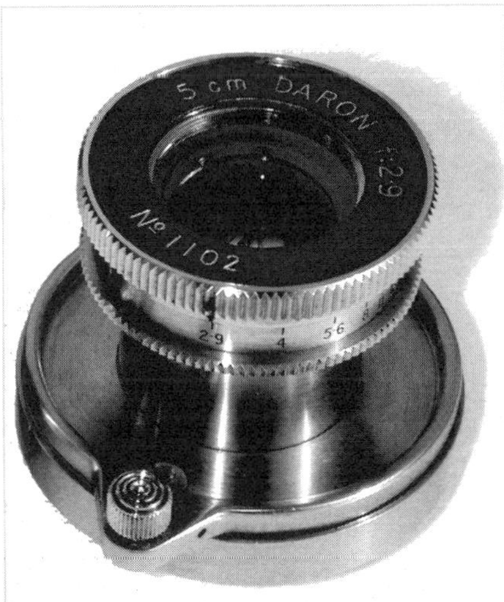

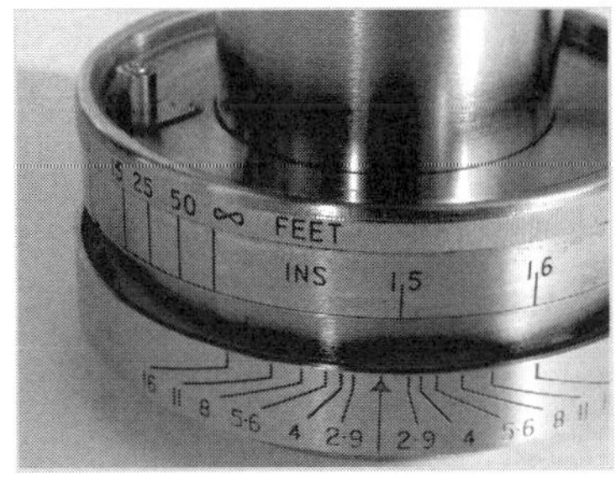

It was fitted in a special focussing mount enabling close-ups to be taken down to 15 in. without the use of extension rings or auxiliary lenses. This was achieved when the detent button was deliberately pressed in enabling the lens to pass a stop and to be unwound further. The focussing was not rangefinder coupled when in close focus mode.

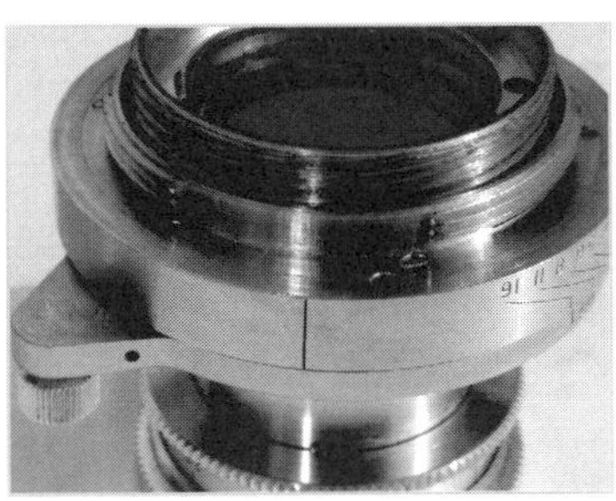

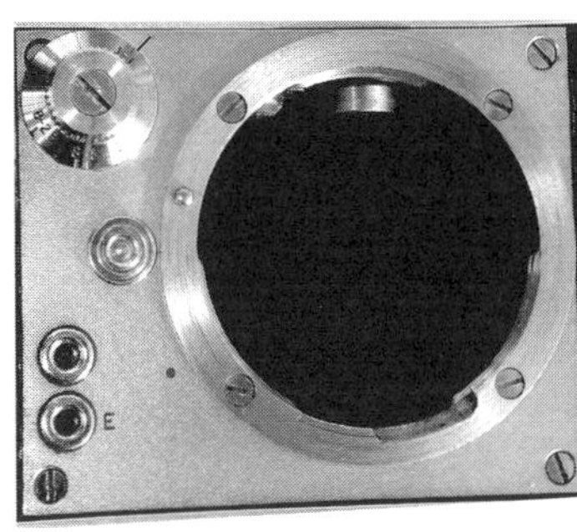

The focussing thread remained completely masked at all times, thus preventing dust or grit creeping in.'

The lens had a 39mm. thread. It was unique in that it used an interrupted screw thread which was cut away in three places, to enable a fast bayonet release and locking mechanism. Additionally it still allowed Leica screw mount lenses to be screwed in conventionally thereby extending the range of suitable lenses considerably.

It was securely held in place by a spring-loaded pin in the lens flange of the camera body, which locked into a recess in the back of the lens. In this way the lens would not come adrift accidentally.

This lens was difficult to manufacture by the small company of Northern Scientific Equipment Ltd. even with the lens grinding equipment that Ilford had supplied to them. It was also not as fast as required and only a small number were made.

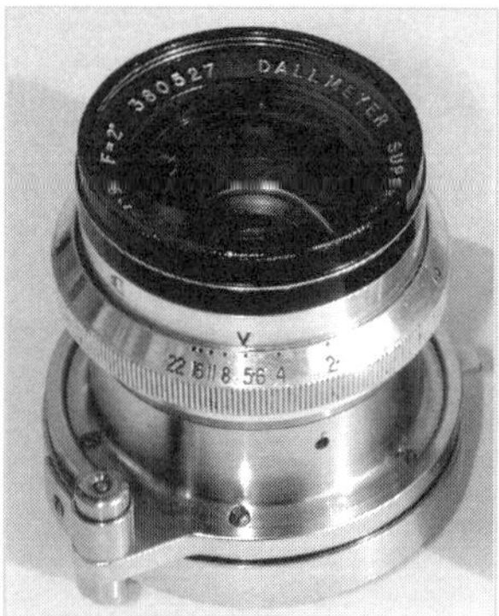

Most of the production from Peto Scott used the 2" Dallmeyer f/1.9 Anastigmat Super-Six lens.

However all the handbooks were printed with the original DARON specification and were either changed by hand or had a correction notice stuck to the inside page.

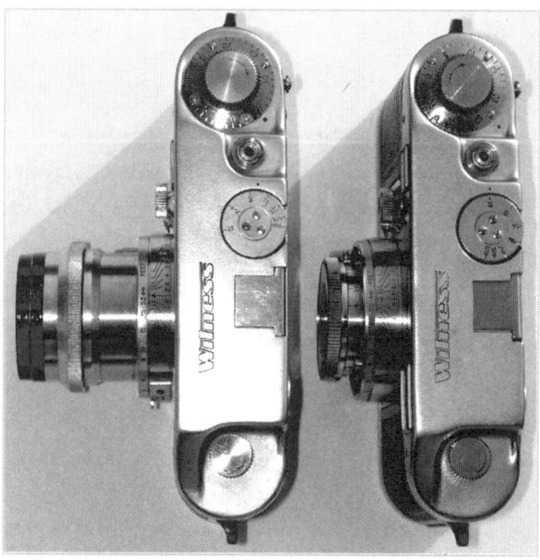

This picture shows the Dallmeyer Super-Six lens on the left and the DARON lens collapsed, to the right.

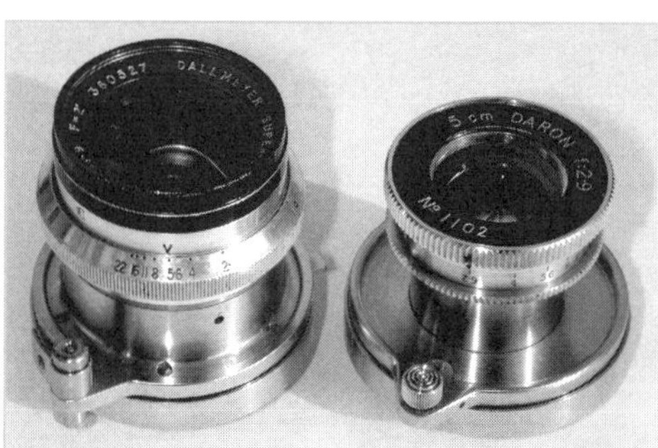

This picture shows the Dallmeyer Super-Six lens on the left and the DARON lens on the right, extended.

Instruction Manual

The instruction manual was, I have been told, written by Bill Pendlebury who was one of the U.K.'s main Leica repairers and a friend of Rothschild. It had been written when the project was under the original control of Rothschild before it was transferred to Peto Scott. I would guess that it had also been printed at this time as it contains details of features that were never brought to market with the final production camera. Details about the Sternberg designed lens and the film cassette system were printed as shown in the following pages.

Here is the layout of the camera taken from the handbook showing the DARON f/2.9 lens:

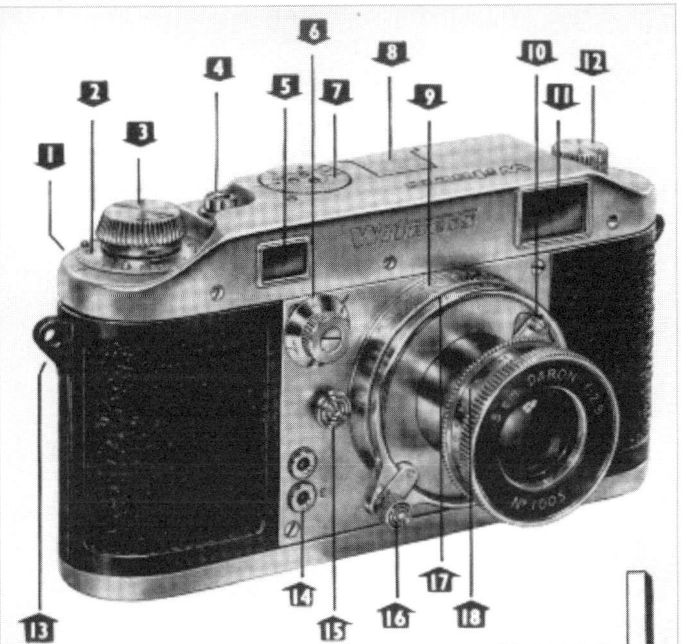

FIGURE 1

1 Rewind Button.
2 Exposure Counter.
3 Winding Knob.
4 Shutter Release.
5 Rangefinder Window.
6 Slow Speed Dial.
7 Fast Speed Dial.
8 Accessory Shoe.
9 Depth of Focus Scale.
10 Near Focus Catch.
11 Combined View Finder & Range Finder Window
12 Rewind Knob.
13 Lanyard Lug.
14 Flash Contacts.
15 Lens Release Button.
16 Infinity Catch and Focusing Knob.
17 Distance Scale.
18 Aperture Setting Ring

THREE

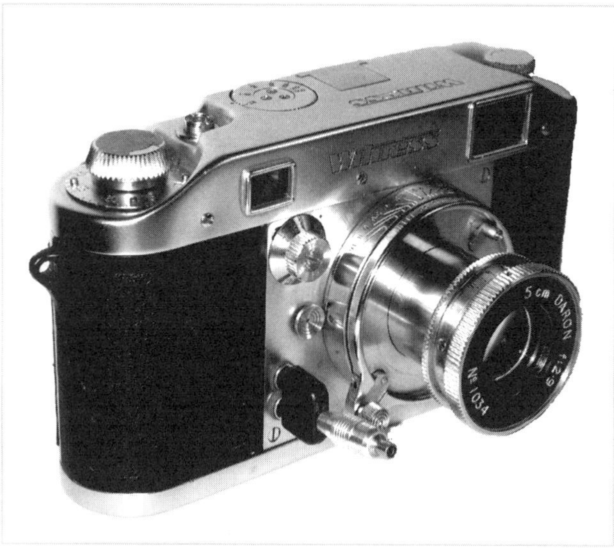

This example has a DARON lens and also a special adapter to connect a flash co-ax cable to the Witness body. (The lens and attachment are both recent additions to the camera body)

Cassette System

The instruction manual also details a unique film cassette system that was also dropped from the final specification.

In some instruction manuals, passages that referred to the special Witness film cassette were deleted by hand; many however exist where these paragraphs are unaltered.

The cassette that was described, but never produced, was intended to be loaded in the darkroom and consisted of three parts; the spool, inner shell and outer shell. When the camera back was closed the inner shell of the cassette was locked while the outer shell remained open.

The words in the manual state that, "This action automatically opens the mouth of the cassette, thus allowing the film to be drawn from it without friction, completely eliminating risk of scratching".

The original design also facilitated the use of two special Witness cassettes (similar to the Contax system introduced many years earlier). The manual stated, "The 'Witness' takes any standard cassette of 36 exposures or less and provision is also made for a special reloadable cassette. There are those who make a practice of taking photographs until the end of the film is reached, its attachment to the spool then preventing any further exposure being made. This practice sometimes leads to considerable embarrassment because the film occasionally comes away from the cassette spool and, unless two cassettes are used, a darkroom becomes necessary to unload the camera. The 'Witness' design is such that two cassettes can be used thus obviating the need to rewind, but when only one cassette is used, the film must be rewound into the cassette before removing the back."

Identification

The camera never had the Ilford logo (although the leather case did) nor had it any reference to the company or Peto Scott in its handbook except for a few notable examples.
Some of the early Witness cameras had the following inscription inside:

Made by PETO SCOTT Ltd. (ELECTRICAL INSTRUMENTS)
FOR DAROTH Ltd.
DISTRIBUTED BY Ilford Ltd.
British Made

The Witness Arrives

• THE WITNESS ARRIVES •

The new Witness is a precision built 35 mm. Camera, a combination of rigid pressure die castings ensuring that the very precise alignment of the various components remains undisturbed during normal use. The back and bottom cover of the camera is completely removable so that thorough cleaning can be carried out when required. Shutter speeds range from Q to 1/1000 sec., and can be set irrespective of whether the shutter is wound or not. The shutter can only be released when fully wound so that partial exposures or over-lapping of exposures are impossible. The 5 cm. f/1.9 Dallmeyer "Super-Six" Lens is mounted on the camera by means of a quick change bayonet arrangement of special design combining the rigidity of a screwed mounting with the ease of change of a bayonet. The coupled range-finder is combined with the viewfinder and is of the coincident image type. Built-in Synchro-flash contacts are provided which can be adjusted by dial to suit any type of flash equipment.

PRICE £121 16 8 Including Tax

Ever Ready Carrying Case £5 5 8

Amateur Photographer, August 13th, 1952

Reviews of the camera first appeared in 1951 under the heading, "**The new Ilford Witness camera**", although in fact it did not reach the market until 1953 because of the manufacturing difficulties. The Amateur Photographer Magazine of 13th August 1952 had three adverts for the camera and a 'price war' had already started. Dunscombe Ltd. in Bristol were advertising the camera for £115 18s 8d while Williamson (Photographics) Ltd. were advertising it for the standard price of £121 16s 8d. Additionally, Pelling and Cross advertised the camera saying that it took 'standard or Leica-type cassettes' The Leica-type cassettes were another feature that never made it to production. Presumably they had been told to expect deliveries of the camera from August 1952.

After acceptable pre-production prototypes had been made, Ilford placed an order for a production batch of 250 cameras.

The total number of Witness cameras made is subject to much conjecture. I believe that about 300 to 350 cameras were manufactured. Research carried out by Dave Todd over a 20 year period on existing cameras, provides the following details:

The following table summarises our known examples of Witness cameras and associated lenses.

The first batch (of probably 250 units) were made with initially the Daron lens and then the Dallmeyer Super-Six.

These were followed at a later time by another batch assembled from remaining parts. The lenses associated with these latter cameras, which have the higher serial numbers, were Dallmeyer lenses but sometimes without the interrupted screw mount. They may have been destined for Leica cameras and not for the Witness.

	Serial Numbers	**Lowest Serial**	**Highest Serial**	**Max. No.**
Camera	08 Un-Known			
	06 Un-Numbered			
	61 Numbered			
	75 in Total	5004	5339	335
Daron	17	942	1106	164
Dallmeyer Super-Six	45 (First batch)	373726	388505	
Dallmeyer Super-Six	13 (Second batch)	437657	484452	

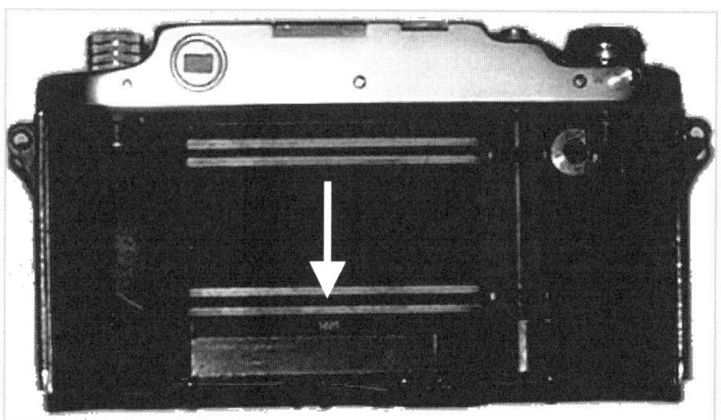

The serial number, if present, appears below the shutter cloth engraved into the metal. Sometimes it has been painted over and is difficult to notice at first.

An ex-employee of Peto Scott told me that a very small number of Witness cameras were sold to government establishments with a 9cm Dallmeyer lens. He seemed to recall that these were used in H.M. Prisons to photograph inmates.

As previously mentioned the first review of the camera appeared in *Miniature Camera Magazine* in April 1951. The camera that was submitted had a Daron lens complete with a chrome lens cap with Witness engraved on the front. The pictures also include one showing the camera fitted with a Contax universal finder.

The review considered the camera to be very exciting and 'heartily congratulated Messrs. Ilford Limited on their enterprise in placing such a beautiful instrument on the market. It is a great credit to all concerned'. They believed that the 'new Leica IIIf', which was about to appear in the U.K., would be selling for £180 so the Witness price of £125 would be reasonably favourable.

The end of the article says, 'we are officially informed by Messrs. Ilford Limited that limited distribution will begin in about a month's time'.

At least another 20 months would go by before the camera was 'readily' available.

The camera was eventually available for purchase in 1953 with a list price of £112.12s.6d. The Wallace Heaton Blue Book advertised it in May 1953 with a 'Final plane shutter'! Perhaps they too were relieved to receive the final announcement that it was now available.

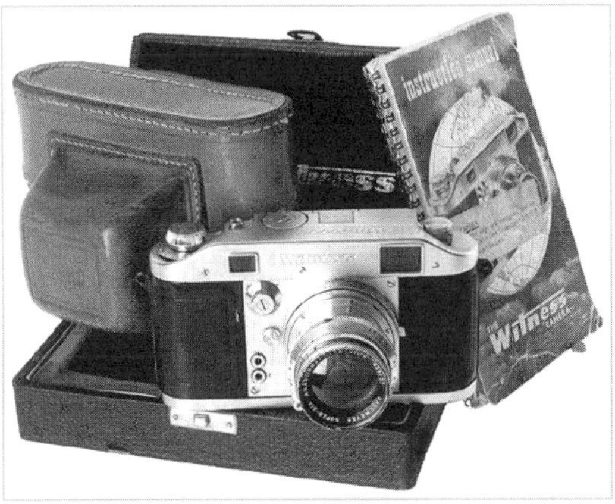

The cameras were sold with a smart purple felt lined ever ready tan pigskin case with Ilford embossed on the front. Reviews stated that they would include lens hood, filters and flash connectors although we doubt if all of these ever were produced. Wooden presentation boxes were also available as shown here.

A review of British Cameras in *Modern Camera Magazine* of January 1953 had the Witness shown with a price of £151 16s. 8d. Whether this high price was a mistake or a price that was quoted to the magazine by an optimistic retailer I do not know.

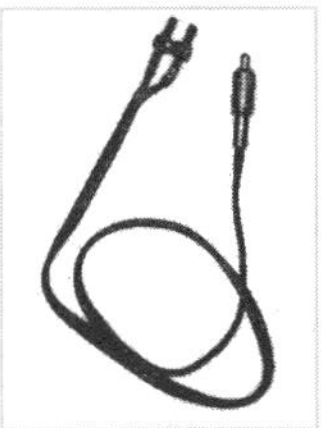

A flash lead was available to connect the camera to electronic and bulb flashguns.

In the *Miniature Camera Magazine* review of the camera in April 1951 they showed pictures of a Witness engraved lens cap. This we believe was never put into production only being available on the review camera.

Guarantee

This guarantee is dated 25th July 1953 and unusually has the manufacturer's name, Peto Scott Electrical Instruments quoted rather than Ilford Limited. I do not believe that any other Ilford cameras assigned the guarantee to the original manufacturer. In most if not all cases Ilford always ensured that any returns, repairs or guarantee problems were resolved in-house and where necessary they employed specific staff to take on this work.

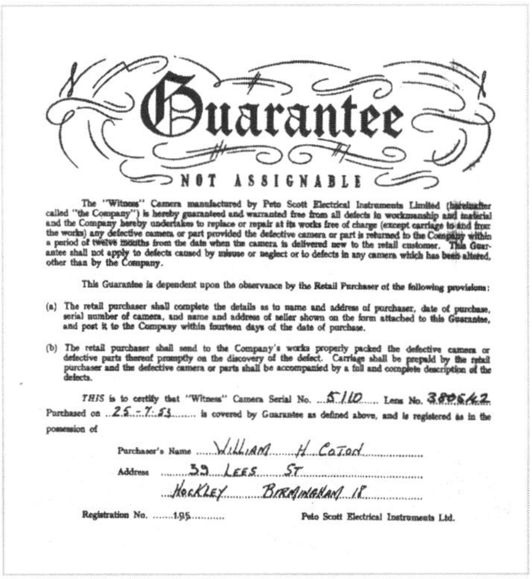

Guarantee

NOT ASSIGNABLE

The "Witness" Camera manufactured by Peto Scott Electrical Instruments Limited (hereinafter called "the Company") is hereby guaranteed and warranted free from all defects in workmanship and material and the Company hereby undertakes to replace or repair at its works free of charge (except carriage to and from the works) any defective camera or part provided the defective camera or part is returned to the Company within a period of twelve months from the date when the camera is delivered new to the retail customer. This Guarantee shall not apply to defects caused by misuse or neglect or to defects in any camera which has been altered, other than by the Company.

This Guarantee is dependent upon the observance by the Retail Purchaser of the following provisions:

(a) The retail purchaser shall complete the details as to name and address of purchaser, date of purchase, serial number of camera, and name and address of seller shown on the form attached to this Guarantee, and post it to the Company within fourteen days of the date of purchase.

(b) The retail purchaser shall send to the Company's works properly packed the defective camera or defective parts thereof promptly on the discovery of the defect. Carriage shall be prepaid by the retail purchaser and the defective camera or parts shall be accompanied by a full and complete description of the defects.

THIS is to certify that "Witness" Camera Serial No. 5110 Lens No. 380542 Purchased on 25-7-53 is covered by Guarantee as defined above, and is registered as in the possession of

Purchaser's Name William H Coton

Address 39 Lees St

Hockley Birmingham 18

Registration No. 195 Peto Scott Electrical Instruments Ltd.

The Final Specification

The camera body was made from precision die-castings, covered on the front, sides and back with black leather. Some early examples had vulcanite coverings, which may have been an experimental covering. The finish of the casting on the outside is perfect whilst the inside is slightly rougher. The camera top, base, front plate and fittings are of high quality satin chrome on brass.

The back was removed by two ½ turn catches on the bottom plate similar to the CONTAX of the time.

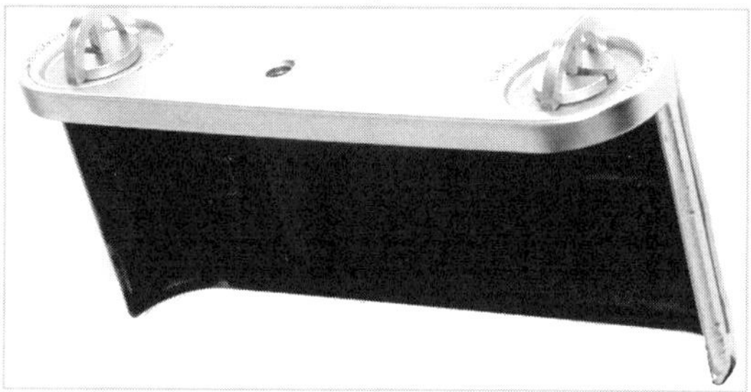

A spring loaded pressure plate in the back holds the film against two film guides in the body.

It had a Leica derived horizontal cloth focal plane shutter timed between 1 and 1/1000th second with bulb and time facilities. The speeds are 1 second, ½, ¼, 1/8, 1/25, 1/50, 1/100, 1/250, 1/500 and 1/1000. It ran on 200 very small ball bearings and was very smooth in operation.

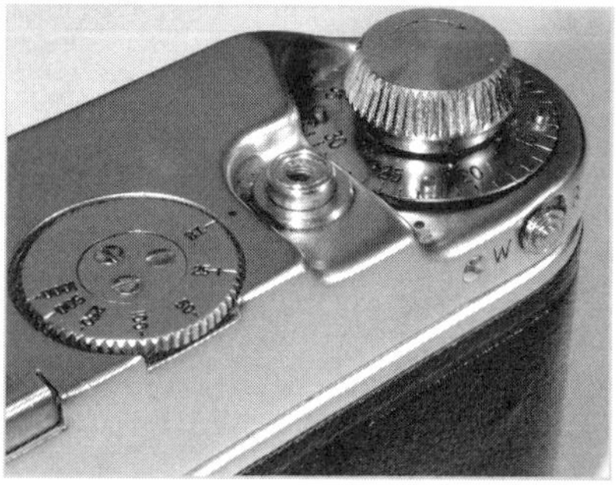

Click stops locate the marked speeds although intermediate speeds can also be set. The fast shutter speed dial is positioned on the top plate so that the knurled edge protrudes just over the edge, which makes adjustment very easy with the thumb.

The speeds can be set before or after winding as the dial is non-rotating. A slow speed dial is fitted on the front plate (upper left, facing).

The film advance and rewind knobs are recessed into the sloping shoulders of the top plate giving a very sleek appearance without any prominent parts. Below the film advance knob and exposure counter, is the wind/re-wind button.

A coupled shutter wind and film advance prevents double exposure.

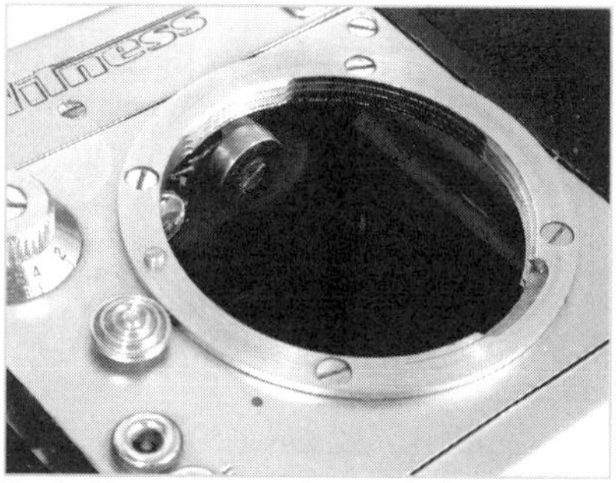

The lens mount used an interrupted screw thread system and would also accept Leica 39mm. screw thread lenses. Because of the interrupted thread a simple 1/12th twist would fix or remove the lens. The lens was held in place by spring-loaded pin to prevent accidental separation. The front of the camera had a push button to release the pin.

Red alignment marks made it easy to fit the lens.

The Dallmeyer Super-Six f/1.9 F2 inch lens could be focused from infinity down to 18". The DARON lens could be focused down to 15". Each lens type had mounts made from chromed brass.

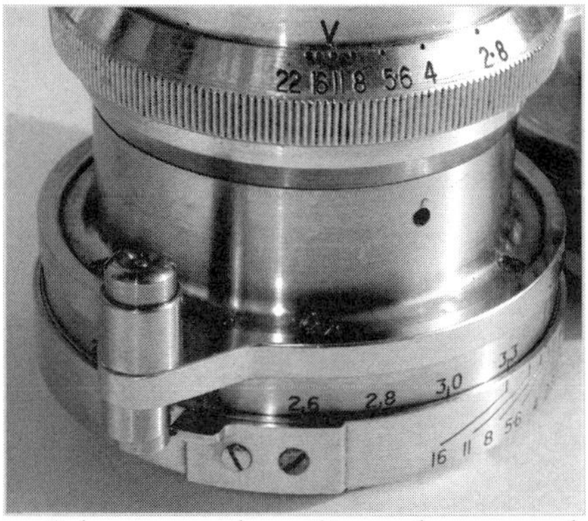

These closer distances were possible by pressing a spring-loaded catch, which allowed the lens to be advanced even further.
The rangefinder however would only operate down to 3 feet.
Built in syncro-flash contacts led to a two-pin socket on the front plate. The lower socket is marked 'E' and is the earth connection for when electronic flash is used.

It has a very long 65mm. base, coupled rangefinder of the coincidence type giving an image almost 90 per cent of the full viewfinder image, using a pair of beam splitting prisms. The interface between the prisms is coated with gold in order to increase the contrast between the images.

On the inside of the camera on the base of the body there is a numbered dial which can be set to adjust the time lag between release of the shutter and firing of the flash. This is adjustable from 0 to 30 milliseconds. Being on the inside of the camera means that you have to know what flash bulb you might use before closing the back with the loaded film.

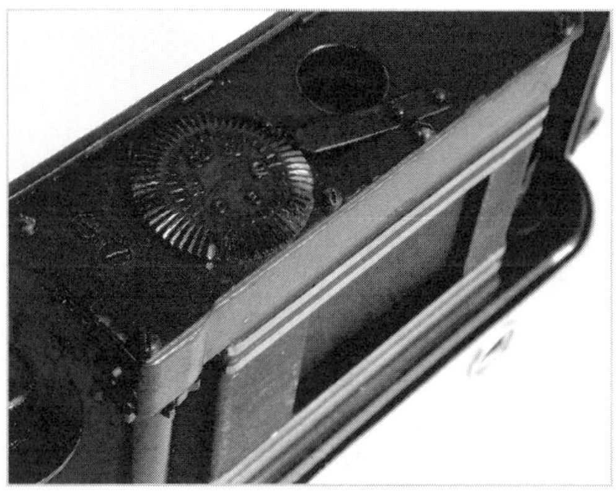

The manual had a table of various types of flash bulbs that can be used against the required setting of the dial and the maximum shutter speed. The following Flash bulb types are listed: GEC No. 22, GEC Speed Midget, Philips P.F. 14, 25, 45 and 56 and Electronic Discharge Tubes.

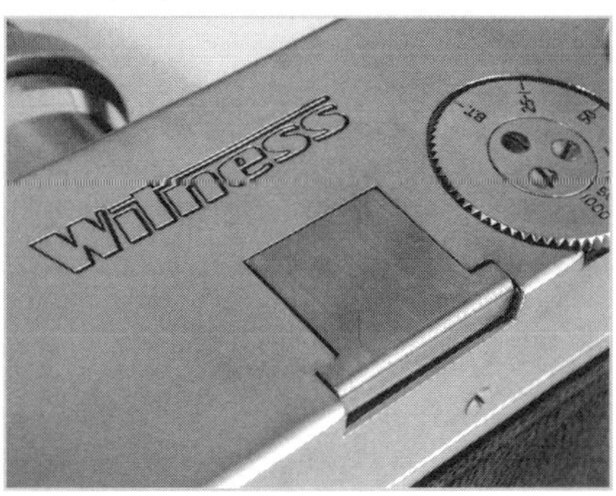

The accessory shoe on the top plate had a nice refinement; a spring-loaded dust cover was built in, "which could be depressed to allow entry of the various accessories such as supplementary viewfinders, etc". This further enhances its sleek appearance.

End of Production

Despite the production difficulties Ilford continued to distribute the Witness, but had less chance of influencing matters with Peto Scott than with Rothschild. Additionally Dallmeyer could not provide lenses in the necessary quantities to support a production of worthwhile size and Ilford was unable to locate an alternative supplier of lenses.

As I write this history what surprises me most is not that the camera took so long from initial design to manufacture but more that Ilford tolerated such a lengthy time.

- Sternberg's original design was drawn up between 1936 and 1945.
- The financing and initial prototypes started around 1944.
- Initial discussions with Ilford started late in 1946.
- The first prototype camera (from Daroth Ltd.) was produced in 1949.
- Further prototypes were created by Peto Scott in 1950.
- The camera was announced to the photographic press in 1951 but did not materialise until 1953.

A tremendous amount of frustration would have built up in this time by potential customers and importantly camera dealers, who no doubt would start to look elsewhere. Ilford's board would also have been frustrated by the lack of return on their investment for some 3 or 4 years.

In 1948 Ilford created a new department to handle camera inspection, which was established and run by Jim Edwards. Jim Edwards and Albert Ninim worked for my father and their task was essentially a simple one. Do the cameras work? Do they perform as expected? Are they up to standard?

It was believed that as Peto Scott had all of the plans, the equipment to make the camera, the required suppliers and all of the parts, constructing the camera would be a relatively simple task. This was not so however. They had many difficulties and as this was their first (and only venture into camera production) they had no experience in dealing with and resolving the problems encountered. Jim Edwards was dismayed that he had to return the majority of Witness cameras back to Peto Scott as they failed the initial inspection tests. It wasn't that the tests were too high but that the cameras were not initially fit for purpose. Correcting production faults would also contribute to the small number of cameras that were actually made.

Production was too small to meet demand. The camera was also appearing in adverts in the Amateur Photographer in July 1953 alongside the Series 2 Advocate, which was selling for £24. 16s. 11d. or an Agiflex II for £84. 0s. 0d.

Finally, Ilford ended the project and sold off the remaining cameras to Dollands for just £67 to retail at around £80. Their list price in 1953 when they eventually came to market was £112.12s.6d. This significant price reduction produced complaints from photographers who had bought a Witness for £112. 12s. 6d and so Ilford generously refunded £40 to every purchaser who had paid the higher price if they could produce the original receipt.

Stereo Witness

Sometime during the 1950's an optician in Lowestoft, by the name of D.A. Evans who was a superb craftsman, allegedly converted 2 Witness cameras on a bar for stereo photography. He also incorporated click stops on the iris diaphragm - a nice refinement to an otherwise superb camera.

Second-hand value

The camera shown on page 44 was purchased second hand for £68 10s 0d. in January 1955. Second hand value in the 1980's was between £500 and £1000. In 2006 a Witness with ever ready case, original box and instruction book was sold for £2640 at Christies. Collectors have a high regard for this significant and rare camera and even its instruction manual can fetch a high price on its own.

In November 2004 a Witness instruction manual was sold on Ebay for £104.52 ($192.50) when 6 people placed 8 bids for it.

The advert said that the manual was an optional extra and therefore was rarer than the camera, although I have never seen it listed as such.

A few weeks later an Ilford Witness leather case was sold for $75.45.

Some Witness cameras today have Dallmeyer Septac lenses. Some of these, we believe, were made up in the 1980's to provide a 'cheap' lens for Witness camera bodies, which did not have a lens. They fit the camera but do not focus on the film plane!

In September 2006 a Dallmeyer Super-Six lens (serial number 388493, one of the last of the 1st batch) was sold on Ebay for £1270.

So why were there so few made?

Some people have made the comment that Ilford did not fund the project suitably and, like many great British ideas and products it eventually was overtaken by other events and pressures. This may be true to a certain extent, but Ilford quite reasonably wanted a return on their investments.

The Witness project had stumbled along for several years without any return at all. This was not their 'fault', circumstances and suitable available manufacturers of both lens and camera body were not easily resolved. Bear in mind also that Ilford was a sensitised film maker and cameras were not their main activity or concern. The camera business had to be able to stand on its own, otherwise the camera business would be closed down.

Even today (probably more so) any commercial project requires sales volume and consistently good product. The volumes of sales is dictated then as now by, a) production availability b) marketing c) the competition and d) the price. If any one of these key items fails or falters then the project is put at risk. The availability of suitable lenses was one of the main deciding factors, together with the limited production volumes coupled with the high quality control rejections. Additionally the Witness camera was Ilford's first camera (post war) and the company did not have any previous experience to draw upon in providing solutions to the problems raised. This project would have provided them with a lot of knowledge about how not to approach camera marketing and manufacturing in the future.

Why Peto Scott?

Before I end this section on the Witness camera I pose the questions,
"Who were Peto Scott Electrical Instruments?"
"What skills did they have to make such a fine camera?"
"Did they make any other cameras?"

For many years I and other collectors would be able to tell you that the Witness was designed by Rothschild and Robert Sternberg and it was manufactured by Peto Scott. This has been common knowledge. I have never heard anyone pose the questions I have raised above. So some research was required.

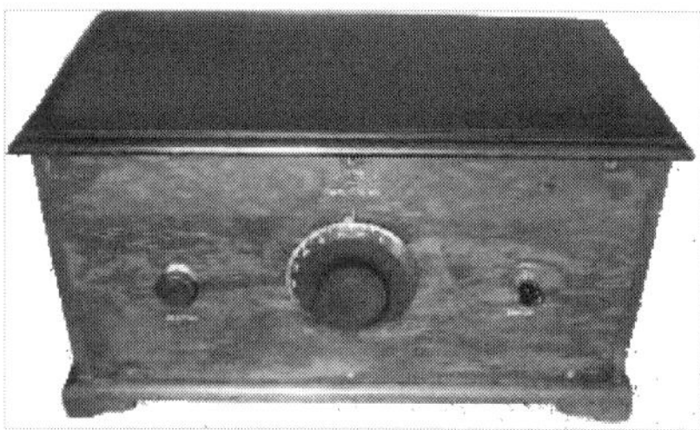

Peto Scott were makers of radio and then television sets, tape recorders and television cameras.

Originally they were named Peto-Scott Company Limited with their head office at 14 High Holborn, London WC1. Later, when they became Peto Scott Electrical Instruments, their premises were in Addlestone Road, Weybridge, Surrey.

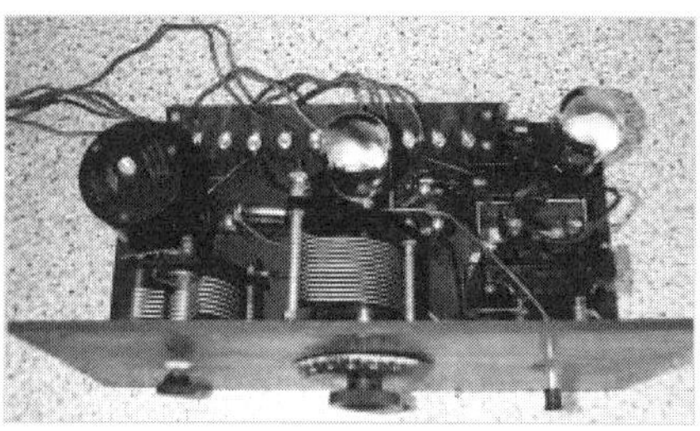

In the 1920's they sold radio receiver kits including the chassis, valves, knobs, dials and wires for radio enthusiasts to build at home.

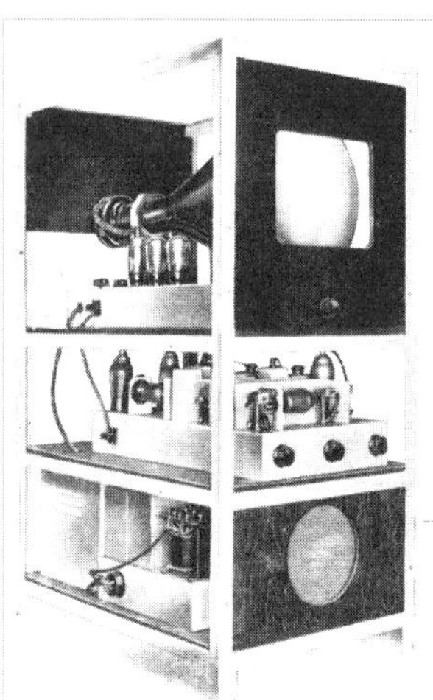

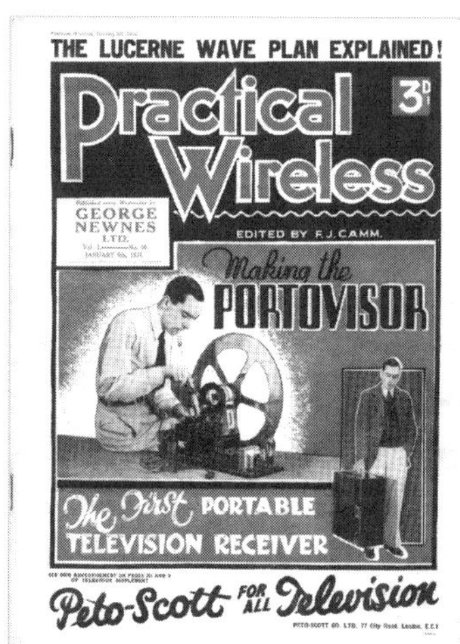

Some time in their history they developed a relationship with Phillips.

Peto Scott sold their equipment alongside Philips (and were also Philips agents in the U.K.) and many of their items were either very similar or scaled down versions. Philips would make the high-end professional models, Peto Scott would make a similar version but with a reduced specification.

Peto Scott did however also make a lot of professional equipment. The BBC used their Reel-to-Reel tape recorders in the making of the Dr. Who television series.

In 1958 they became wholly owned by Philips who have retained their name as a Trade Mark.

In the 1960's Peto Scott television cameras were at the forefront of colour television along with others. These cameras were their only other cameras that they made.

So how did making radio sets help a company to even consider making a very highly specialised miniature camera?

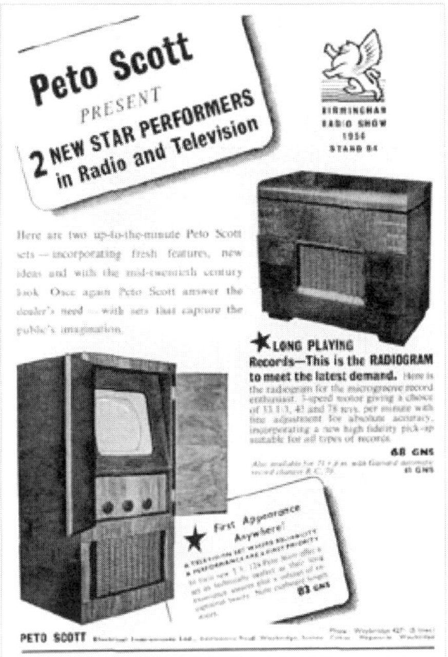

At the time of the Witness production they were also making radios and televisions sets like this.

I can only guess why Ilford choose Peto Scott to complete the camera. Maybe making metal radio chassis would provide the skills and machinery for making camera body parts.

Certainly, the radios of the time had tuning knobs that ran in ball bearing hubs and so they would have no difficulty with the focal plane shutter assembly. Additionally they had been making aircraft instruments during the war, which would have given them additional skills.

The lens manufacture was, as previously noted, carried out by other companies.

The basic design specification and drawings were completed by the time they took on the production although as previously stated they made refinements to make the camera fit for manufacture. They had sourced the various components required from outside companies and the final prototype was exceptional. However, sad to relate they were unable to make production cameras fit for purpose first time, every time.

Robert Sternberg

Robert Sternberg was born in Limburg-am-Lahn, Germany on the 19th January 1914. Emigrated to the United Kingdom in 1936. Married an English teacher, Joan Jary in 1942 and moved to Manchester. He went on to design optical scientific instruments, lecturing in optical physics, and working on astronomical spectrometers.

At the age of 45 years he was awarded a First in physics as a mature student at Manchester University.

In 1969 he co-wrote a classic textbook on the subject of astronomical spectrometers.

He finally retired to Norfolk in 1980 where he spent his remaining years. He was a somewhat shy and reserved individual who was most at ease when talking about his professional interests or absorbed in classical music, his life-long love.

He died in 1991. (Extracted from his obituary in the Independent, 5th March 1991, written by Hilary Sternberg)

Werner Rothschild

Rothschild eventually moved his company, Northern Scientific Equipment Ltd. from Bolton to Lymington. He also changed his name again, this time from Vernon Rothschild to Vernon Ryden.

He was a very keen sportsman participating in shooting and had a great love of motorcycles. A photograph of him in his motorcycle leathers used to hang in the office. He keenly attended several Isle of Man TT motorcycle races.

Some time later (after 1979) he then moved to Portugal where he bought a stud farm. Later still he moved to the U.S.A.

Despite many attempts I have been unable to track down any of his descendants to see if further information could be obtained.

Extracts from two patents that Rothschild filed in the U.K. at the same time as the Witness (and Craftsman) were being developed, are shown on pages 239 and 242.

Development Summary

The following diagram shows the complexities of the Witness project.

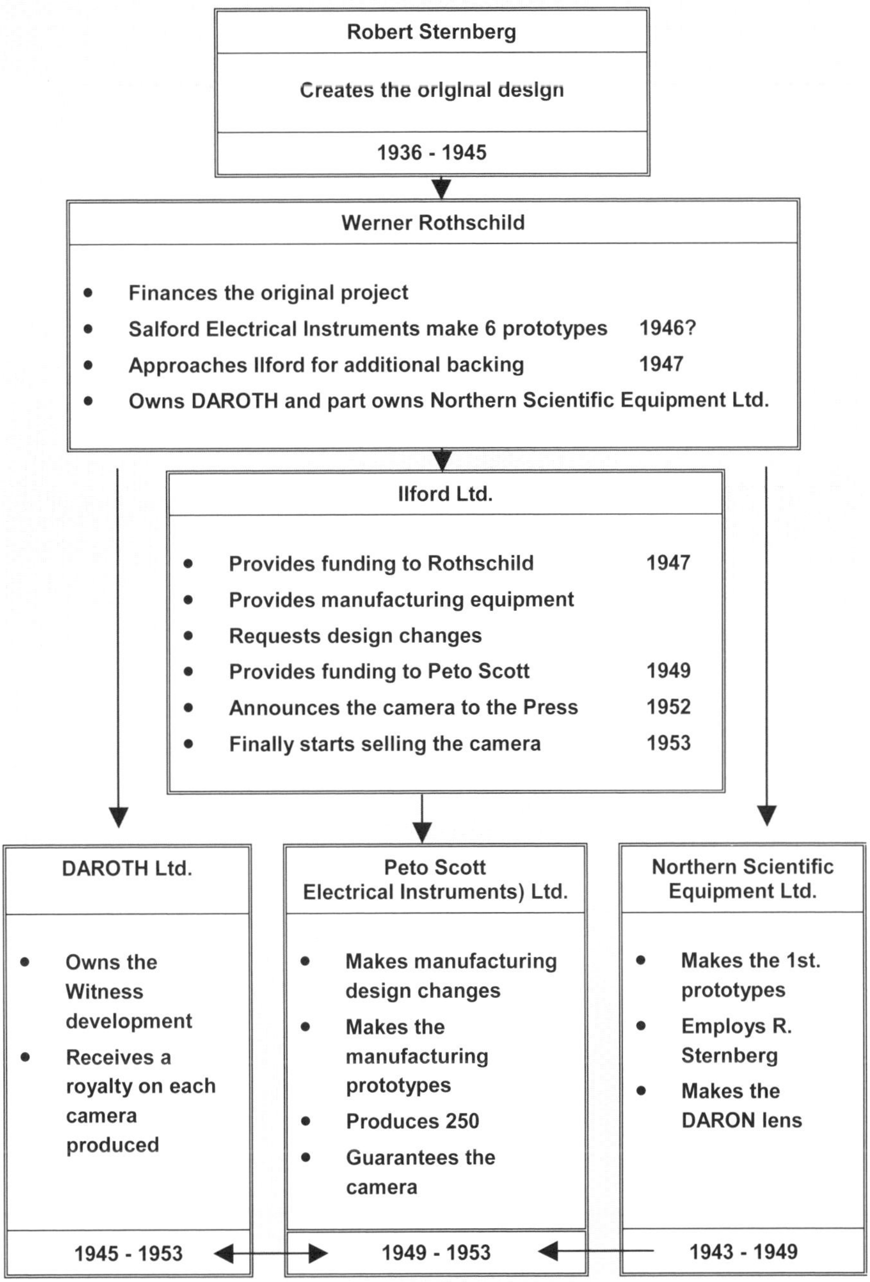

References

My grateful thanks to Dave Todd for his help and contributions to this section and to Jim Edwards for his first hand knowledge of the quality control issues that he had to deal with.

Additional information from the following publications has been referred to within the text.

Miniature Camera Magazine	April	1951
Amateur Photographer	August 13th	1952
Amateur Photographer	April 18th	1952
Modern Camera Magazine	January	1953
Amateur Photographer	1st July	1953
Christies Sale Catalogue	July	1990
Leica Historical Society Newsletter	Spring/Summer	1991
Leica Historical Society Newsletter	Autumn	1991
Independent Newspaper	5th March	1991
Christies Sale Catalogue	15th February	2005

Buyer Beware or Spot the Difference

Always beware of cameras that are being sold with the tags, Rare, Prototype, Unusual etc. These adjectives are often used by people who are not specialists of the particular item being sold. Rare may mean, "I (the seller) have never seen one before" and Prototype may mean, "It is different from others that I have seen". However a true specialist may take a different view. If you have the time and ability you should contact a specialist before you part with your money, especially if it is a lot of money.

Having worked in the violin trade for several years I am well aware that people make new violins to look like old violins. The first owner of a new antiqued violin should be well aware that it is a new violin. However as the instrument gets sold and re-sold there comes a time when a new customer may think that it is an antique violin and the seller cannot dispute this. Is this modern violin now a fake?

If the instrument is supplied with provenance - documentation that says who made it and when, then the instrument is not a fake. If it is sold without provenance it is up to the buyer to check out any statements and 'adjectives used' accordingly. The seller may truthfully believe it to be an old violin and needs educating if it is not. There are hundreds of violins with an Antonius Stradavari label inside which were made in the 1900's not the 1700's.

In a very similar way, cameras that are sold using the words Prototype and Rare need to be treated with caution.
Here is a photograph of a Witness camera and its lens that I was sent.

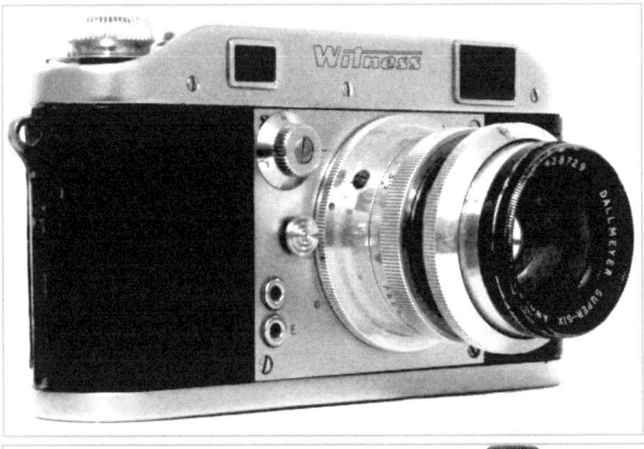

The seller told the owner that as the body did not have a serial number it was probably a Prototype and that as the lens was different from others associated with the Witness it too was probably a prototype.

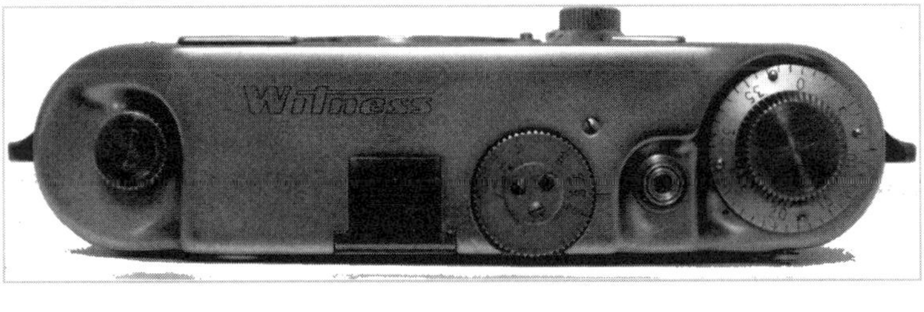

On close inspection the following points are revealed:

There is an extra screw in the top plate beside the speed dial. This spoils the clean lines of the top so is either a repair, or a late mod. At first we believed it was a repair, as the top looks a bit lumpy as if it has been removed and replaced not too subtly. But we then looked at the instruction manual and there is a similar screw in the same position that was not present on the production cameras. So it could be a prototype or a camera faked to the manual, which was inaccurate in several respects to the final production version.

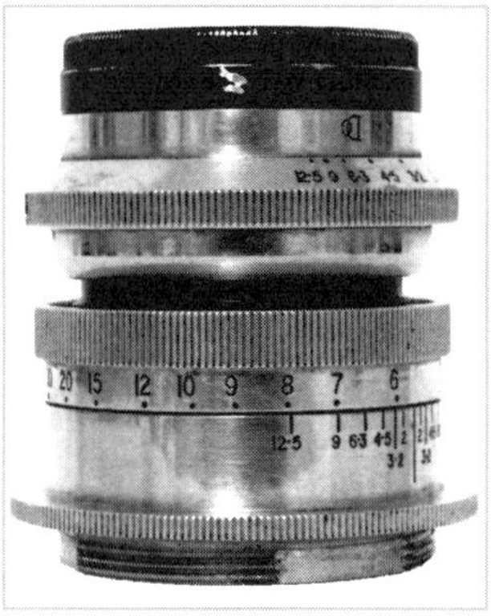

The slow speed index has a crude line at 3 o'clock, not a neat red engraved line/dot at 1 o'clock.

The lens serial number indicates that it was produced after the initial batch of Witness Dallmeyer lenses.

The lens mount is completely different, just having a knurled flange. It has no close focus or indeed a Leica type focusing lever/infinity lock, let alone the nice Witness concealed helical thread.

The aperture engravings are Leica increments 6.3/9/12.5 not the usual Witness 8/11/16/22.

The interrupted screw mount looks crude and was probably added later.

The lens looks like it is of alloy construction, not the lovely chromed brass usually found.

We would suspect this to be a late camera, assembled from the remaindered spare parts that never had its serial number engraved.

The lens we think is a much later one, designed to fit a Leica, which has been modified and added to a late Witness body.

Is this camera a Fake? Was it worth the price paid for it?

It is still an interesting camera and because of the points noted above has 'uniqueness' about it. Only the owner can say whether it was worth the sum he paid for it.

The points raised are also relevant to every other camera in this book and in your own collection. Take advice and whenever possible compare your camera to other examples, photographs, articles and the instruction manual.

Ilford Craftsman - 1949

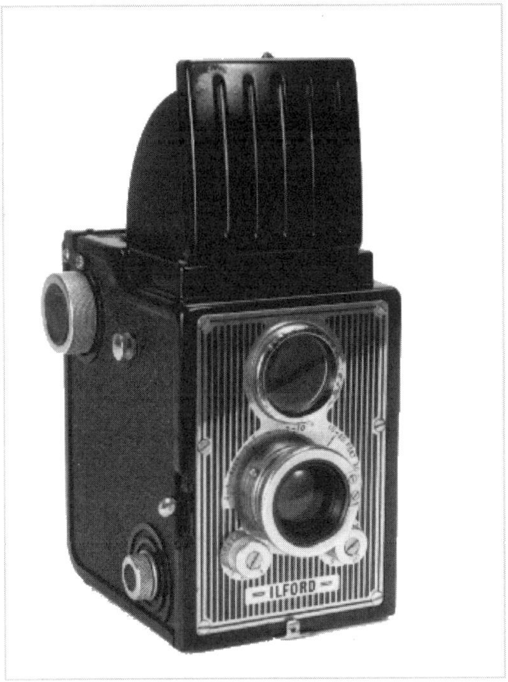

The Craftsman was one of two, twin-lens reflex cameras marketed by Ilford (See also page 210). It was made available very shortly after the Advocate was announced and designed to meet the needs of young people interested in photography.

It was made of shockproof plastic with chromium-plated fittings. It took roll film in 120 or 620 sizes. The brilliant viewfinder showed an image nearly as large as the actual picture obtained.

The two-component lens worked at two apertures - f/9 and f/18 and could be focused from 4ft. to infinity by rotating the lens mount.

Mrs Hawarden, an ex-employee of Vernon Rothschild at Northern Scientific Equipment, told me that the lenses arrived as blanks. These would be polished and have the edges chamfered. Then they were measured with a micrometer prior to cementing them with balsam and baked overnight.

Two shutter speeds, 1/25th and 1/75th sec. were available together with provision for brief time or 'bulb' exposures.

It had a two-pin socket for connecting a flashgun located on the left side edge of the camera body. The Craftsman's flash lead also fitted the Advocate Series II.

It sold for £7. 10s. 6d with an ever-ready case at £2. 1s. 3d and filter mount for 8s. 8d.

This camera was designed for Ilford by Rothschild (who also worked on the Witness) and manufactured by his company Northern Scientific Equipment in Bolton

It was a camera of distinct styling. The front plate was made of chrome with vertical stripes in black, all parts were of exceptional solidity.

By 1952 Rothschild had to ask some employees to leave as they were short of orders.

Chambon Ltd.

The moulds to produce the Craftsman body were made by Chambon Limited. They also supplied automated film packaging machinery to Ilford. The simulated leather finish was particularly fine.

Early in 1948 Chambon Ltd, wanted to build seven factories in Hemel Hempstead on 33 acres of land it had bought two years earlier. This would move them from their premises in London to cleaner surroundings in the emerging Home Counties. This was before the new town of Hemel Hempstead in Hertfordshire had been announced to the public. After many delays they eventually moved to their new premises.

They are still in operation today, although under French ownership as Komori-Chambon.

One thing that has remained constant throughout Ilford's changing history has been the need for packaging and printing machinery. Chambon appear to have survived well.

Ilford Advocate

The Advocate was designed and made for Ilford by David Kennedy (Engineers) Ltd. who would later become Kennedy Instruments, a wholly owned subsidiary of Ilford Ltd. In a similar way to their relationship with Rothschild and the Witness, Ilford financed new equipment and had the controlling interest with a 75% share in the company.

Mr. David Kennedy had an association with Mr. James Mitchell, one of Ilford's Directors and may have met at school together. James Mitchell, who had been the editor of the Ilford Manual for several years, was given the task of forming the Ilford camera and equipment division.

To fully appreciate the Advocate camera and its design requires some knowledge of the company and the personalities involved in its construction. This understanding is also aided by knowing about the Kennedy family and its various business interests prior to the design and development of the Advocate. The following information has been very kindly supplied to me by James Kennedy who, as a child went with his father, Walter Kennedy, into work on Saturday mornings and later ran the business up until it was sold in 1985. David Kennedy was his grandfather.

David Kennedy Engineers

The Kennedys were originally high-class motor engineers and David Kennedy established the company in 1906. In the very early days they worked out of premises in Pembury Road, South Norwood, London, SE25 mending bicycles. Later moving to purpose built premises at 213-215 Selhurst Road, South Norwood.

The firm, David Kennedy Engineers, was later incorporated. David Kennedy was an Associate Member of the Institute of Automobile Engineers. In those days the car was a rarity and thus mending them was a new adventure requiring sophisticated processes including coach building, machining and foundry work. David bought chassis', engines and transmissions from De Dion Bouton in Paris and constructed the coachwork etc. David Kennedy was the first firm in the London area to sell Petrol from a metered pump. The business thrived and during this time David started and pursued his hobby interest of photography and cinematography.

David Kennedy was apparently a clever design engineer (a trait that many of his descendants also share) and design of machinery and equipment was quickly the product of the works because the machinery and skills were there.

Walter Kennedy was born on the 12th August 1911, and would go onto run the company and design the Advocate.

When the Great War started in 1914, hand made car production was stopped and the firm turned its attention to the manufacture of engineered supplies for the war effort. The company was at this stage starting to diversify the products it produced and specialising in general engineering and motor engineering. Later the Garage business became the poor relation and David pursued general engineering products as the profitable way forward.

During the war the company produced mine fuses, gyroscopes for torpedo guidance systems and a host of basic items, like box spanners and other tools. This shift in skills also moved the firm into general precision engineering.

Walter Kennedy went to school at Stanley Technical College in South Norwood and later studied engineering, I believe, at a Polytechnic in London. Later he worked for the Solex Carburettor Company in Acton.

If David Kennedy was a good engineer then Walter was brilliant. It was David's interest in photography that lead Walter to study the growing and popular opportunity for photography for the masses. Working together and sometimes not always too harmoniously, they worked on many schemes. At this time they formed an association with Cherry Kearton for whom they built a camera for aerial photography.

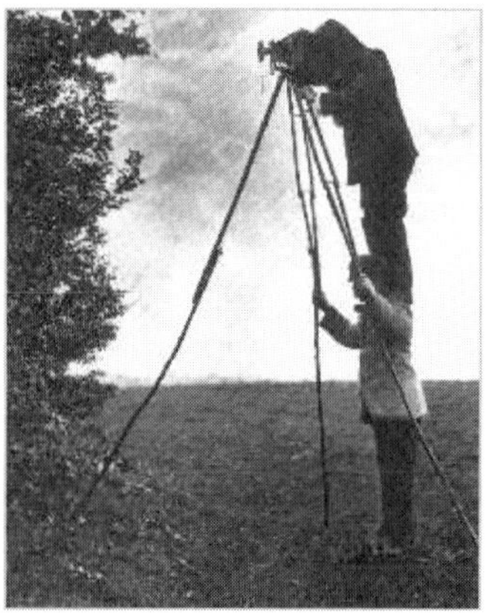

Cherry Kearton standing on his brother's shoulders.

Richard and Cherry Kearton were brothers who were brought up in Thwaite in Swaledale. Both worked for a time in the same London publishing house, but they both had a strong interest in natural history and they left to become full-time naturalists. Richard popularised his passion for ornithology by writing and giving public lectures on the subject. Cherry became a wildlife photographer, using his photographs to illustrate his brother's books. Their first collaborative work, British Birds' Nests, was published in 1895. They were pioneers of bird photography.

Cherry later became the first person to make an aerial photographic record of London, taking his views from an airship. He also photographed and described the wildlife of Africa on the Serengeti and in the Congo, both in still photographs and in early cine films such as *Wild Life across Africa*, *In the Land of the Lion* and *My Dog Simba.*

Before World War II David Kennedy and Walter Kennedy designed a camera for aerial work for the explorer. Kearton who was famous for flying his De Haviland Moth over the African plains photographing wild animals from an angle nobody had previous seen. The basis of the camera was used for aerial reconnaissance during the war and the whole topic was very hush-hush, the hardware being used extensively throughout the war.

Cherry Kearton was always demanding something new, first as a customer of David Kennedy and then later as a friend of Walter's. We believe that there was more to the aerial camera that they designed before the war than any of us will ever know about!

In recognition of Cherry Kearton's pioneering photography in the early 1900's, the Royal Photographic Society to this day, awards a "Cherry Kearton Medal and Award", *'For a traveller concerned with the study or practice of natural history, with a preference for those with an interest in nature photography, art or cinematography.'*

The company was also involved in the making of large aerial cameras for the early ordinance survey mapping of the U.K. These, I have been told were about 3 foot tall and 1 ½ feet wide.

When World War II started, once again the Kennedys turned their attention to the war effort. The Garage Division nearly failed during this difficult period.

During the war, Walter was in a reserved occupation however he quickly signed up for the Local Defence Volunteers - the Home Guard; later to become Captain of an AckAck Battery at Anerley in South London. Although Walter was a Captain in the Home Guard he was no Captain Mainwairing of Dad's Army repute.

It was during his time as the battery commander he realised that AckAck was not being used as a precision weapon but was really devised to frighten the enemy out of the sky rather than shoot them down.

To improve matters he developed and built a hand held 'computer', which would allow a fairly deftly trained gun layer to calculate the exact location of an enemy aeroplane in advance of its arrival.

With this device the gunner was able, by a neat algorithmic expression, to predict the projected position of the aircraft; this predicted pinpoint allowed the fuse setting and trajectory of the round to be prepared with some time in hand. The system worked but was more successful with the introduction of anti-aircraft rockets. For this work Walter received a Citation from King George VI and the MBE.

Kennedy Instruments

David Kennedy (Engineers) Ltd. was created in August 1942. Kennedy Instruments was established on the 17th March 1948, as a wholly owned division of David Kennedy Engineers. It had as its first directors; David Kennedy, Ethel Mary Kennedy and Walter David Kennedy. The company was registered at; 5 Howden Road, South Norwood, London SE5.

By 1948 the company took on two more directors also from the Kennedy family; Herbert Alexander Kennedy and Eugene Winifred Pauline Kennedy. Walter Kennedy was recorded as the works manager, David Kennedy was engineer.

Ilford agreed to buy into Kennedy Instruments on a 75 / 25 arrangement on the 18th August 1949 with the Managing Director as W.H. Dimsdale who, in later years, would go on to become joint managing director with James Mitchell of Ilford Ltd.

Before the Advocate production started the Kennedys were already involved with Ilford in the making and supply of items for Ilford's accessories catalogue including test strip holders, metal printing frames, a Design award winning tripod and a colour processing machine.

The Design of The Advocate

Walter Kennedy devised the concept and set out the design. The shutter development was in place before the War and the associated design was built around that technology. We believe that the original shutter may have been designed to meet a requirement requested by Cherry Kearton in the 1930's.

The Advocate body was made as a die-casting of aluminium silicon alloy and finished in very distinctive stoved ivory enamel. This made the camera quite different from others of its time and a choice that contributes significantly to the fact that most of these cameras are instantly identifiable today.

Walter used a pressure die-casting , which produces an absolutely stable body that would not bend or warp. This process allows components to mate perfectly but makes the paint layer critical, probably only a couple of microns thick. If the paint were too thick then the body shell would not close.

The body components have a tapered leading edge, which allows the parts to mate with no light leakage.

The sand castings were made by H.J. Mayberry and the pressure die-castings were made by Fry's.

The stove enamelling was done by Kennedys at Weir Road both for the cameras and for the 35mm. filmstrip printers that they also made. The main person responsible for this work was a Polish man called Bernard Rimmer. The bodies were first hand sprayed with a special black 'undercoat', which was a requirement for the ivory enamelling, and then baked in an oven. The ivory enamel was then hand spayed onto the hot bodies and then baked again. The black undercoated finish was also the final finish for many of the Advocate specials.

The Advocate is also distinguished by its aluminium film advance and rewind knobs. The same knobs were used on the 35mm. filmstrip printers. These were made by Kennedy and then sent to LHT Anodisers Ltd. for treatment that stops them oxidising.

The early cameras had a chromium plated film pressure plate, which was eventually replaced by a black painted plate. The use of chrome was a good idea but in practice would impose too much drag on the film even though it was a perfectly smooth and polished surface. Additionally if a film was left inside the camera for a long period then the film would stick to the pressure plate and require a great deal of effort to wind on the film with the result that the sprockets in the film might tear.

To resolve this the chrome plate was replaced with one that had a black painted surface. This would allow a good air layer between film and plate but still provide the drag to permit a uniformly tensioned spooling. Going to a painted surface probably saved 1s 6d as well!

The original black painted versions might not have provided the drag required to spool on the film with the right tension. So they increased the tension by increasing the interference between the plate and film. They would have required a shim perhaps a couple of thousandths of an inch to solve the problem.

The solution may have been in the brown paper that they wrapped the casings in. The plates were probably painted and laid down on brown kraft paper and allowed to dry. The matt paint would have been an air-dry paint not stove enamel.

When the paint was dry the plate was cut free from the paper leaving the paper behind and there you have a Pressure Plate Assembly of a precision standard. (This would explain the presence of brown paper on the back of the pressure plate, which until this information was providcd was a bit of a mystery.)

David Kennedy's daughter Joan was born in 1919. She became an artist and designed the David Kennedy logo and later the David Kennedy (Engineering) logo. Joan's husband made the maple wood box for the Advocate as a prototype.

The factory employed around 50 people in total. The camera bodies would be delivered from the die-casting company and enter the workshop. Each camera body was then cleaned up and then had some 20 or so screw holes, each to be carefully drilled and tapped. From here the bodies went to be enamelled and then on to the assembly line. Ilford supplied the Dallmeyer lenses and the viewfinder and all the other parts were made in-house.

The completed cameras were passed over to Ilford's camera inspection department for examination by Jim Edwards and Sid Woodland. Relatively few of the cameras failed their inspection. Most of the Dallmeyer lenses were very good but the Wray lenses, used later in production, did cause a few problems with more than an acceptable number being rejected on inspection.

The company made a total of 10,000 cameras in two batches of 5000. At its height, production was increased from 200 to 500 cameras per week under the direction of Arthur Marshall who was first the machine shop supervisor and then development engineer. Final inspection was performed by Mabel Miller.

David Kennedy died in 1946 hence the election of; Herbert Kennedy, Walter's cousin, to the board. He was another very clever engineer and brains behind the Beer Tap we see in use today in pubs. Herbert was also Managing Director of J Kennedy Ltd.

Post Advocate (and the Kennedy Instruments Monobar)

Walter Kennedy had ideas by the score and was always keen to tackle new and varied problems. He produced designs for other cameras including that of a compact camera with a self-winding mechanism and in February 1956 he was working on the design of a 5 x 4 Monobar camera. A scan of the original engineering drawing is shown on page 252. However Ilford were imposing cost pressures on him to which he could not respond. The main problem was the cost of and consistent quality of the lenses from Dallmeyer not the price or quality of the camera. Kennedys only received £5 5s. for each camera supplied to Ilford Ltd. Walter believed that given more resources he could bring the Advocate to a world market, undoubtedly with design improvements a-many. The pressures and demands placed on the company by Ilford would eventually end their relationship.

The Kennedys were superb engineers but had no control over the production of the lenses, which was held as the main stumbling point for any future development. Ilford also wanted to consolidate and relocate all of their smaller businesses to their main factory at Basildon. The staff at Kennedys visited Basildon and the factory and were asked to either re-locate or to go their own way. Some decided to move, others decided to stay.

Ilford closed the business in Balham and moved it to their works at Basildon. Walter lost heart and all interest in cameras and their associations. He retrenched to South Norwood in 1956/57 taking with him the staff that did not want to go to Basildon. Sad to relate but Walter Kennedy never looked at another camera again. However, being the superb engineer he was, he quickly turned his attention to other products. He never looked back after 1957 and went on to create further successful businesses that are still active today including the manufacture of Towel Cabinets and Continuous Towel Washing Machines. A successful business that is a world leader today under the name Kennedy Hygiene Products Limited. The innovative work of the company's founder being continued. The UK patents database lists many patents in this area. I have listed some of the Kennedy patents on page 245.

Ilford finally bought out the remaining shares in Kennedy Instruments on the 15th July 1960 marking the end of this remarkable company and its products.

In 1985 David Kennedy (Engineers) Ltd. was sold to the Davis Group and then again in 1987 to MAJ a company run by three French brothers named Le Duc. They took the company to a turnover of $1 billion per year.

David Kennedy (Engineers) Sales Ltd. was dissolved on 15th December 1987. David Kennedy (Engineers) Ltd. was dissolved on 7th June 1988.

Advocate Announced

Early in 1949 Ilford held a luncheon for London and Provincial photographic dealers to announce the imminent arrival of the Advocate to be closely followed by the Craftsman. At the meeting several Advocate cameras were handed out for inspection. Mr. James Mitchell said, "he was pleased to announce the first Ilford camera was now in production". It is interesting to note that his statement does not acknowledge either the Falling plate camera of 1902 or the Witness camera of just a few years earlier.

The first advertising leaflet for the Advocate, produced in May 1949, stated, "The Ilford Advocate Camera is not a copy of a camera of foreign origin but represents a new development native to this country."

The Advocate was first put on sale in June 1949 and a review in the B.J.A at the time made the following comment:

"The Advocate is a landmark in British camera construction. It brings the precision miniature camera into the medium price class and gives a lie to the assertion that we cannot hope in this country to compete in the miniature market."

The reviewer was correct that British camera construction could be good but unfortunately time has proved him wrong in that Britain could compete in the miniature market.

Ilford Advocate - Series 1 - 1949

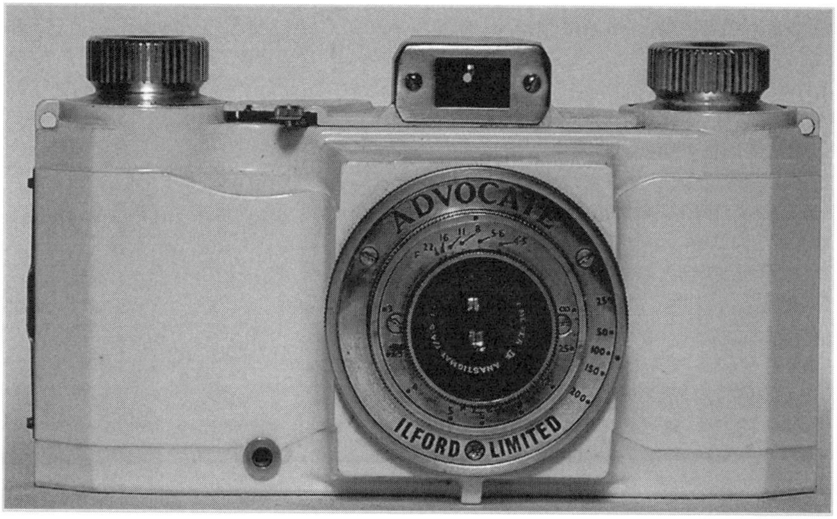

The Advocate body was made as a die-casting of aluminium silicon alloy and finished in very distinctive stoved ivory enamel. The lens was a bloomed Dallmeyer Anastigmat working at f/4.5 with the short focal length of 3.5 cm. giving exceptional definition and depth of field. The lens could be focused between 3 feet and infinity.

The shutter operated at 1/25, 1/50, 1/100, 1/150, 1/200 of a second and bulb and was released by lateral pressure on a lever at the top of the camera.

Combined film wind and shutter setting eliminated double exposure, and the direct vision viewfinder gave a clear and accurate view of the field covered.

The shutter showed considerable engineering novelty, the various speeds being controlled by the sequential flexing of a leaf spring. It was very silent in operation to the point of being a disadvantage as there was little or no audible indication that the shutter had actually been fired.

There was a comprehensive selection of accessories for the Advocate including; case, filter mount, lens hood, supplementary lens, etc.

Ilford believed that the performance of the Dallmeyer lens was quite exceptional being more than equal to the Leica 35 mm cameras of the time.
The Series 1 did not have any flash connections. It sold for £22 11s. 6d.

The lenses had a serial number on the front, clearly visible. The camera body also had a serial number, engraved by hand using an electrograph pen, in the inside. This can be seen when the back plate is open and you look at the bottom of the camera (See overleaf). The number appears above the tripod bush.

All serial numbers started with 1919 – followed by a number. The exceptions to this were the 'Series 3' models, which started 1919W. The W referring to the Wray lens and to a few which were suffixed with an E to indicate they had been factory synchronised for use with Electronic Flash.

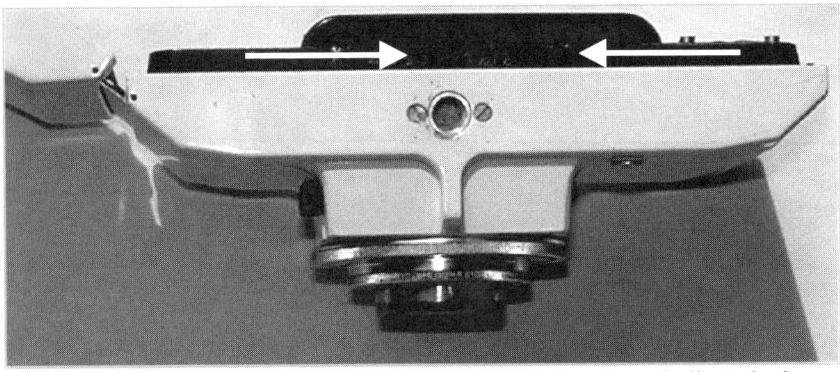

The location of the camera serial number is found as indicated above, between the two arrows.

Advocate Manual

The 16 page manual that came with the Series 1 camera was also very distinctive and probably quite expensive to produce. All of the photographs of the camera were, so the manual said, taken with an Advocate camera. The printing was very exceptional as all of the bright metal parts appear nearly like a hologram and stand off from the pages very noticeably.
Here are two pages from the manual.

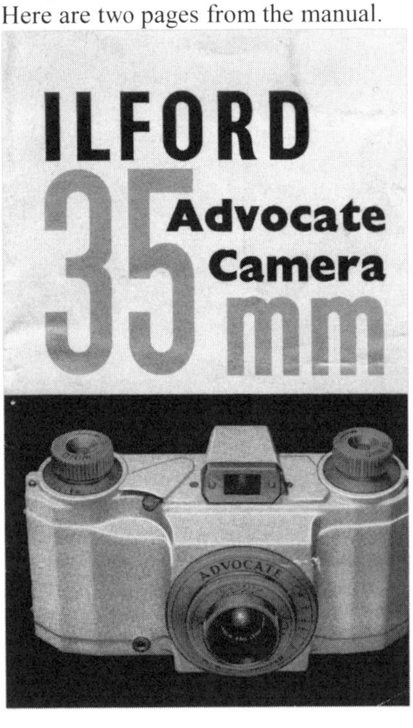

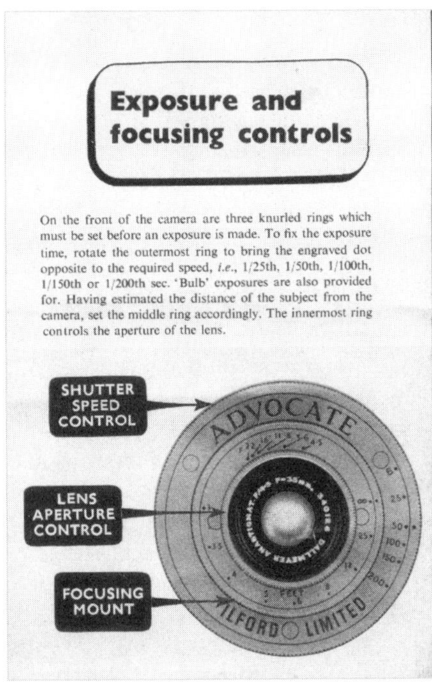

Exposure and focusing controls

On the front of the camera are three knurled rings which must be set before an exposure is made. To fix the exposure time, rotate the outermost ring to bring the engraved dot opposite to the required speed, *i.e.*, 1/25th, 1/50th, 1/100th, 1/150th or 1/200th sec. 'Bulb' exposures are also provided for. Having estimated the distance of the subject from the camera, set the middle ring accordingly. The innermost ring controls the aperture of the lens.

Ilford Advocate - Series 2 - 1952

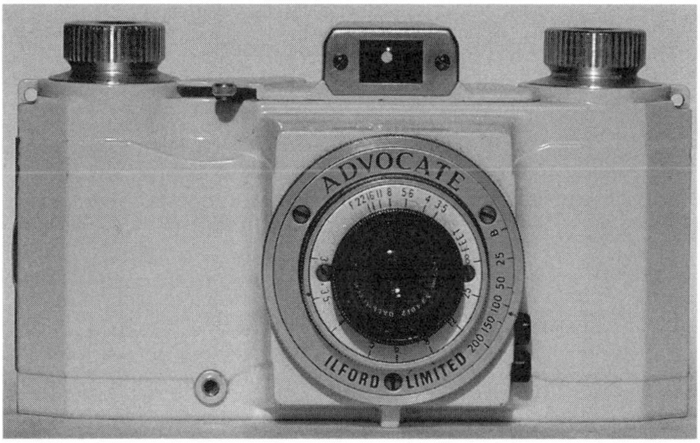

The Advocate was revised during 1952 and launched in December 1952 as the Series II. It was given a bloomed Dallmeyer f/3.5 four-glass anastigmat lens to replace the original f/4.5 lens, more suitable for colour photography. Built in flash contacts were provided via two sockets on the side of the lens mount. It had more legible scale markings on white instead of a polished background on the aperture ring, a new design for the body closure and minor changes in the internal mechanism.

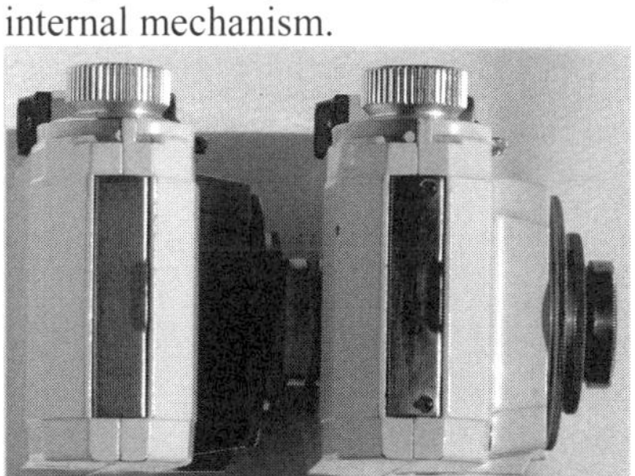

The Series 1 back plate was locked by an aluminium catch, which went over two locating pins (Photo on right). The Series 2 had a similar catch but it was locked onto an edge bar fitted to the side of the body. (Photo on left)

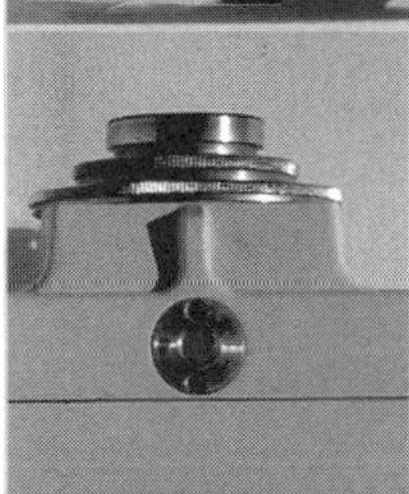

Early Series 1's had a large inset tripod bush, made of aluminium and attached to the body with 2 screws which were in line with the lens. The bush being fitted from the outside of the body. This was changed during the life of the Series 1 to the smaller bush as shown below.

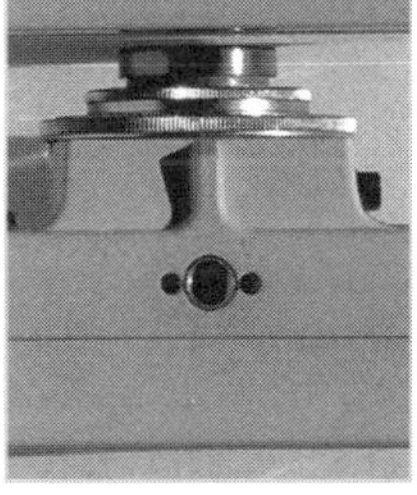

The Series 2 had a smaller bush that was fitted from the inside of the body, with the fitting screws in line with the film plane.

The first 1600 or so Advocates (Series 1's) had a chrome finished film pressure plate thereafter they have a matt black finish.

The metalwork on the front of the viewfinder on early Series 1's was of a nickel finish. Later models used aluminium. Also the metal for the shutter dials was changed from the nickel finish to an aluminium grey.

When you open the back of a Series 1 you can see two levers, one at the top and one at the bottom, between the film plane and the shutter leaf. The top one attached to a spring cocks the shutter whilst the lower one releases the shutter. The Series 2 changed both of these mechanisms so that the levers and springs were out of sight.

The viewfinder rear aperture was increased in diameter from 3mm to 5mm in the Series 2.

In most other respects the Series 2 looked and operated like the Series 1. The system of concentric rings for focusing aperture and shutter speed control, the hinged cassette pivot for easy loading, and the linked shutter and film transport mechanism to prevent double exposure were all retained plus the distinctive die cast aluminium alloy body, finished in ivory enamel.

In 1955 the camera was priced in the Ilford Photographic Materials, General Catalogue as £24 16s. 11d. However in the back of the catalogue is an errata page which reduced the price to £19 17s. 6d. (including purchase tax).

Early Series 2 listed accessories in the manual of; filter mount, lens hood, combined lens hood and filter mount, leather case, supplementary lens (allowing focusing between 12 ¼ and 16 ½ inches from the back of the camera), lens cap, transparency viewer, transparency Holders and miniature film slide storage cabinet.

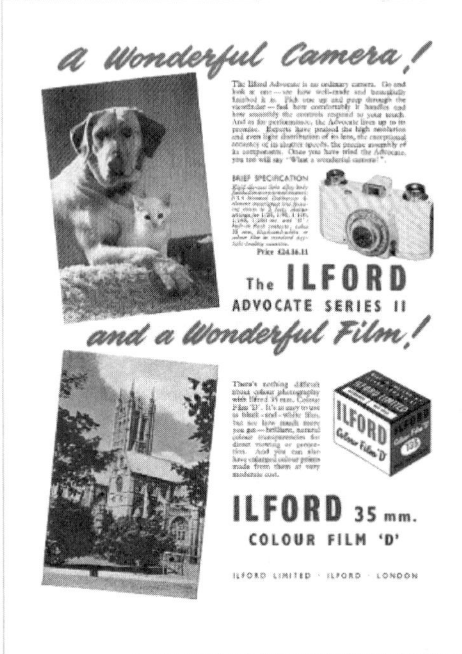

I know of several Advocate Series 2 owners who have a short wire lead with a pair of connectors for the flash sockets on one end. They look like someone has cut off the lead from a flashgun. Strange to relate but this was how they were supplied. This short connecting lead enabled you to wire up to a flashgun that you might already have. I can back-up this conjecture as I have an internal Ilford marketing pamphlet, which lists all of the other accessories, and a, 'Flash Lead: A lead for fitting the flashgun. Price 6s 11d.' This lead was also provided for the Craftsman camera.

Later on the Series 2 was shown with an Envoy Minor Flash Gun or with an Envoy Zing Flash Gun – which has an 8-inch reflector' allowing the use of large flash bulbs.

Some of the marketing leaflets for the Series 2 say, "The standard model is synchronised for use with flashbulbs, or a model can be supplied at the same cost suitable for use with electronic flash." Additionally, Ilford were advertising the Advocate as being available for electronic or bulb synchronisation in AP dated 7 Dec 1955.

This statement on its own was a bit confusing as I am not sure how one would identify one version from the other from an external inspection or indeed from an internal inspection. Flash firing is achieved by one of the pins attached to the shutter blades running in an arc-shaped slot and touching a thin copper strip as it reaches the point where the shutter is fully open. The shape of the copper strip would probably be different in an X and M synchronised camera so that the contact was made slightly earlier for M than X.

However, the Series II manual was later updated with the text:

"The flash gun is connected to a two-pin plug socket in the side of the lens panel and upon release of the shutter, the circuit is momentarily closed and the flash bulb fired. Class F and M flash bulbs, used at a shutter speed of 1/25 second, are suitable for the type of synchronisation employed.

Electronic Flash Models suitable for use with electronic flash at all shutter speeds are identified by the letter E after the body serial number."

Conquest of Everest

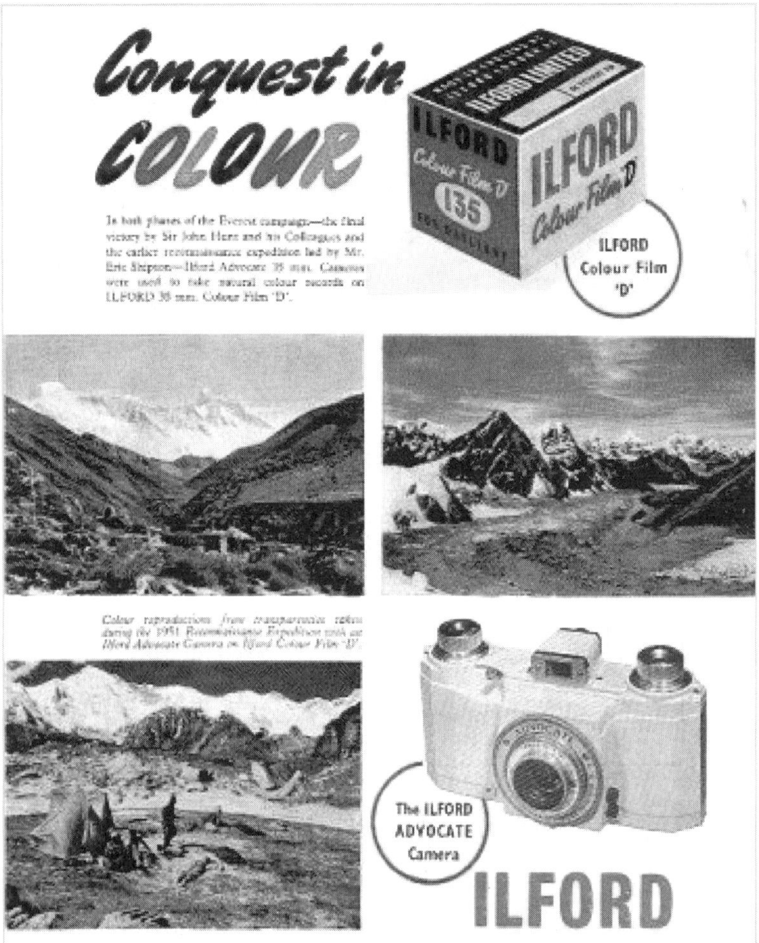

The advert says:

"In both phases of the Everest campaign – the final victory by Sir John Hunt and his Colleagues and the earlier reconnaissance expedition led by Mr. Eric Shipton – Ilford Advocate 35mm Cameras were used to take natural colour records on Ilford 35mm. Colour Film 'D'."

Ilford Advocate in Presentation Box

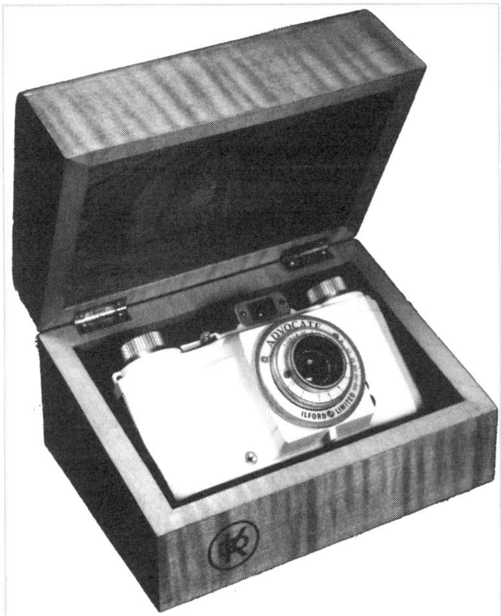

Here is a picture of an Advocate Series 2 in an exceptionally fine presentation box made from maple with David Kennedy's initials/logo on the front.

The presentation case was made by Islwyn Davies who was the husband of Walter Kennedy's sister Joan.

Image courtesy of Colin Harding – National Museum of Photography, Film and Television.

Advocates were sold to the public in an attractive simulated snakeskin finished box as shown below.

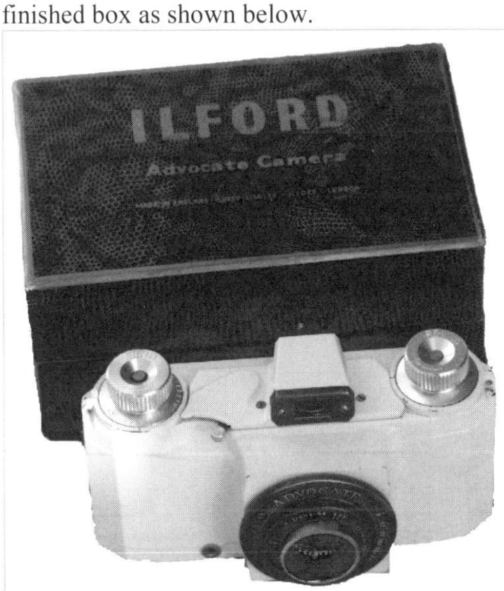

Ilford Advocate - Final Variations

Ilford was always very demanding of its suppliers to produce high quality and consistent goods at the right price. The performance of lenses was always high on their quality control demands.

The lenses supplied by Dallmeyer were of very consistent and quite high quality with regard to optical performance and focal length. However, their output was limited (history repeating itself from the earlier Witness difficulties) and so Ilford approached the firm of Wray Optical.

Wray's output was found to be extremely variable ranging from lenses of very exceptional quality of the right focal length (only a small variation being tolerable within the Advocate design) to those of very poor optical performance. Ilford was thus unable to obtain the economies of larger scale production that had been expected.

However Wray were able to help and for this reason some of the Advocate's have a Wray Lustrar f/3.5 35mm lens instead of the Dallmeyer.

Ilford Advocate - Ross Lens

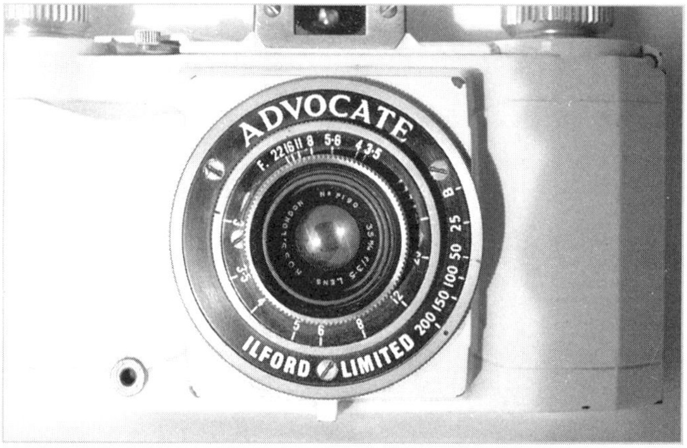

Image courtesy of Wally Morley.

Ilford also approached Ross to see if they could supply suitable lenses. This was also an unproductive route as far as general production was concerned. I do not know the technical reasons why the lens was not suitable however I have found one example of the Ross lens as shown above. Note that this lens is fitted to a Series 1 body, perhaps using an old body to try out the new lens.

Ilford Advocate - Wray Lens

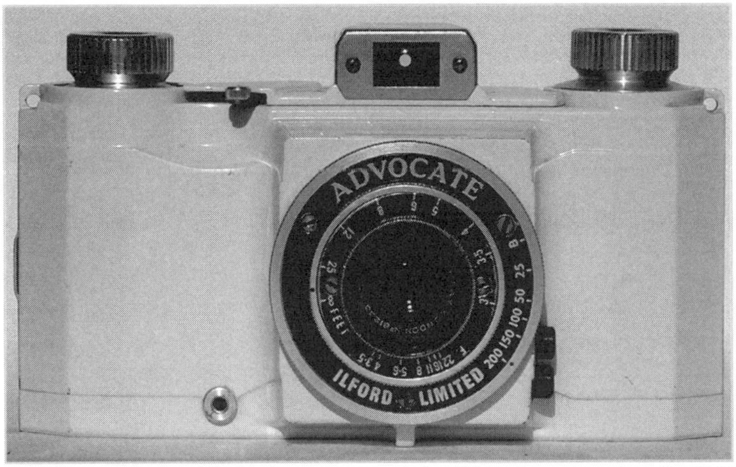

The cameras with the Ross lens and the Wray lens are visually different from the previous Series 1 and Series 2 because of their black enamelling on the aperture and shutter rings. I usually refer to these variations as 'Series 3' although Ilford never marketed them with this name. Additionally, Ilford never produced any advertising showing the new black faceplate as far as I am aware.

Visually the ‘Series 3’ is very good and has lasted well over the years, the black lens and shutter rings with silver lettering, which further enhanced the legibility of the markings.

All of the examples of the camera fitted with the Wray lens come from a batch of cameras taken from the Series 2 range. This deduction is made by examining the serial numbers. The numbers also have a suffix of W to indicate the Wray lens. This information also indicates that the 'Series 3' was made at the same time as the standard Series 2 or at least was earmarked for this variation for a later time. Therefore its lack of publicity is to say the least, unusual. Maybe the variable production quality of the lenses deterred the company from formally announcing this stylistic change although they could have updated the Series 2 using the Dallmeyer lens and the black faceplate had they wished. Why this was not done is just another mystery/fascination within this research.

Ilford Advocate - Summary

So far I have presented the following Advocate variations:

<table>
<tr><th></th><th colspan="2">Series 1</th><th>Series 2</th><th>'Series 3'</th></tr>
<tr><td>Flash</td><td colspan="2">No</td><td>Yes</td><td>Yes</td></tr>
<tr><td>Knobs</td><td colspan="2">Aluminium</td><td>Aluminium</td><td>Aluminium</td></tr>
<tr><td>Shutter release</td><td colspan="2">Aluminium</td><td>Aluminium</td><td>Aluminium</td></tr>
<tr><td>Tripod bush</td><td colspan="2">Aluminium Externally fitted. Screws In line with lens.</td><td>Aluminium Internally fitted. Screws in line with film plane.</td><td>Aluminium Internally fitted. Screws in line with film plane.</td></tr>
<tr><td>Viewfinder rear aperture</td><td colspan="2">3mm</td><td>5mm</td><td>5mm</td></tr>
<tr><td>Viewfinder plate</td><td colspan="2">Nickel</td><td>Aluminium</td><td>Aluminium</td></tr>
<tr><td>Back catch</td><td colspan="2">Located on pins</td><td>Located on edge bar</td><td>Located on edge bar</td></tr>
<tr><td>Film pressure plate</td><td>Chrome</td><td colspan="2">Black</td><td>Black</td></tr>
<tr><td>Internal levers and springs of shutter release and cock</td><td colspan="2">Visible</td><td>Hidden</td><td>Hidden</td></tr>
<tr><td>Lens and Shutter dials</td><td colspan="2">Nickel</td><td>Aluminium</td><td>Aluminium</td></tr>
<tr><td>Lens and Shutter enamelling</td><td colspan="2">Black lettering on nickel</td><td>Black lettering on aluminium</td><td>Aluminium lettering on black</td></tr>
<tr><td rowspan="2">Lens</td><td colspan="2" rowspan="2">Dallmeyer 4.5</td><td rowspan="2">Dallmeyer 3.5</td><td>Wray 3.5</td></tr>
<tr><td>Ross 3.5</td></tr>
<tr><td>Serial numbering</td><td colspan="2">1919-nnnn</td><td>1919-nnnn</td><td>1919W-nnnn</td></tr>
</table>

From the above table you can see a progression of enhancements made to the camera. This neat order has been recently 'disturbed' by the discovery of two cameras, which are hybrids of some of the above features.

Ilford Advocate - Variant - Wray Lens / Series 1

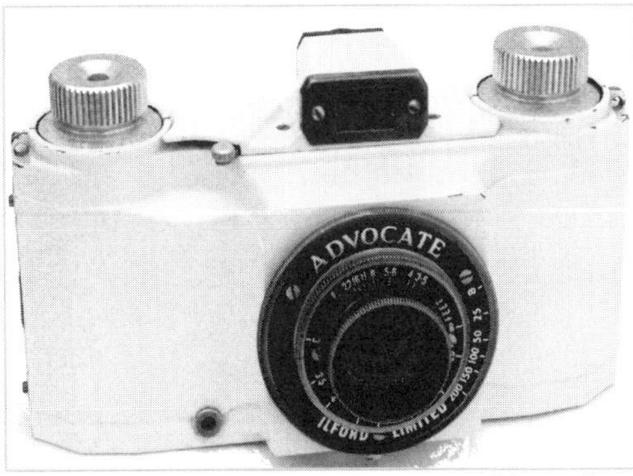

We have seen several of these variants. At first sight they look like a Series 3 Advocate with the black and aluminium dials. This one has a Wray lens and a serial number of 1919-4619W.

However on closer inspection you will see that:

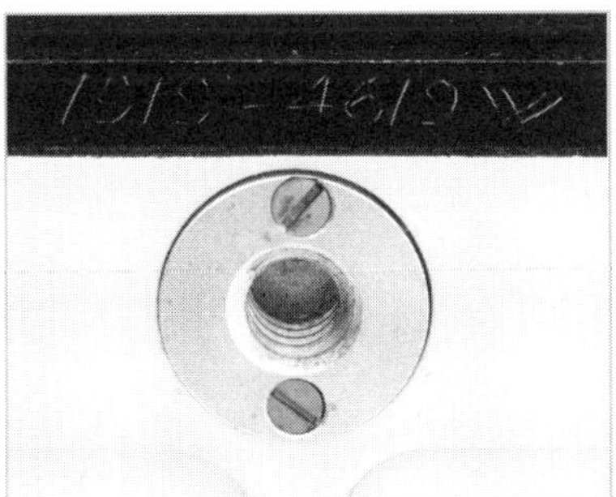

- The body is a Series 1 – no flash connections.
- The viewfinder front metal work is of the older Series 1 nickel finish.
- The tripod bush is an externally fitted Series 1 type.
- However, it has a Wray lens and a serial number indicating this. The Wray lens and the black faceplate were only fitted to a batch of the Series 2 bodies.

The engraving of the serial number has the following oddities when compared with the serial numbers on the majority of cameras:

- The number 4 is like the one typed here '4' - a single line is used to make up the number. Usually a 4 is drawn from two lines, i.e. an L with a vertical line through the horizontal line of the L.
- The W is made up of two overlapping 'V's whereas W's are engraved as a one single line. (others have a more conventional W)
- The 9's in the serial number have a rounded vertical stroke like this 9. 9's on all other 90 inspected cameras are made up of a circle with a straight vertical stroke, like a P reversed.
- All of the inspected serial numbers would indicate that all cameras were engraved by the same person or at least using the same font.
- Of the 18 Series 3 cameras we know about with a W, only 4 have the W at the end of the serial number, all the others have it after the 1919.

So, our conclusion is that this camera was engraved by someone other than the person who engraved the standard run of cameras. We would also suspect that the lens/shutter assembly was fitted to an older body and probably to use up the remaining components. I personally believe that this would have been done by Ilford service engineers who left and set up on their own, using parts to build complete cameras and giving them serial numbers in the process.

It is certainly an unusual camera. Whether this work was done at the factory or later in its life we cannot say. A list of reasons why this might have occurred is provided on page 18.

Advocate Serial Numbers

Body serial numbers provide vital clues to several pieces of information. They can be used to deduce the volume of a particular model produced and sometimes give insight as to when a particular model was produced.

David Gardner has carried out a detailed survey of Advocate serial numbers with the following results:
If the serial number includes a:
W as in 1919W - 6527 then it had a Wray lens fitted.
E as in 1919 - 10055 E then it can be used with Electronic flash.

The only know example of an Advocate with a Ross lens has no serial number, which indicates that it was a test camera that, as noted previously, never came to production.
The following statistics are based on a surveyed sample of 152 Advocate cameras.

	Earliest Known Marketed Date	Latest Known Marketed Date	Marketing Life Span Years	Body Serial Number Lowest Number Found	 Highest Number Found	Possible Maximum Number of Cameras Produced
Series 1	June 1949		4	1919-23	1919-4948	5000
Series 2	May 1953 From Handbook	May 1956 From Catalogue	3	1919-5082	1919-10055	4500
	With electronic flash sync			1919-7162E	1919-10005E	?
'Series 3'	With Wray lens		?	1919 W-6290	1919 W-6660	370

At this point I must thank David Gardner for his significant contribution to this section on the Advocate.

All of the serial numbers start 1919. The only reason we can ascertain for this number was that it was the birth year of his daughter Joan. All the drawings and reference numbers for the camera were preceded by '1919'. The serial numbers were 'scratched' onto the back of the body by hand. Had they been more formally engraved; the engraving would have been costly and largely irrelevant. The engraving process would have raised the surface of the metal around the numbers making the case closure unreliable, because of the interference between the shut faces of the case and may have allowed light to ingress. By hand engraving, only the paint is removed retaining the integrity of the closed components.
This was the final job at the end of inspection and testing.

The serial numbers were passed onto Ilford and in the normal manner linked to the retailer and then the owner of the camera, should any later repairs or servicing be required. Some Advocate camera have unusual serial numbers or no serial number at all and most of these can be put down to cameras that were either made for employees of the company or were used as development cameras. The Ross lens cameras would fall into this category, as would the six black crackle finished bodies that were made for some of the staff.

Ilford Advocate - Basic Body

The most distinctive feature of the Ilford Advocate, especially against other cameras in any collection, is the ivory enamel finish. However, other colours were considered. Various methods mostly of different paint finish were assessed in an attempt to give the camera a black and chrome appearance but they came to nothing.

At one time several bodies were produced in six different enamel colours, Red, Green, Blue, Brown, Yellow and Black, and presented to the Ilford board for consideration. These were rejected by the board.

I came tantalisingly close to seeing several of the original bodies some years ago. When Ilford disbanded the Amateur Products Division several employees decided to set up on their own as camera repairers. Ilford allowed them to have many of the spares and tools that they used. The technician who had originally worked on the Advocate coloured bodies still had them, but was unsure exactly where they were in his house. Luckily he did have the black and a brown body to hand which he gave to me. Sadly, he died a few years ago and the whereabouts of the other camera bodies is now lost.

These two bodies I sold in 1997 at Christies with all the other cameras I had in my collection. Then, in 2005 I went, purely by chance, to a very large antiques fair at Swinderby in Lincolnshire and came across these same 2 bodies and my old Advocate Hospital special which I promptly bought back.

Advocate Specials

The Advocate, particularly because of its robust die cast construction and short focal length, was a useful basis for specialised cameras. This picture shows a black body. Black bodies were used by the company for several 'specials'.

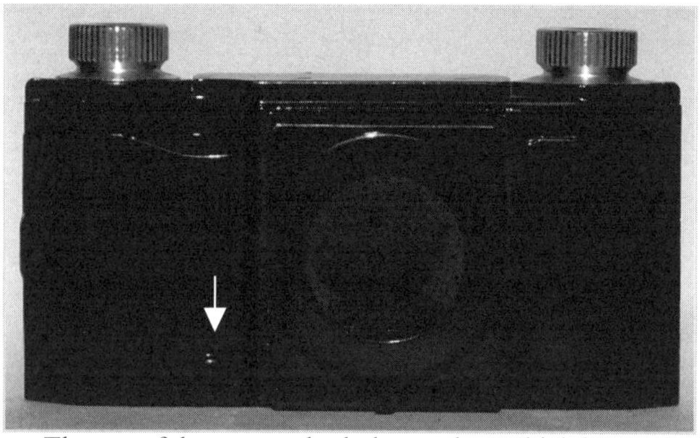

You can see from the picture that the hole for the cable release (lower left to the lens mount) is filled in with a plug, which could be drilled out if required.

The top of the camera body has a plate which is attached to the main body by two screws and the shutter release has been reversed so that it is on the back of the camera rather than on the front. The only identification to be found is that the rear plate has, "Made in England" as part of the casting. This is identical to all other production bodies.

The rest of this section is concerned with Advocate 'Specials'. By Specials I mean adaptations to the basic Advocate body that were made by other companies in association with Ilford, who supplied them with the bodies.

Apart from the Princess Elizabeth special that is shown overleaf, Kennedy Instruments had little or nothing to do with any of these specials. They would have supplied the 'special' body to Ilford who then dealt with the outside companies. They would no doubt have discussed the design plans and intentions. As Kennedy Instruments were a wholly owned subsidiary, any income generated from these adaptations would have been a welcome addition to the balance sheet along with the supply of the standard Advocate cameras to Ilford.

Most, if not all of these specials, are likely to be one-offs or at the very least part of a very small production run.

How many specials still exist today is impossible to say. They do not have any standard identification (apart from any lens or shutter identification) and only someone who recognises the shape of the body and the film advance and rewind knobs would be able to identify them as Advocate specials. To many eyes they are simply 'a strange old/odd camera'.

For me, they are fascinating, as you never know what you might discover next and what you need to research. In trying to understand these cameras my research has taken me from underwater photography to aerial photography, from hospital operating theatres to police scene of crime evidence recording.

Ilford Advocate - Princess Elizabeth Special

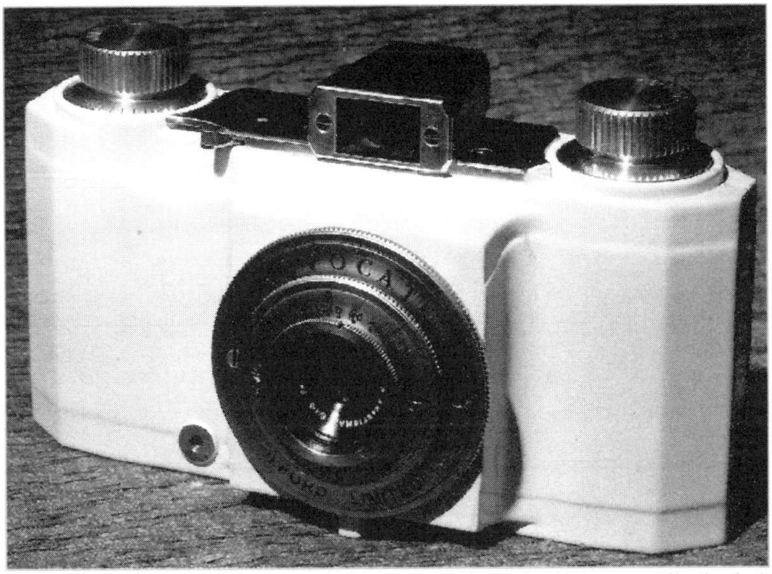

Perhaps the most famous of these specials is the Princess Elizabeth Special. This was presented to the then Princess Elizabeth and the Duke of Edinburgh by the Borough of Ilford in March 1948. The camera was a wedding gift from the people of Ilford. (An article about the gift can be found in the Ilford Recorder Thursday March 25th 1948)

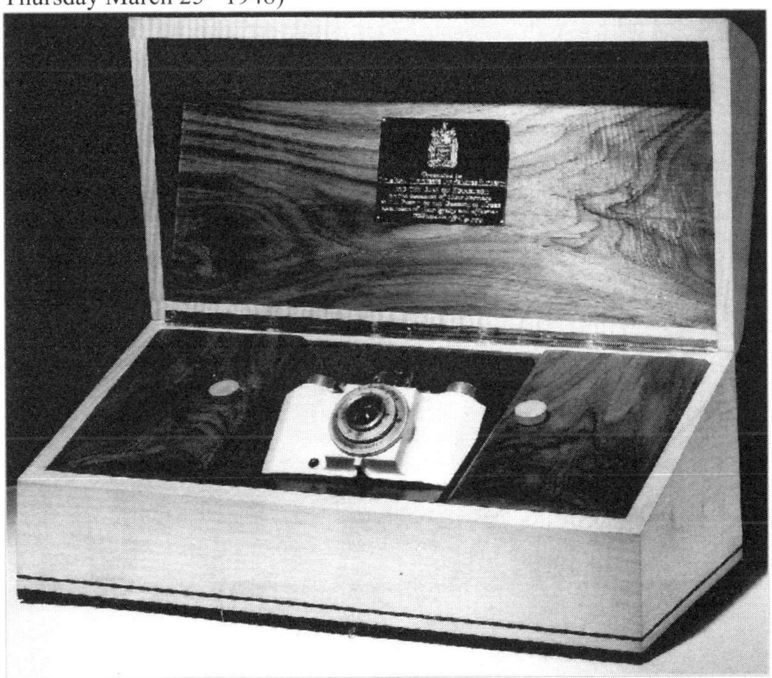

The camera was a pre-production prototype Series 1. It had a casket of solid mahogany veneered with sycamore and walnut, inlaid with ebony and contained in addition to the camera, a carrying case of suede with silver fittings and a selection of filters and films. The casket had a silver hinge and bore a silver plate with the Borough (of Ilford) coat of Arms and inscription, "Presented to Her Royal Highness The Princess Elizabeth & the Duke of Edinburgh on the occasion of their marriage by the people of the Borough of Ilford as a token of their loyalty and affection 30th November 1947". Four other manufacturers had been associated with Ilford Limited in its production. The presentation case was made by Islwyn Davies who was the husband of Walter Kennedy's sister Joan Kennedy.

All of the cameras, knobs, and viewfinder mounts, top plate and control rings were made of silver. The cost of the camera and casket was £340.10s. which was collected from public subscription including a large number of schoolchildren.

In April 1948 the Mayor of Ilford, Alderman G. Colvin, received a thank you letter from the Princess:

" Dear Mr. Mayor,

We are both delighted with the camera which Ilford has so kindly given us as a wedding present. It is beautifully made, and extremely simple to operate. I have not, of course, yet had an opportunity of taking films or of trying the various filters, but I have no doubt whatever that the camera will produce excellent results and that we shall both make constant use of it.

I should like to say how charming I think its sycamore case, and how glad the Duke of Edinburgh and I are that the people of Ilford should have chosen such an extremely acceptable present with which to show their good wishes for our happiness. I hope you will tell all those who subscribed to the camera, including the large number of school children who, I am told, contributed, what very real pleasure their generosity has given us.

Yours sincerely,

ELIZABETH."

Some years later this camera was sent to the Ilford customer service department for repair. My father happened to have gone into work that Saturday morning and was called over by the technician who was working on repairs. He recognised it as the presentation camera and the police were called in.

It had been stolen and changed hands several times until the unsuspecting 'owner' sent it in for repair. It was duly repaired and returned to the now Queen Elizabeth II.

Ilford Advocate - Hospital Special

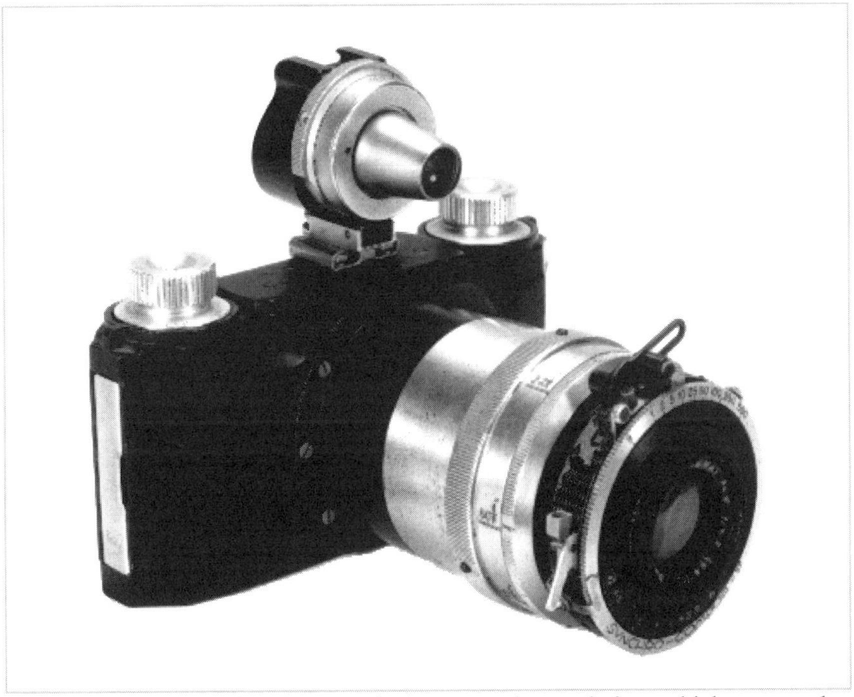

The Hospital Special photograph shows another variation, which was made primarily for use in hospital theatres, to take, so I have been told, photographs of operations in progress.

It has a Dallmeyer Anastigmat 4 inch f/4.5 lens (Serial number 464195), which is fitted with a Synchro - Compur - P shutter. The film advance knob is linked to the shutter cocking lever via an internal linkage rod.

The lens barrel is fitted to a plate, which is attached to the body by 6 screws.

Focusing is achieved by turning the barrel, which is marked with very specific distance markings: 50 5/8", 41 5/16", 32" and 22½.

These markings are unusually specific and make me ask the following questions. Were these distances actually requested? or Did the engineer making the lens barrel, simply unwind it a bit, mark it, determine the focussing distance and then unwind it a bit more and so on?

Why would a distance of 41 and 5/16th inch be required?

A Wray adjustable optical viewfinder is fitted in place of a normal optical finder, which was never fitted to the specials.

The body is slightly different to a 'standard' body. The front half of the body uses a different casting. It does not have a cable shutter release hole neither does it have the casting 'plug' which could be pressed out as shown on the black and brown bodies on page 79. Instead the plate has a semi-circle extension over the cable release hole. This is part of the left (facing) plate, not an additional item. This is interesting, as they made no attempt to hide the original cable release hole location.

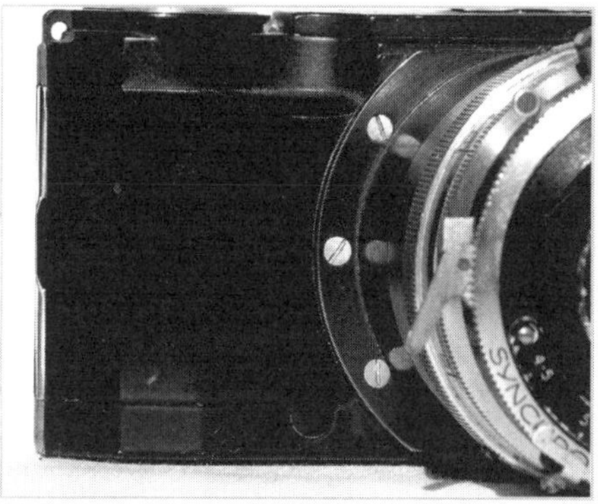

Additionally the body of this special does not have (nor require) the square shaped lens attachment block found on all standard Advocates. The lens assembly is fitted to a plate, which is then screwed onto the main body obviating the need for any additional extension.

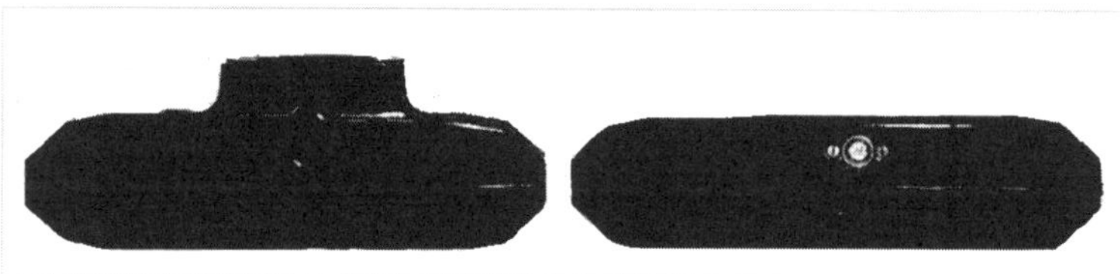

Left Image: Standard body with rectangular shaped lens attachment block

Right Image: Hospital Special without the rectangular extension

Kennedy Instruments occupied premises in Weir Road along with scientific instrument makers and Weir Hospital. Based purely on conjecture on my part, maybe this Hospital special was made for the local hospital?

Ilford Advocate - Police Special

A Police Special was produced in prototype form for police officers at crime scenes. This outfit included an Advocate with a lens pre-set at a fixed (short) distance. It was housed in a hood which was fitted with lights either side of the camera. The unit was placed over fingerprints, which had been dusted, and on contact with the table surface a micro switch fired the lights and the exposure was taken.

Ilford Advocate - Meter Reader Special

A Meter Reader Special was made for reading gas and electricity meter dials by door to door meter reader men. This too used a contact micro switch to take the exposure.

Ilford Advocate - Cathode Ray Tube Special

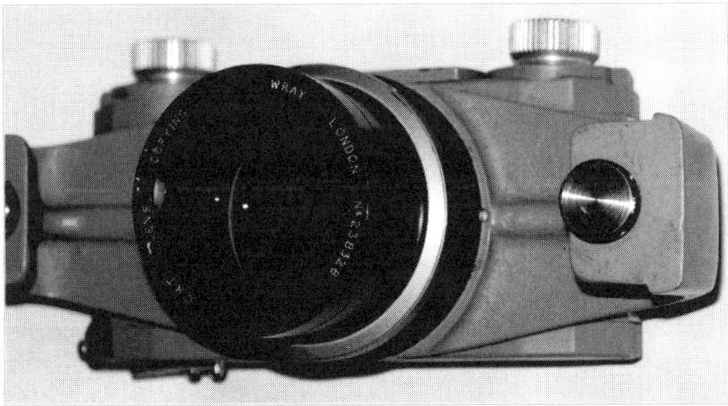

This special, I believe was fitted to an oscilloscope to take pictures of a trace on the cathode ray tube.
The lens is marked; WRAY, LONDON, Nr. 238328, 2in. f1.0, C.R.T. LENS COPYING, 4:1
The camera takes half-frame vertical format negatives.

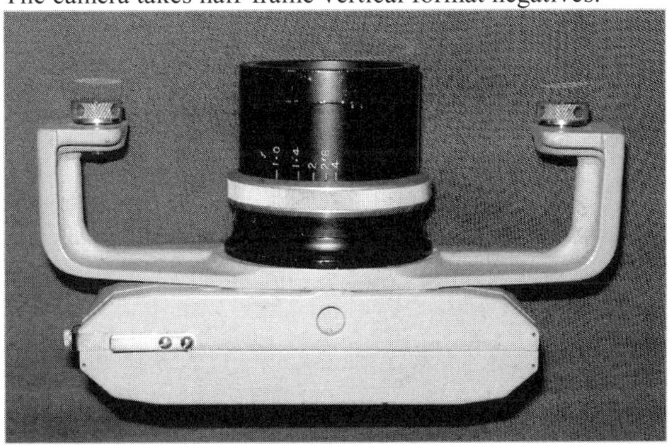

The body is painted grey and is similar to most other specials except that it has an additional catch, which needs to be pressed before the side catch is unlocked and the rear plate can be opened.

The top of the camera has a name plate: Made By Kennedy Instruments Ltd. 12a Weir Rd Balham S.W 12. This is the only Advocate special (or indeed any Advocate), which I have seen which has Kennedy Instruments identification.

I have found information relating to the very fast lens as follows:

"This was a Gauss design with heavy element glass designed for oscilloscope recording at 4:1 ratio. The colour correction is therefore optimised in the blue/green region associated with period cathode ray fluors. It is essentially a Unilite with two glasses behind the iris, but extra glasses at the front. It was used on Shackman and other cathode ray tube recording cameras, for RAE (Farnborough) and Edgerton et al. Boston, USA."

Ilford Advocate - Photomicrography Specials

Ilford supplied the basic Advocate body to a number of makers of photomicrography equipment.

The camera has a body without a viewfinder and with a blanking plate screwed to the top of the camera body. The shutter leaver is reversed so that it functions from the back of the camera instead of from the front. The units have a removable lens and shutter attachment .The end of the attachment is fitted to the eye-piece end of a microscope to enable photographs to be taken of the object slide under the microscope. Instead of an optical viewfinder, the lens/shutter assembly has a focusing eyepiece that is at right angle to the lens axis. This looks onto a prism called a beam-splitter inside the assembly. You can then see and focus onto the object slide. The light can also travel through onto the film in the camera.

These photomicrography cameras can be identified by the provision of a dark slide. The slide would be re-inserted prior to the removal of the unit to prevent the film from fogging. This would then leave the main photomicrography unit still attached to the microscope. The film could then be rewound or the body taken into the dark room for processing.

Overleaf are several examples of these cameras.

Ilford Advocate - Beck/Epsilon Photomicrography Special

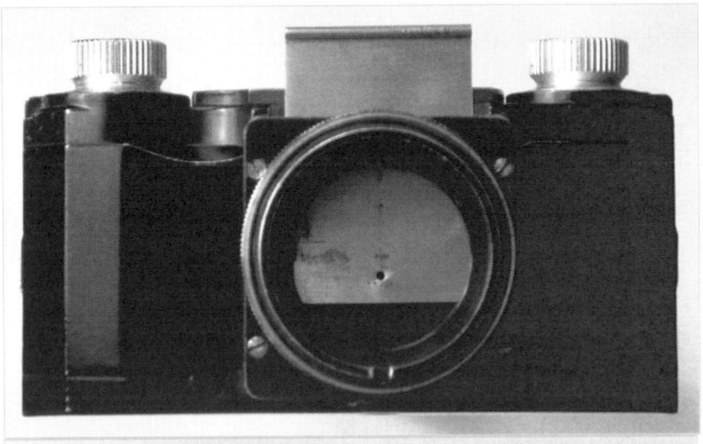

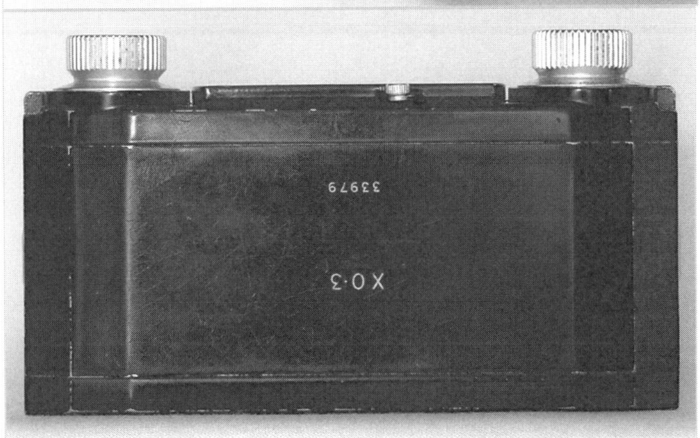

This example is black with the shutter release leaver reversed so that it is projecting from the back of the camera and it has a blanking plate on the top as there is no need for an optical viewfinder. There is no tripod bush fitted in the base.

The back can be completely removed as each side has release catches without a hinge (instead of the single catch and hinge). The outside of the back cover has engraved: X 0.3 and 33979. (These are upside down)

The lens/shutter body block has been replaced by a square plate that is screwed to the body with 4 screws.

Between this plate and the body is the dark slide. This is a thin strip of metal, which has been wrapped around a pin to provide the removal 'handle'.

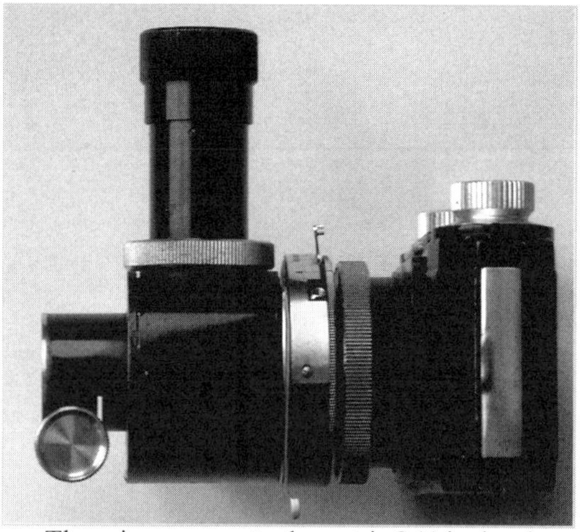

The front plate has the lens/shutter attachment ring. This is a trapped, free rotating chromed knurled threaded ring, which allows the camera to be attached to the lens/shutter assembly. The unit is kept in the correct alignment as it has a slot that matches a locating pin in the body.

The microscope attachment is 3 ¼ inches in overall length with a diameter of 2 ¼ inches. It is engraved BECK LONDON.

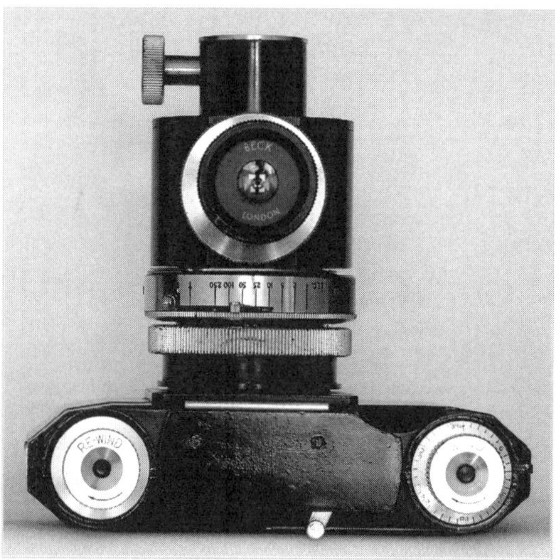

The shutter is an Epsilon with a chromed steel, time marking band fitted around the outside of the shutter. The markings are 1, 2, 5, 10, 25, 50, 100, 250, T and B. The original, front facing, engraved timer markings are retained (but unseen when the unit is in place).

Immediately behind the time marking band there is the shutter cocking lever. In front and below the shutter there is a thin metal shutter release leaver. The shutter also has a cable release connection point. The shutter release that is fitted to the camera in the reverse position at the back, is there to prevent double exposures

The Beck lens assembly is made up of a cylinder that is fixed to the shutter assembly. This contains the lens (at least 1 in the front of the assembly) and a beam splitter prism within the main body. The prism directs the image to an eyepiece tube that is fitted to the assembly at right angles. This is also held in place by a trapped, free rotating chromed knurled threaded ring. The tube can only be inserted in one orientation as it has a slot in the tube that connects with a locating pin in the body of the main unit.

The eyepiece tube has a lens at each end with the outer one being used to adjust the focus. Internally there is an engraved grid, which is seen when looking through the unit. The top of the eyepiece is also engraved, BECK LONDON.

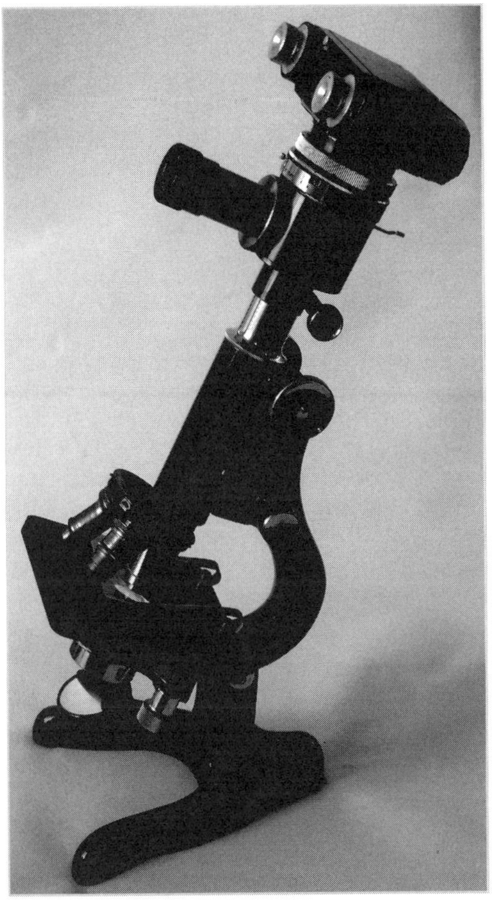

The end of the unit that attaches to the microscope has a 26 mm. diameter attachment with a locking knob. There is an aluminium blanking plug for the attachment hole when the unit is not connected to a microscope.

The camera has a finely made mahogany case with green felt lining the compartments for the camera body, lens/shutter attachment and with 'stops' fitted to the hinged lid to hold the parts securely in place.

Here it is shown attached to a contemporary Beck microscope as all photomicrograph cameras would be.

Ilford Advocate - Watson Barnet Photomicrography Special #1

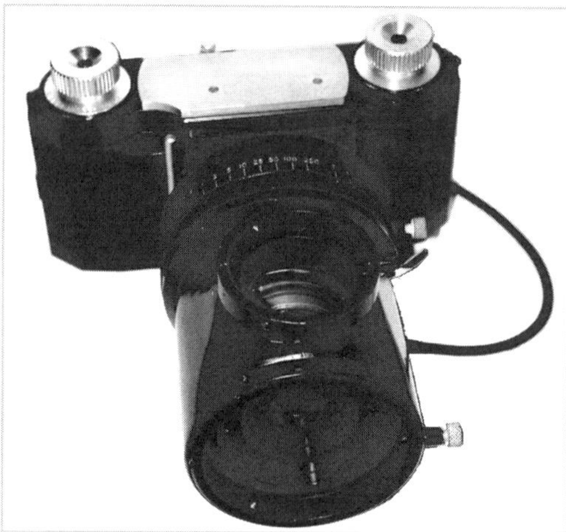

This example uses a Watson Barnet attachment. Watson's had a factory at Barnet and equipment from this location was identified with 'Watson Barnet' engraving as opposed to just Watson. This move occurred around 1957.

Image courtesy of Doug McKee.

In the usual way for such a unit an eyepiece would be fitted to the upper hole and the microscope attached to the front aperture. It has a beam splitter that directs the image to the eyepiece. This particular example, like many of these units does not have its eyepiece tube or the microscope attachment plate that fits to the front end.

The large round engraved ring next to the body is the shutter and is marked, Sec 1 2 5 10 25 50 100 250 B T. The shutter is cocked by a leaver on the side of the unit and it is provided with a cable release.

I have a very similar unit which is engraved just 'Watson' and is identical except that the grip screws that hold the various components together have a longer knurled end that assists attachment.

Ilford Advocate - Watson Barnet Photomicrography Special #2

This example also uses a Watson Barnet attachment but with several notable differences.

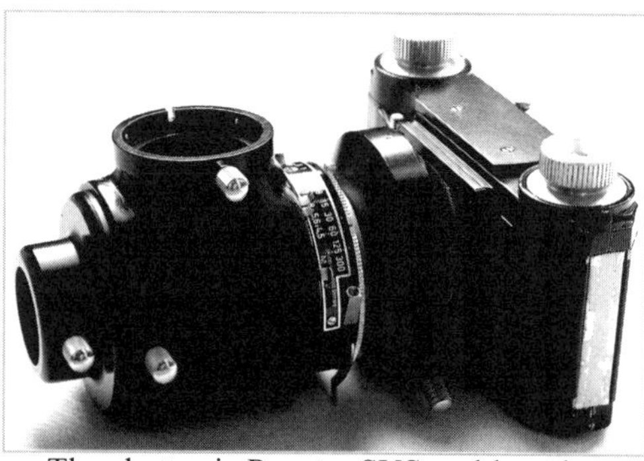

When the unit is tightly locked onto the camera body with the side screw, the body and photomicrography unit can still be rotated freely. This would enable the picture to be aligned with the object on the slide.

The shutter is Prontor-SVS and has shutter speed markings of B 1 2 4 8 15 30 60 125 300. In addition it has a slider marked M and V.
The aperture can be set to; 22 16 11 8 5.6 4.5. It has a flash connection with a switch for setting electronic or bulb flash and a cable release socket.

Ilford Advocate - Beck/Compur Photomicrography Special

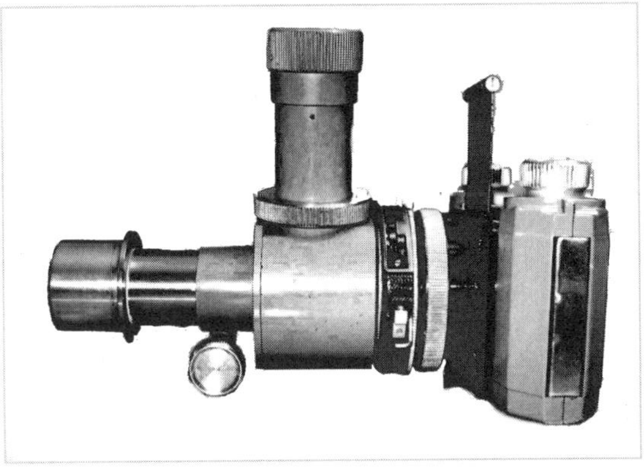

This Photomicrography camera is based on an Advocate and was made by R.J. Beck. Beck also used the Sportsman as a basis for a photo-micrography camera, which is described on page 166.

Image and text courtesy of Dr. Chris Lord.

This camera has a serial number of 36224, and is labelled X 0.3 on the back plate.
It has a Compur leaf shutter with speeds B & 1s, & 1/25s - 1/500s.

The body is based on the standard special body but unusually is finished in ivory enamel rather than the usual black.
The shutter release button has been reversed in common with other specials.

The back plate has been changed to be completely removable with two side catches rather than being hinged.
The microscope assembly is screwed to the body by 4 screws.

It is fitted with a dark slide that lies between the shutter and the body can be raised or lowered by pulling the aluminium edge to the slide.
The aperture is determined by the microscope objective, not the camera.
The focal ratio is 2/na where na is the OG numerical aperture.

(OG - Optical Gradient, NA - Numerical Aperture For a lens the resolving power depends upon the wavelength of light being used and inversely upon the numerical aperture. The N.A. is the product of the refractive index of the medium (1 for air, 1.5 for immersion oil) and the sine of the angle, i, the semi angle of the cone formed by joining objects to the perimeter of the lens. The larger the value of N.A., the better the resolving power of the lens. Most objectives have their N.A. Value engraved on the barrel.)

In use the camera is slotted into the eyepiece tube of any standard optical microscope (23.5mm fitting).

You focus the focusing eyepiece on its framing graticule, and then focus the microscope until the image is sharp on the graticule.

You then cock the shutter (independent of the camera) and wind on, pull back the dark slide to expose the film, and open the shutter.

You can wind on a fraction of a frame. Unlike the standard Advocate the wind on and shutter cocking mechanism are not linked.

You can deliberately multiple expose, and/or wind on only a small amount instead of a full frame if you so choose.

Ilford Advocate - X-Ray Special

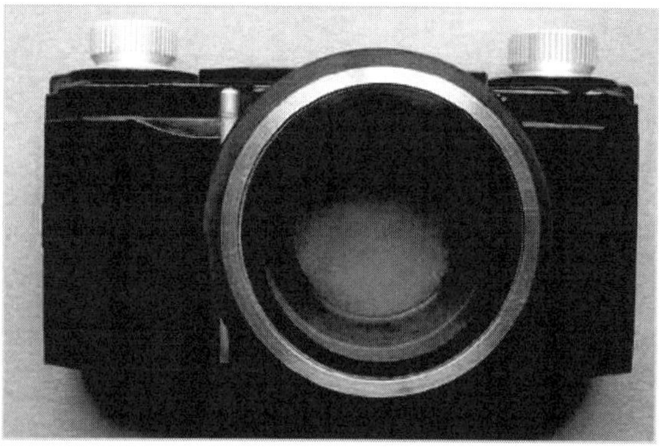

In McKeown's *Price Guide to Cameras* there is the following statement relating to an Advocate *X-Ray camera:*
Advocate-X-Ray c1956. Black enamel version of the Advocate with sheath-shutter for X-ray photography.

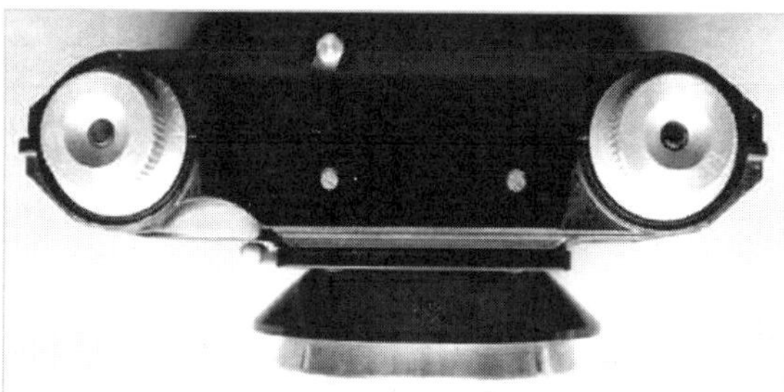

This statement has caused some confusion. I believe that the only reason that this camera was identified as an X-Ray camera was because the body (as shown here, without any lens or shutter assembly) has a dark slide. This is similar to X-Ray plates that require a slide to be removed to allow the film to be exposed. In this camera example a similar arrangement would also be required.

However in all complete examples of Advocates, which have the dark slide, they are without exception fitted to cameras designed for photomicrography. The body would need to be removed from the microscope leaving the photomicrography unit in place and prior to doing so, the dark slide would have to be re-inserted to prevent the film from fogging.

The image of the camera body shown in the previous example has X 1/3 engraved on the lens attachment flange. This is identical to the engraving on the Advocate - Watson Barnet Photomicrography Special shown earlier in this section.

Having said this, a camera designed for photomicrography could be used with an X-Ray source and Ilford did have 35mm X-Ray film. Whether a specific camera was designed for use with X-Ray seems, until I find such an example, unlikely in my opinion.

Ilford Advocate - Aerial Photography Special

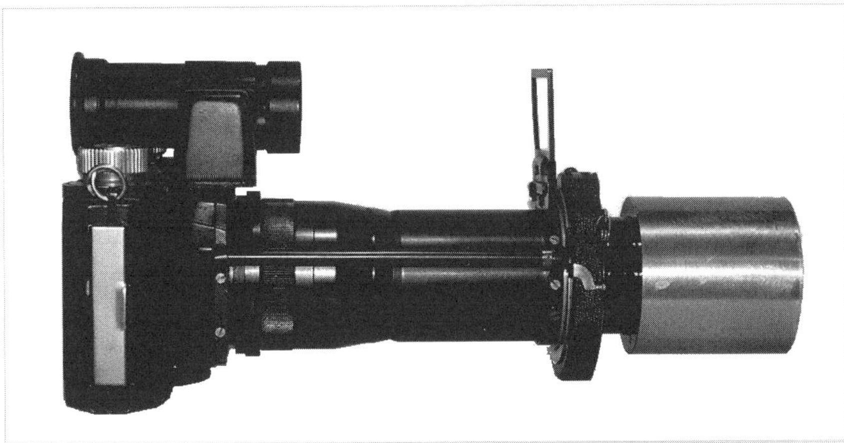

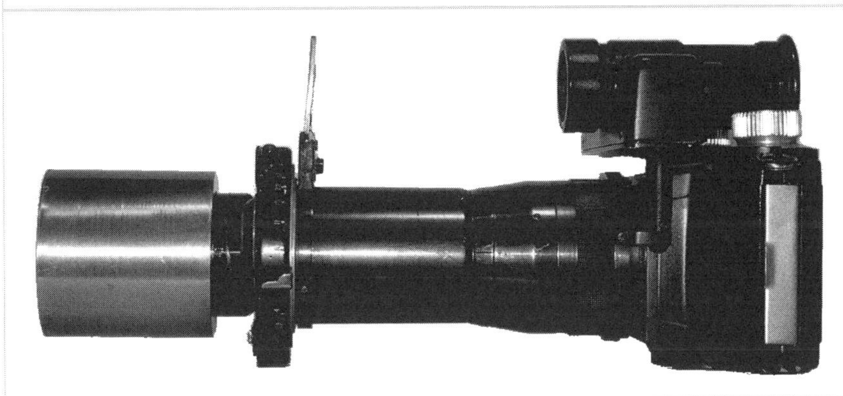

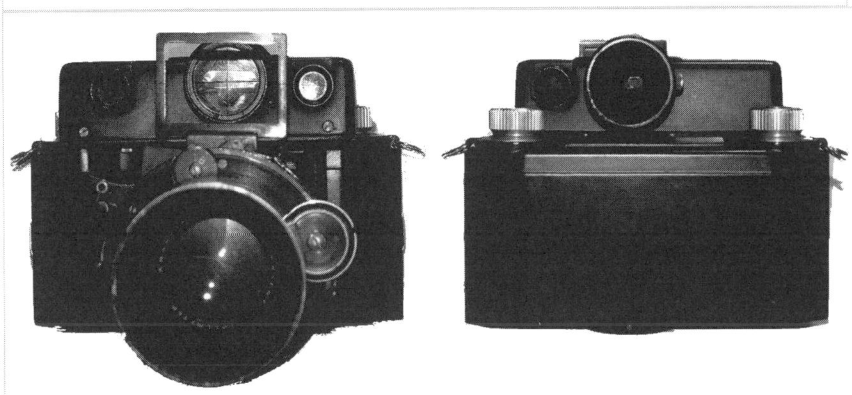

This Advocate special is a formidable piece of equipment.

The camera uses a standard black Advocate body with the exception that the back cover is not hinged. Both sides to the back have standard Advocate release catches allowing the back to be completely removed.

The front of the body where the cable release connection would be is blanked off with a cast plug. This arrangement is neater than the method used on the Hospital special.

The top plate of the camera is part of the viewfinder/rangefinder assembly and not a simple plate as found on other specials.

The lens assembly is fitted to the body by four screws on an attachment plate. Immediately in front of the attachment plate is the focussing ring. Just behind this is a cam that goes around the barrel. As the barrel is turned the cam pushes a follower, which in turn alters the rangefinder setting.

The barrel has engraved markings, which are very hard to read even under ideal lighting. They are as follows: 8 (infinity), 50, 38, 28, 24, 20, 18, 16, 14, 12, 10 and 0

The shutter assembly is 4 inches away from the body when the focusing is set at infinity and 4 ½ inches at full extension.

On the left (facing) side there is an external linkage, which connects the film advance leaver to the shutter. To cater for the extension of the barrel it has a rod inside the connecting tube. This is then attached to the shutter release. A release trigger is fitted to the end of the linkage near the camera body. The film advance knob is released by the Advocate shutter release lever, which is fitted in reverse so that it is on the front of the camera just above the release lever. The lever does nothing more than to allow film to be advanced. The shutter has to be cocked by hand as there is no connection between the camera controls and the shutter-setting lever.

The shutter is a COMPUR dial shutter (Serial 43864) with settings of Time, Bulb and Instantaneous and with speeds of 1, 5, 10, 25, 50, 100 and 200. On the left side is the lens aperture setting leaver, which is marked; 3.4, 8, 11, 16, 22, and 32.

The lens is a Dallmeyer Anastigmat F= 6" (Serial number 361167). Attached to the lens is an aluminium lens hood, which has parallel sides and is 2 inches in length.

Fitted to the back of the lens assembly is a rectangular sighting frame. This has an adjustment lever to fine-tune the vertical positioning of the frame. It has a locking screw to fix the adjustment.

The viewfinder assembly is connected to the body by 2 screws on the top of the camera. It has a large central viewfinder tube directly over the lens barrel. This has a cross-wire in its front glass and the rear eyepiece has an adjuster that moves the viewing hole a few millimetres left or right of the axis. On removing the rear eyepiece one sees that there is nothing between the eyepiece and the front glass.

Fitted at right angles to the viewfinder tube is a rectangular section. This has two glass windows, one at each end of the section. Directly under the right window there is a rod that is connected to the cam follower, which is adjusted when the focussing barrel is turned. Behind this window and to the left of the eyepiece is the rangefinder window.

There are no other markings or identification on the camera apart from those already noted (shutter and lens).

The camera was obtained direct from Agilux when the company was closed down and sold off in 1969.

Agilux Ltd was a subsidiary of Aeronautical & General Instruments Ltd (AGI) that made cameras for military use during the Second World War and continued to make a range of civilian cameras in the late 1940's, through to the early 1960's. (See also Ilford's additional involvement with AGI, detailed in Phase 3 on page 122).

AGI were based at Purley Way, Croydon, Surrey. A company called Negretti Aviation, which was part of the Meggitt Avionics group of companies, acquired the AGI camera business in 1969 and are now based in Fareham, Hampshire.

Ilford Advocate - Underwater Special

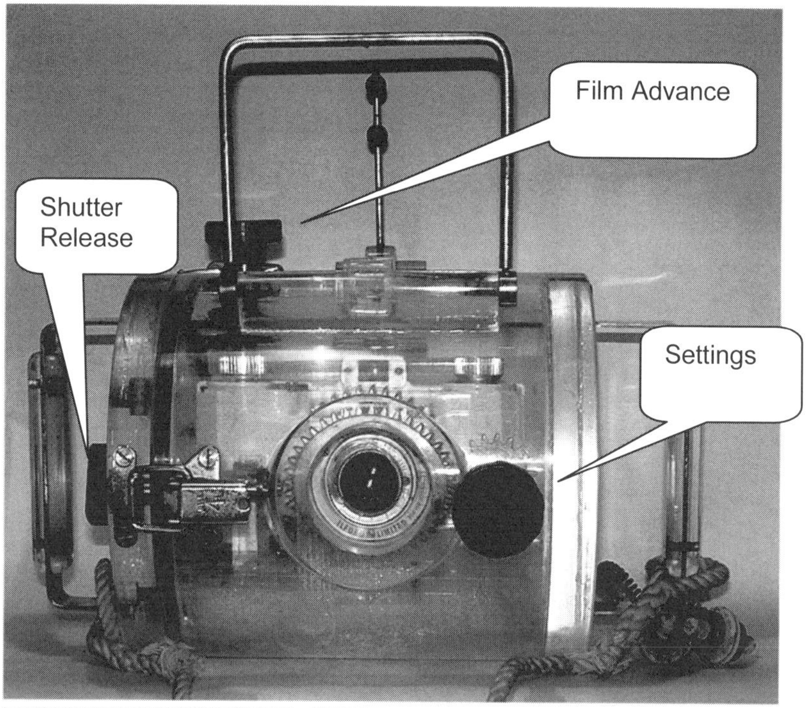

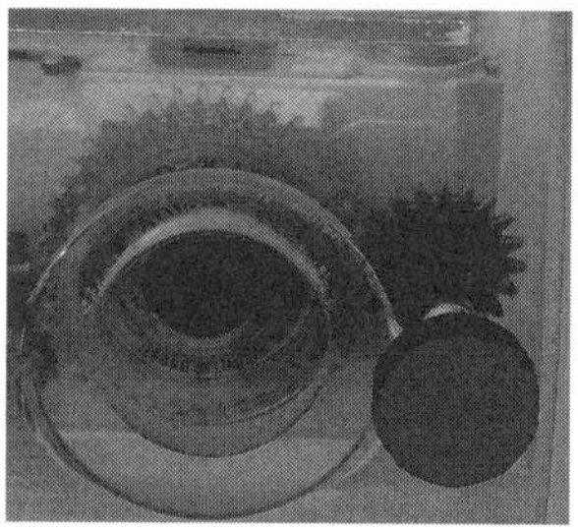
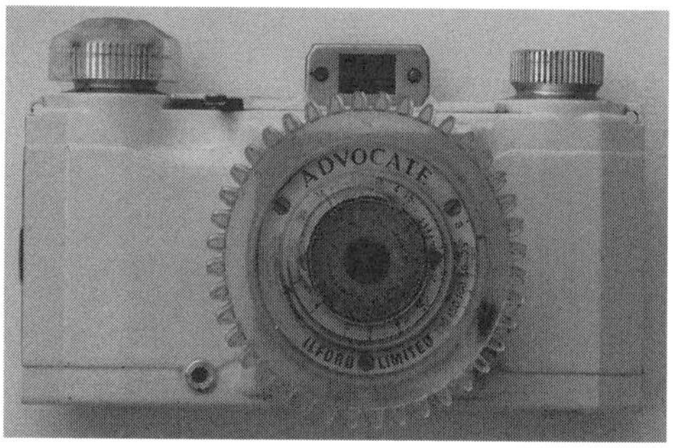

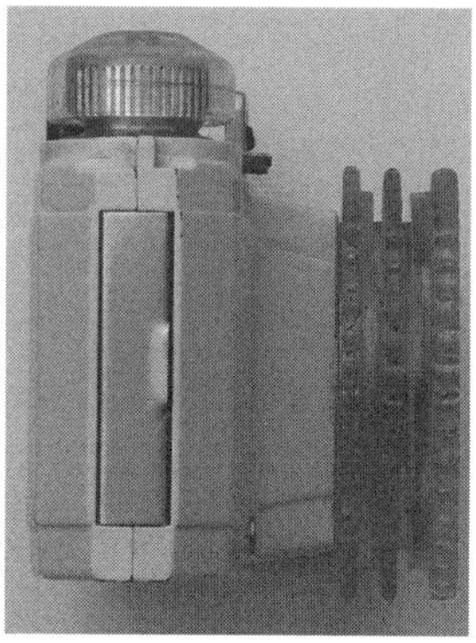
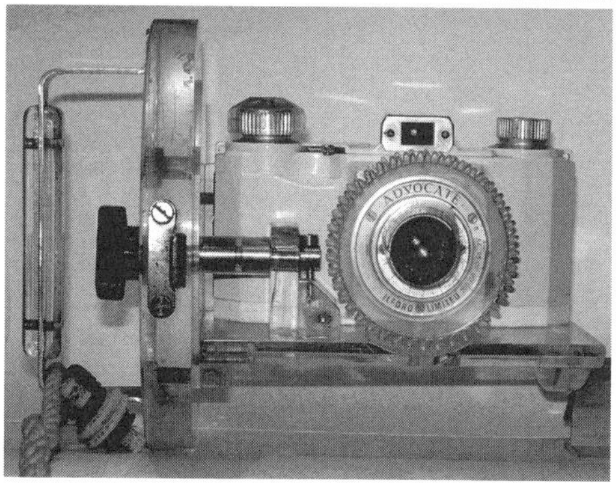

This underwater housing has been made specifically for an Advocate Series 2 camera. James Kennedy has told me that, "the underwater variant was in Walters Kennedy's office at Balham and, as a small boy I was allowed to hold it. It weighed a ton, I seem to remember. That would have been in about 1955/56/57"

The housing is made from Perspex. The main body has an overall length of 177mm. The thickness of the Perspex is 21mm. The internal diameter is 107.7mm.

The camera is fitted to a plate and located by a lengthened 'case' screw. The plate is at right angles to one of the end plates that have an inset rubber O-ring and three clamps to secure it to the main housing. The O-ring has a diameter of 121mm and a thickness of 6.5mm.

When the camera is locked onto the plate, you have to locate a release mechanism pin into the cable release hole on the front of the camera. The release mechanism is connected by a rod and linkage to the external shutter release knob.

The camera's film advance knob has a Perspex cap that is a push fit onto the camera knob. It has a slot to enable the external knob to be connected to the film advance knob on the housing,

The aperture, distance and speed setting rings on the camera have individual Perspex gears push-fitted onto the rings. These connect with a single gear fitted to a knob on the front of the housing. You are then able to manually withdraw or push in the knob so that its internal gear connects with the gears on the aperture, distance and speed setting gears.

The three knobs (film advance, shutter release and settings) have 7.5mm shafts with an O-ring fitted on each shaft. The shafts pass through a tube that is 10.5mm in diameter and these are set into the Perspex housing and end plate.

Two handles are fitted on the side of the housing to hold the unit. A flip-up viewing square at the front and a sighting post at the rear allow for framing. It has a lanyard fitted to the handles.

The camera lens is very close to the Perspex housing, which is thinner at this point being about 10mm thick.

There is no identification on the housing except that the lock catches are stamped WBE 4 (being the make and size of the catch).

Ilford Advocate - 50mm Ross Xpres/Epsilon Special

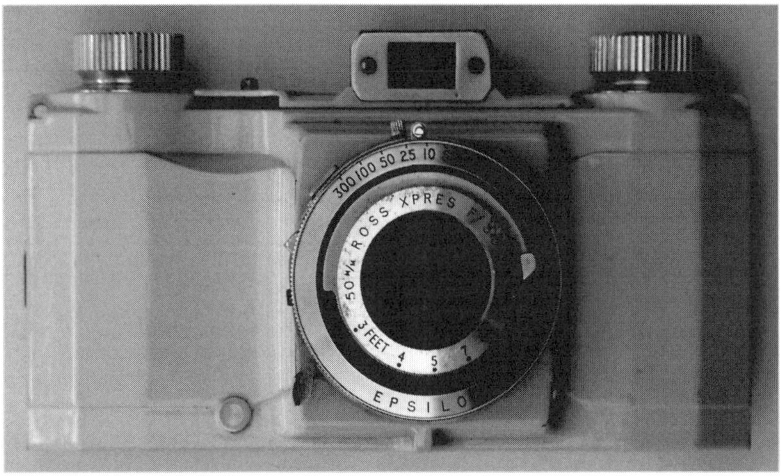

This Advocate Series II (Serial number 1919-5473) has been modified by the removal of the standard lens and shutter, which have been replaced by an Epsilon shutter and a 50mm Ross Xpres f 3.5 lens.

We do not know for certain whether this was an 'official' Ilford/Kennedy modification or performed by a private individual. Either way it has been converted very professionally. The lens/shutter assembly were contemporary with the camera although the 50mm Ross Xpres lens is a rare item to be found on any camera.

The modifications made are as follows:

The shutter cable release connection and the side flash connectors have been plugged with well engineered aluminium plugs. The shutter release lever has been removed. An aluminium knob has been fitted into the top of the shutter release cover, which acts against a spring and releases the film wind on mechanism. The front on the viewfinder has had a piece of black card inserted, which reduces the vision of the finder. The lens and shutter assembly fits well onto the body. The diameter of the unit being about 4mm less that the original leaving an obvious sign that the assembly was never originally intended to be fitted to the camera. Inside the camera, between the film guide and the lens there is the standard plate with its rectangular hole. This hole has been enlarged and some scribe lines are visible. The tell tale sign that this was probably not a factory made conversion is that the edges of this enlarged hole have not been blackened, leaving them shiny.

The shutter has the following settings: T, B, 1, 2, 5, 10, 25, 50, 100, and 300. The lens aperture settings are: 3.5, 4, 5.6, 8, 11 and 16. The focusing numbers are: 3 feet, 4, 5, 7, 10, 20, 40 and Inf.

The shutter is cocked using the lever on the front assembly, which is moved from 12 o'clock to 9 o'clock. The shutter is fired by pressing the side lever (left facing) on the assembly. It has a cable release connector and a synchronised PC flash connector also on the left side.

Ilford Advocate - Black Crackle Finish, Employee's Special

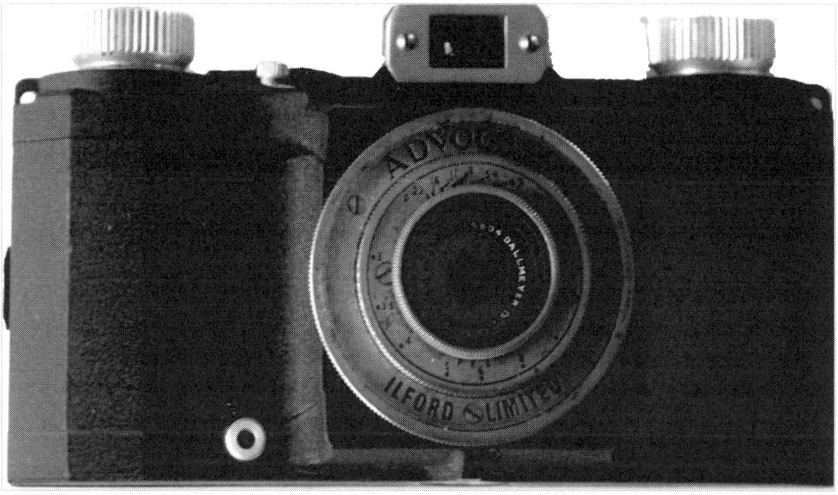

Approximately six of these Advocate Series 1's were made by employees of Kennedy Instruments for their own use. They were not finished in the standard black smooth finish but had a slight crackle finish applied. This particular example is owned by Arthur Marshall who was their machine shop supervisor and was very extensively used throughout its working life. Another employee modified the shutter of his black Advocate to enhance the speed from 1/200th up to 1/500th so I have been told. This would have been a useful extension to the range, had development continued.

Ilford / Kennedy Instruments Monobar - 1954

The Kennedy Instruments Monobar was originally launched in 1954. The Monobar had been jointly designed by practising medical photographers, Charles Engel and Dr. Peter Hansel and it was originally intended for medical work.

Kennedy Instruments, as previously noted in the Advocate section, became a wholly owned Ilford subsidiary. The K.I. Monobar was sold both under the Kennedy name and later in 1958 under the Ilford name although it retained the KI Monobar title. The marketing of the camera was extended to include scientific and engineering businesses as well as the medical profession.

Two versions were produced; the Type U and the Type F. The Type U was the 'full' version whilst the Type F was a simplified version of the Type U, which was designed for special applications such as photomicrography where the full range of camera movement was not necessary.

Ilford / Kennedy Instruments Monobar - Type U

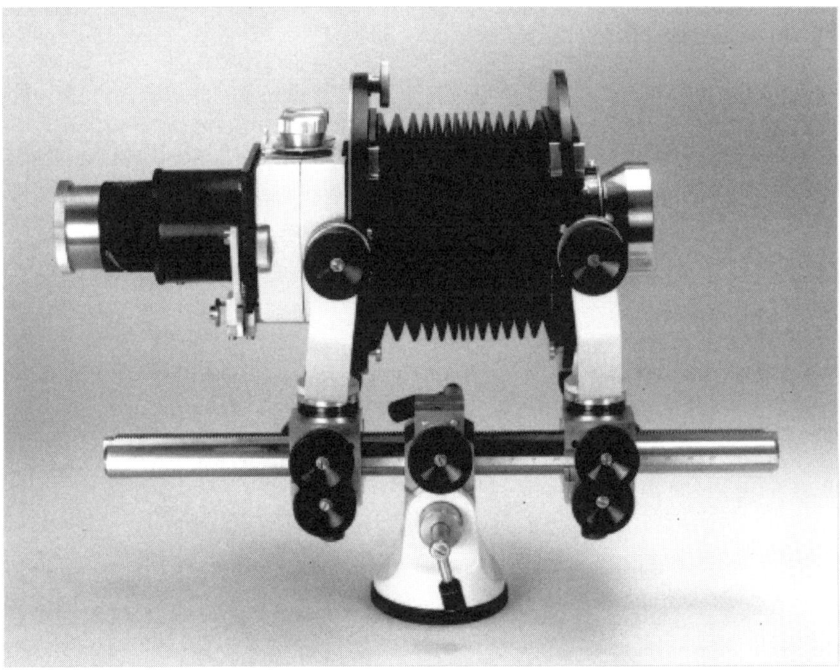

The Kennedy Instruments Monobar Type U was a superb and unique 35 mm monorail field camera, with full control over focusing and tilting.

A large cream enamelled tripod head supported the unit. This had two locking levers for setting the horizontal and vertical angles of the complete unit.

Above the tripod head a round section 12" long monorail supported ten adjustment controls. A millimetre scale was fitted to the length of the Monobar enabling readings to be made against index marks on the front and rear panel-bearing blocks.

The central control knob moved the complete unit forwards and backwards along the geared rail. The front four knobs controlled the lens panel; forwards and backwards, for focusing and swing control for imaging. Both had two separate locking knobs.

The rear four knobs provided the same controls for the film plane. The swinging and tilting movements could be moved through 30 degrees on either side of the centre and vertical positions.

Mounted on the front and rear plates were two ivory enamelled yokes, which held the front and rear panels. These panels each had two adjustments for tilt control of each plane. Both the front and rear yokes had a friction fit adjustment for controlling the rising/falling adjustments.

The front panel provided location and fixing for a lens mounting plate. Several plates were available for a wide variety of lenses. The example shown has a Schneider-Kreuznach Super-Angulon 1:8/65 mounted on a Synchro-Compur shutter.

The rear panel held a square section bar, which supported a ground glass optical viewing system. To view the picture area this section would be pushed up against the rear plate and was locked by a detent button engaging a slot on the square bar. The picture could then be composed using the other control knobs. A final adjustment knob on the top of the rear plate allowed the viewing/film plane to be rotated 360 degrees around a central axis. Once the picture was composed the viewing assembly would be withdrawn to the end of the square support bar. The gap produced would now accept the film holder and be fixed by another detent catch on the support bar.

The film holder was die cast and finished in ivory enamel with aluminium knobs. Access to the film was achieved by turning two slotted thumbscrews on either side of the holder. A standard film cassette could be inserted with the film being taken round the back and onto the take-up spool. This was very compactly constructed. Rewind and film advance knobs were placed on the top of the holder.

Double exposure protection was achieved by a small catch at the base of the film advance knob. To permit the film holder to be removed from the camera without fogging the film a large black, flush mounted wheel controlled a gate which when raised exposed the film area and when shut provided a light tight cover.

Connecting the front and rear panels you could use either a standard square section bellows unit or a leather bag bellows. Bag bellows enables the use of wider-angle lenses so that the standards can be closer together to achieve correct focusing whilst retaining movement as well.

The specification of this camera was very impressive and many are still in use by commercial, industrial and architectural photographers.

Using the controls provided this 35 mm camera allowed for: Rising and falling front, Rising and falling back, Cross front sideways movement, Swinging and tilting camera back, Swinging and tilting lens panel and Revolving film back

Ilford / Kennedy Instruments Monobar and Accessories

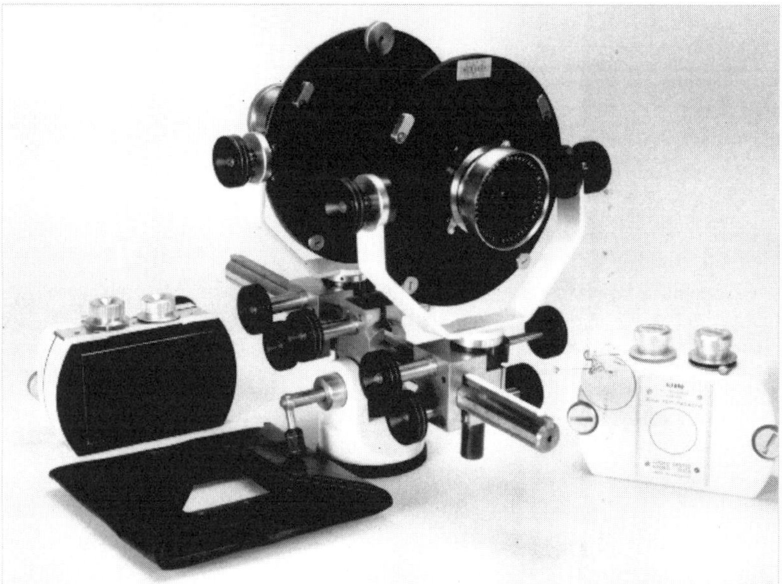

This picture shows the complete unit. To the left is a leather bag bellows and either side are two cassette magazines. The magazine on the right is marked Ilford on its nameplate.

The cassettes used the same knobs as used on the Advocate and indeed the finish of the enamel on the camera and the cassettes was the Advocate white finish.

One of the advantages of this camera in addition to the fact that it was a 35mm. camera with the movements normally found in large format field cameras, was its size. It is about 12 in. long, and the height without the rises is 9 in. It weighed about 9 lb. In scientific work, the manoeuvrability of the camera and the ease with which it can be incorporated into practical settings is a great advantage. Similarly in photomicrography and photomicrography where the full range of movements are not required (the Type F being the preferred variant) this was also an advantage.

Ilford / Kennedy Instruments Monobar - Type F

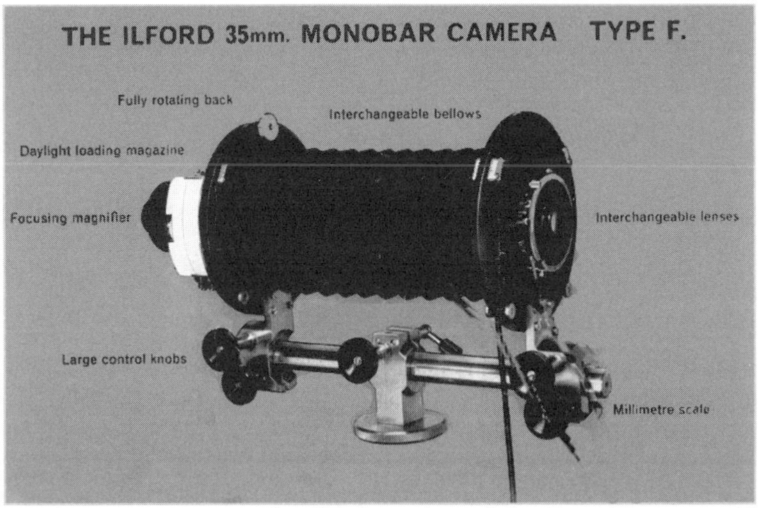

The Type F was a simplified version of the Type U camera. This was designed for special applications such as photomicrography and photomacrography where the full range of camera movement was not necessary.

The front and rear panels are rigidly mounted on bearing blocks and with the monobar, are fitted with focusing movements and locking devices. The back is fully rotating with index marks for the vertical and horizontal positions.

A suitable range of lenses, each lens mounted in an XM synchronised Compur shutter with cable release, was available for each camera. Each lens being in a Monobar lens panel, which is attached to the front of the camera by locating, studs and locking clips.

Interchangeable magazines accept the standard 20 or 36 exposure daylight loading cassettes. Each magazine has an exposure counter and a manually operated sheath and is instantly fitted or removed from the camera.

Black square bellows were supplied with each camera; bag bellows being available for wider-angle lenses.

The lenses, bellows and magazines were fully interchangeable between the Type U and F cameras. The cameras were supplied complete with one magazine and one lens blank panel.

Monobar Prices and Options

Prices and options available at the time were recorded as follows:

- Ilford 35mm Monobar Camera, Type U with one blank lens panel and one magazine. £180 0s 0d.
- Ilford 35mm Monobar Camera, Type F with one blank lens panel and one magazine. £120 0s 0d.
- Lens 2 in. f/3.5 Dallmeyer in Compur shutter with cable release and mounted in Monobar lens panel. £29 0s 6d.
- Lens 3 in. f/3.5 Dallmeyer in Compur shutter with cable release and mounted in Monobar lens panel. £30 18s 10d.
- Lens 4 in. f/4.5 Dallmeyer in Compur shutter with cable releases and mounted in Monobar lens panel. £30 18s 10d.
- Lens 2 3/8 in. f/6.5 Dallmeyer W.A. in Compur shutter with cable releases and mounted in Monobar lens panel. £26 19s 10d.
- Extra magazines £30 0s 0d.
- Extra blank lens panels £1 10s 0d.
- Annular flash attachment (300 joules) Flash head only £25 0s 0d.
- Right angle focusing attachment £10 0s 0d.

Film Strip Printers by Kennedy Instruments

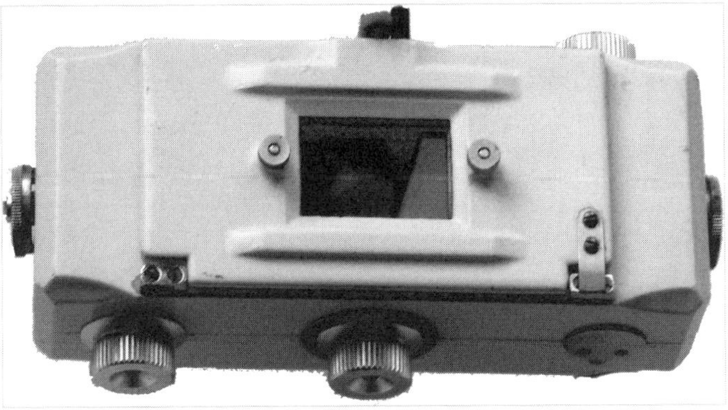

To complete this section about Kennedy Instruments I have included details of two Film Strip Printers, which Ilford marketed.

In the December 1955 General Catalogue, Ilford presented a film strip printer finished in stoved ivory enamel:

"A printer for the preparation of film strips, either by contact or by projection. The printer holds up to 10 ft. (3 m.) of film or paper on the feed spool. Correct spacing between frames is assured. The design enables the sequence of frames on the negative to be altered and also sections from different negatives to be printed on the same strip.

Two masks are provided – full frame (24 x 36 mm.) and half-frame (18 x 24 mm.) – and it is possible to print two half-frames side by side in a strip which otherwise consists of full frames.

The case is of cast metal, finished in stoved ivory enamel. A storage case is available."

The original prototype of this printer was made by Walter Kennedy and Arthur Marshall with very few engineering drawings apart from a few notes and 'sketches on the back of a cigarette packet' (a practice that annoyed their draftsman considerably!). It was left at the factory on a Friday but was stolen during a robbery that weekend. The unit was to have been shown to Ilford on the following Monday. They had to rebuild another unit in super-quick time referring to the various notes they had made and memories of decision taken when the first prototype was put together.

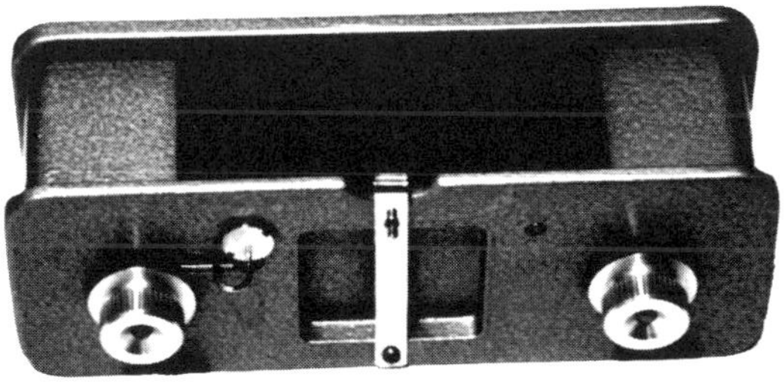

In May 1960 the printer was revised and simplified and looked like this:

This unit is of cast metal, finished in aluminium hammered lacquer but retains the original Advocate knobs.

PHASE 2 (1950-1956)

The implementation of Phase 1 was not without it's disappointments. Ilford continued to distribute the Witness, but had less chance of influencing matters with Peto Scott than with Rothschild and Daroth. Additionally Dallmeyer could not provide lenses in the necessary quantities to support a production of worthwhile size and Ilford was unable to locate an alternative supplier of lenses.

There were no such problems with the Craftsman but Ilford was probably reluctant to continue to give financial support, as this was not within the plan. Possibly the most potent factor was the relatively high price asked for a beginners camera, so further production orders were not placed.

As regards to the Advocate the main disappointment was again partly a lack of suitable lenses (at an advantageous price), but the opportunity to follow this up by investigating German sources was not taken or not taken in time. Also many people sincerely thought that the Advocate had an "un-camerary" appearance against the worldwide standard of black leather and chrome plate. And so, Ilford expanded its options by simply entering into additional arrangements with other suppliers. This phase includes the following products:

Prentice & Envoy Box	Kershaw Soho (Sales) Limited
Envoy Wide Angle	Photo Developments Limited
PIM Monorail	P.I.M. Limited

Ilford Prentice

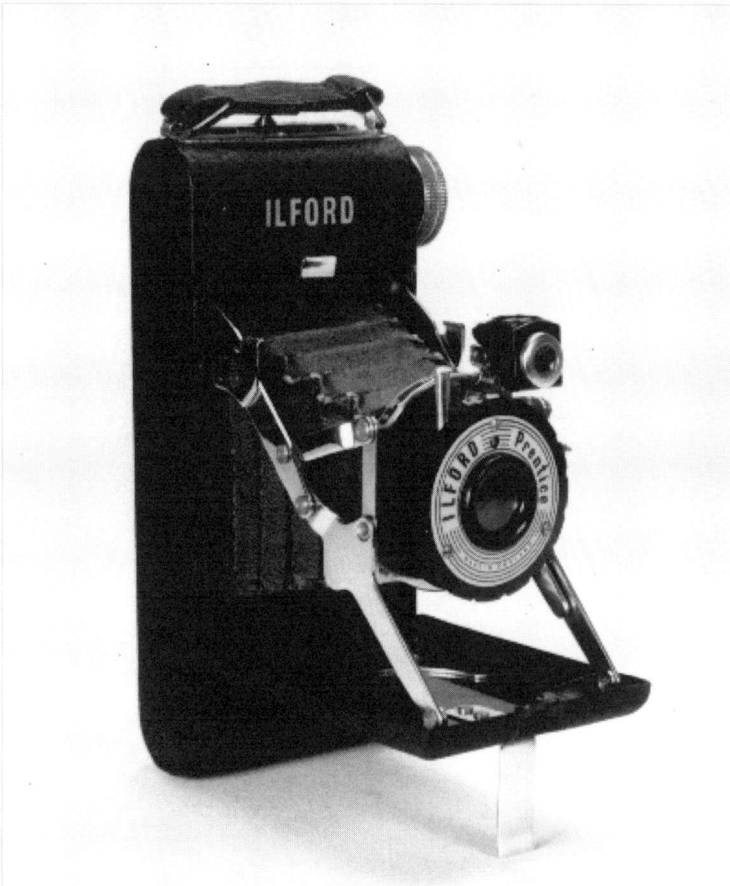

The Prentice was made in 1950 for Ilford by Kershaw Soho (Sales) Limited. This was the equipment side of Soho, the film side of the company had already found its way into the Ilford empire.

The Prentice was basically a re-modelled Kershaw Eight-20 Penguin folding camera. It took 8 exposures on 120 film.

David Gardner, has examined an Ilford Prentice and come to the following conclusion as to its construction.

“Looking at the Prentice I see it is not actually Penguin clone, it is a hybrid of the Penguin 'front end' (the lens, shutter, focussing mechanism, waist-level viewfinder assembly) the King Penguin 'back end' (all body parts and lens support etc) and the Curlew (winding knob). The finish also has the black paint finish of the Penguin rather than the leathercloth panels stuck on a metal body as on the King Penguin. So when the camera is closed it looks like a bald King Penguin and when it is open the first impression is that it's a Penguin! It looks a bit like Kershaw had a bag full of surplus parts and decided to make a camera from them.”

The body was made of pressed steel finished in black crinkle enamel with chromium plated small parts.

The lens was fitted with a 3 point focusing scale, 6ft., 10ft and infinity, focus being set by a lever on the top of the shutter behind the lens. Two apertures were provided, f/11 and f/16, these were set by a 2-position lever on the left-hand side of the lens.

The shutter also had instantaneous and bulb settings, indicated by a pointer which can be seen from above when holding the camera in the taking position, and also by the letters I and B appearing in a small windows just above the lens on the front face. The shutter was operated by depressing a long button, which stood high above the lens.

A swivelling brilliant finder enabled horizontal or vertical scenes to be taken.

The camera was opened by a conventional catch on the front face and a pull out strut underneath the baseboard provided firm support for long exposures.

The back was removed completely on releasing a spring catch under the carrying handle. The lower spool holder swings out, for insertion of the new spool. The empty spool was inserted in the usual way by pulling out the knurled metal winding knob.

It sold for £3. 13s. 6d, plus £1. 11s. 1d purchase tax.

Ilford had such success with this camera that Kershaw, feared the effect on the sales of their own version the Penguin Camera, and repeat orders were not accepted by them.

(This is the camera that the book, '*Silver by the Ton*' incorrectly reported as follows, " a cheaper 35 mm camera, the Penguin, was bought for resale ...")

Ilford Envoy Box

The Ilford Envoy (not to be confused with the Envoy Wide Angle camera) was a very simple yet extremely efficient box camera taking eight pictures of size 2 ¼ x 3 ¼ in. on film size 120 or 620. Described as 'an ideal camera for those starting photography and for those who require the maximum number of good snapshots with the minimum amount of thought and trouble'.

Ilford Envoy Box - Model 1

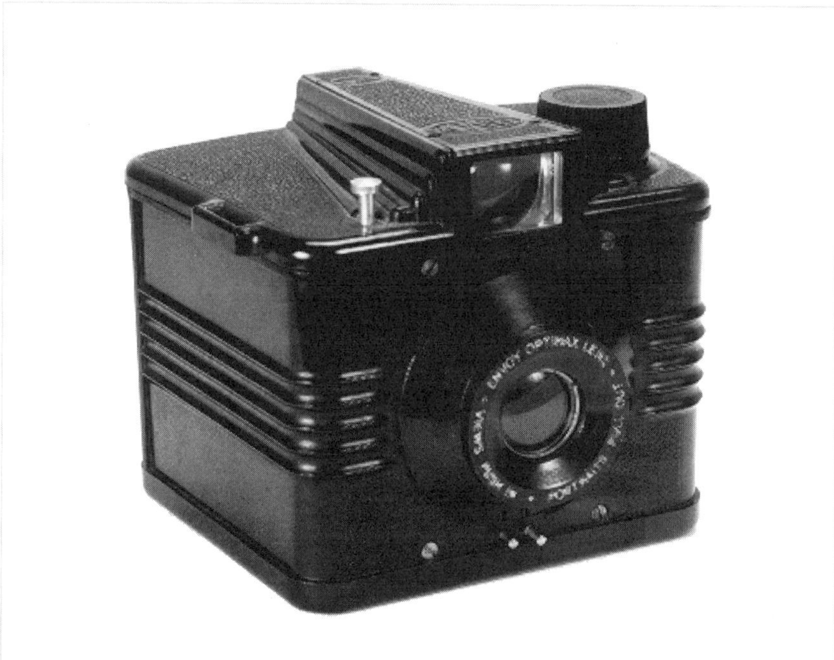

The body was made of glossy black moulded plastic, in two separate parts, held together by a ¼ turn catch on the bottom plate.

It had an Optimax lens with two positions of focus, achieved by pulling out or pushing in the lens mount.

The model 1 had the inscription:

'VIEWS PUSH-IN - PORTRAITS PULL-OUT'.

Ilford Envoy Box - Model 2

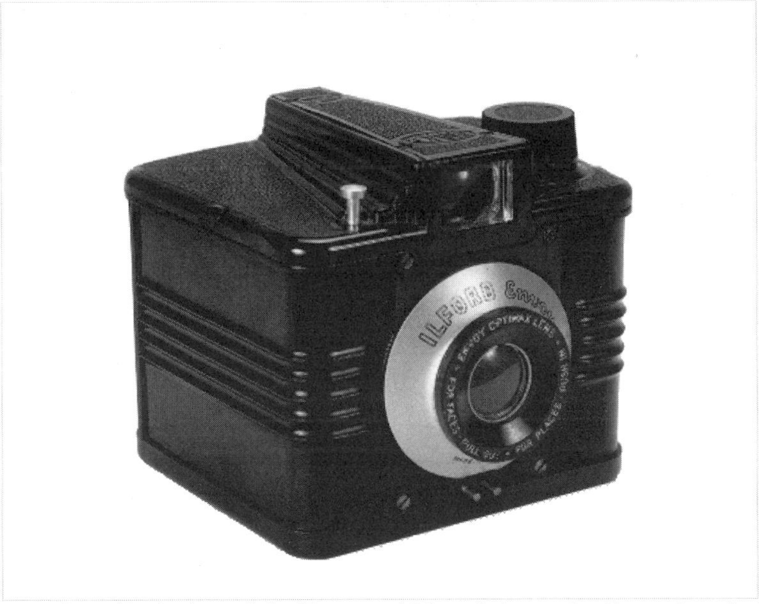

When Ilford adopted the 'Faces and Places' slogan the Envoy inscription was changed to read, 'PUSH-IN for PLACES - PULL-OUT for FACES'. I have called this the Model 2.

Both cameras had an optical direct-vision viewfinder and a simple pushdown shutter release button on the top of the camera.

B.S.S 2-pin Synchro flash contacts were fitted. The recommended flash guns listed in the Ilford Materials, General Catalogue were the Envoy “Major” and “Minor” Flash Guns, the “Black Prince” Dynamic Flash Gun, the Envoy Zing Flash Gun and the Courtenay Cadet Electronic Flash Gun.

In 1955 the camera sold for £1 19s. 9d.

Ilford Envoy Box - Model 3

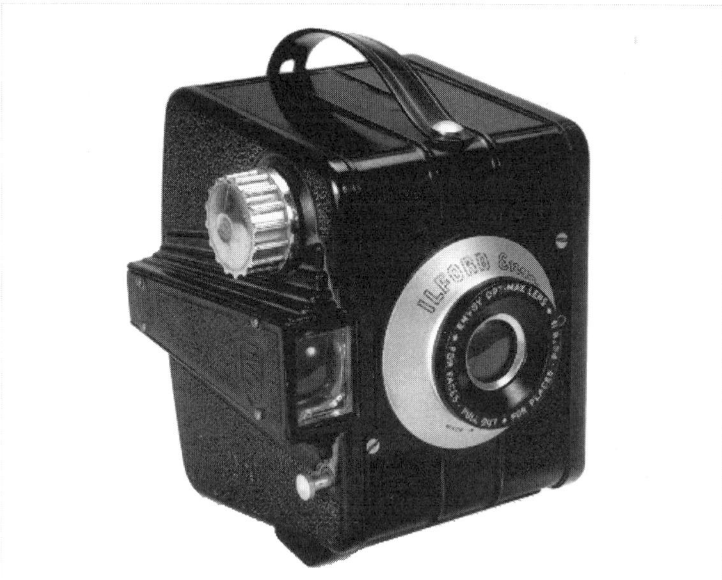

This model underwent one more face-lift for the model 3. Whilst the early models had two plastic slots on each side of the top plate for the use of a neck strap, this proved to be a weak point in the construction. To remedy this, a plastic handle was fitted to the side of the camera, furthermore the inscriptions and nameplate were rotated 90° so that they appeared under the handle when the camera was carried in this way, and two 'feet' were fitted to the side so that the camera could stand up.

Additionally, both the Model 1 and 2 had a 2-pin flash connector. This was replaced on the Model 3 with a small co-axial connector. The company at last falling into line with the standard adopted by most if not all other manufacturers. The camera was sold for £2. 3s. 0d.

The Ilford Envoy was available as an Ilford Gift Outfit No. 1, comprising camera, case and one Selochrome film for £2-14s-2d, or as Gift Outfit No 2 comprising camera, case and one Selochrome film plus flashgun and four bulbs for £3-19s-0d.

Apart from the time when this camera was in production it had little 'claim to fame'. In the late seventies however, it appeared again, not as a production camera but as a 'prop' in an advertisement.

Canadian Club ran an advert in magazines saying, "Its holidays with a difference for Cindy - CANADIAN CLUB - THE UNCOMMON SPIRIT". Next to the girl (presumably Cindy) in the advert was an Ilford Envoy Box camera. I of course assume that they chose this camera to illustrate the idea of something 'good, old fashioned and reliable'.

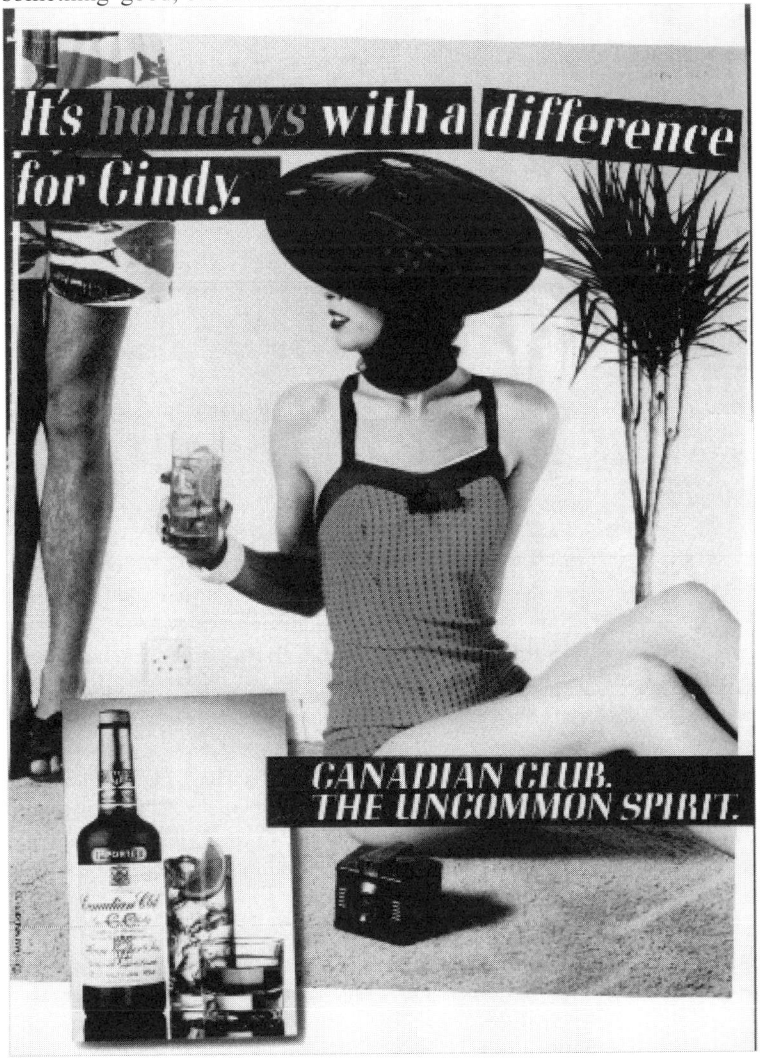

Envoy Wide Angle - Agilox - 1950

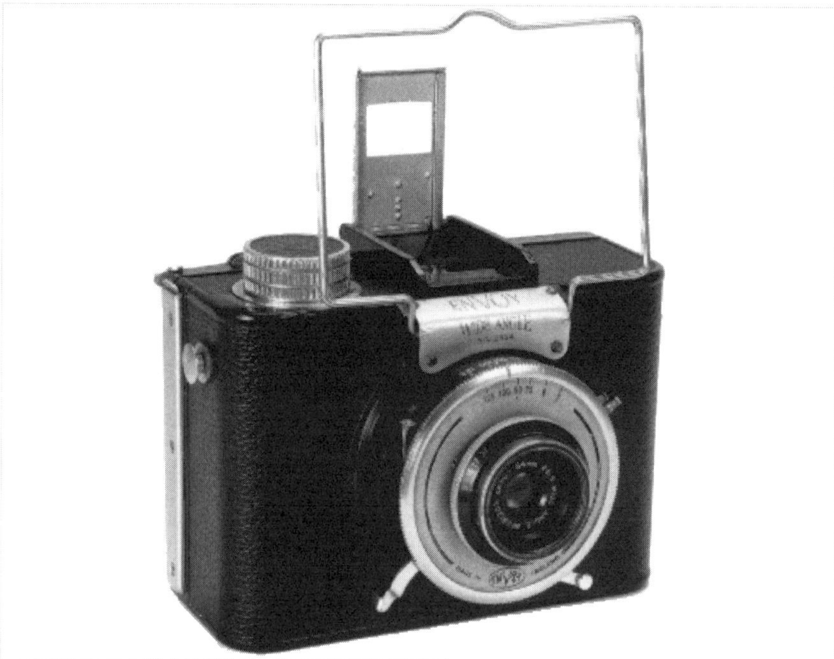

The Envoy Wide Angle camera was not strictly an Ilford camera but one of several Envoy cameras, which Ilford marketed.

It was made by Photo Developments Limited, a company run by one Norman Mousley. He was an enterprising man who ran a chemist shop and after the war he realised that if you could make anything you could sell it. England was hungry for so many goods after the war that any enterprising individual could build up a very good business. To manufacture the camera many tools were hand made by Mousely himself with the same care that was applied to the camera construction.

It was predominately used by Fire Brigades and Police Departments to record wide-angle shots at the scene of incidents. The camera was so good for this type of work that today (1983) the Bedford and Luton Police departments still use their Envoy cameras as there is nothing now on the market with this type of lens giving distortion free pictures.

The camera took flat film in single metal holders or roll films with a special adapter, which slipped onto the body.

The viewfinder was a wire frame type with parallax adjustment on the rear sight.

The lens was a bloomed f/6.3 Taylor-Hobson of 6.4 cm. focal length, of four-element construction, with an acceptance angle of 82 degrees. Focusing and depth of field was controlled by stopping down as follows:-

f/11 - 10 feet to 60 feet f/16 6 feet to 400 feet, f/22 - 4 feet to infinity f/32 30cm to infinity.

The camera was available with at least four shutters; Agilox, Epsilon, Prontor and Synchro - Compur.
Four speed shutter, synchronised at 1/25th and 1/50 sec.
Eight speed shutter, synchronised at 1/25th and 1/50 sec.
Compur X-M shutter, fully synchronised.

The original model was marketed with just the 4 and the 8 speed shutters and sold for £33 4s. 9d and £36 14s. 9d. This is recorded in the Ilford Photographic Materials, General Catalogue of 1952.

After 1952 and before 1955 they started offering the Synchro-Compur shutter. The three models then sold for £36. 3s. 8d, £40. 0s. 8d and £48. 10s. 8d respectively. (These were later reduced to £32 12s. 4d, £36 2s. 4d. and £43 17s. 4d.

The camera was sold as an outfit in a brown leather case containing the camera, 6 flat film holders, roll film holder, hooded focusing back, cover sheath for roll films, flash connector, lens cap, supplementary lenses, lens hoods and other accessories including flash guns were also available.

One of the flashguns that was available was the Envoy Minor. When you ordered the flash you would have to specify the required flash connection; Compur, B.S.S or Ilford connection.

Envoy Wide Angle - Synchro-Compur

The following is a copy of the text from the handbook supplied with the camera. It makes interesting reading if only because of its honesty in the described limitations of the camera and suggested methods of use. The camera shown has the Synchro-Compur shutter.

ENVOY
WIDE ANGLE CAMERA

PHOTO DEVELOPMENTS LIMITED
Leonard Road – Handsworth – Birmingham 19 – England
Telephone: Northern 2237 – Telegrams: Envoy Birmingham

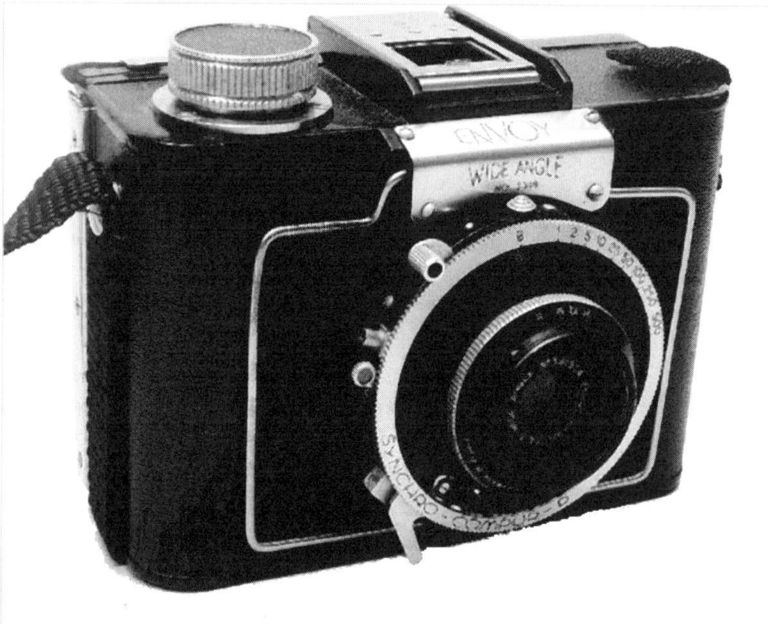

Image Courtesy of Gary Alexander.

This camera has been made to accommodate the long expressed wish of the professional photographer for something simple yet highly efficient. In order to ensure that the performance of the instrument to be as high as possible, the lens has been manufactured by Messrs. Taylor, Taylor, Hobson Limited.

Although it is said that there is limited scope for any wide angle camera, we feel that too few people have explored the field that wide angle can work for. The one bid disadvantage is, of course, restriction to smaller apertures.

Should one be in a position to overcome this difficulty however, by means of flash, or time exposure, the Wide Angle Camera offers numerous advantages over the normal camera. The "Envoy" Wide Angle Camera is fixed focus, this means quick action, and the user of a fixed focus camera can have his next plate in position whilst focussing camera is being set correctly.

The next important point about the "Envoy" Wide Angle Camera, is the depth of field. Having a precision short focal length lens of 64mm (2.4") it is possible by stopping down to f/32 to be in focus from 30 inches to infinity.

Police Departments, Fire prevention Sections, Builders Progress Departments, Industrial, Professional and Estate Agents are amongst the people who will find this camera indispensable. It is especially useful for records of window display and for any type of "shot" where space is limited. In the later case, the camera need only be hung on the wall by the rear sight (bring to the vertical by wedging camera base away from wall) and then expose in the normal manner.

A further interesting feature is the camera adaptability for plate or film (120 or 620)

For film, the cradle is inserted in camera body, paper backing wound on in the usual manner, then push the winding knob home, seeing that the key is correctly located in the spool slot. A counter back is supplied and it must be understood that this cannot be inserted or removed whilst the back (gate) is closed. This is because the rollers not only form part of the format but they also lie in the same plane as the plates.

For plates, remove cradle and use in the normal manner.

Accessories Lens Hood Nos. 1-2 & 4 supplementary
Lens mounted, Cable release

Features

Lens

The lens is a bloomed 64 mm Taylor, Taylor Hobson, of four element construction with eight air-glass surfaces. Angle of acceptance is 82 degrees. f/11 is the largest working aperture stopping down to f/32. It will be noticed that the lens opens up to f/6.5 for use with the ground glass screen when composing your picture. f/11 does not cover fully but f/16 will satisfy the majority. f/32 covers the full negative and has been found to give the highest performance at this stop or slightly lower at f/20.

Shutter

The shutter is of the four speed sectional type fitted with Synchro-flash points for use at 1/25th, 1/50th or open flash. Flash plug adaptor and lead are supplied. An eight speed shutter 1 sec to 1/25 fitted with Synchro-flash points, can be supplied at an extra cost.

Plates

Six plate holders are supplied, that take standard ½ x 21/2 size. Remove cradle when using plates.

Films

Eight on 120/620. Insert counter back. With film already lead round cradle, insert same and then push winding knob home. See the winder key is correctly located in spool slot, then close gate and secure. DO NOT attempt to remove camera back whilst gate is closed, as it is not possible to do so without ripping the pressure plate off.

View Finder

This is the wire frame type, and the rear sight has parallax adjustments incorporated.

Focus

The focus is fixed on this camera eliminating a great deal of time and trouble when in confined spaces. Depth of focus will vary slightly with different cameras. Approximate figures:

f/11 10 ft. to 60 ft.
f/16 6 ft. to 400 ft.
f/22 4 ft. to infinity
f/32 30 in. to infinity

Camera Body

The camera body is of die-cast material. It is leather-covered, and the overall measurements are 41/4 x 33/4 x 21/2 in. weighing 17 ozs.

Case

A good quality strong leather case is supplied which holds all the equipment.

Setting Up

It is essential to have camera upright, failure to do this will give distortion in corners. Avoid camera shake at all costs, as the field of coverage at only a feet distance is extremely wide, and shake is accentuated on wide angle work more so than with a normal lens.

Synchronising

The firing cap on this shutter may be set for one of the three types, GEC/22. (2) P. Range. (3) Electronic.

Landscape work should be taken at 1/32 as infinity is greatest at this stop.

Remember that proximity to your subject will realise maximum strength from your flash.

Envoy Wide Angle - Epsilon

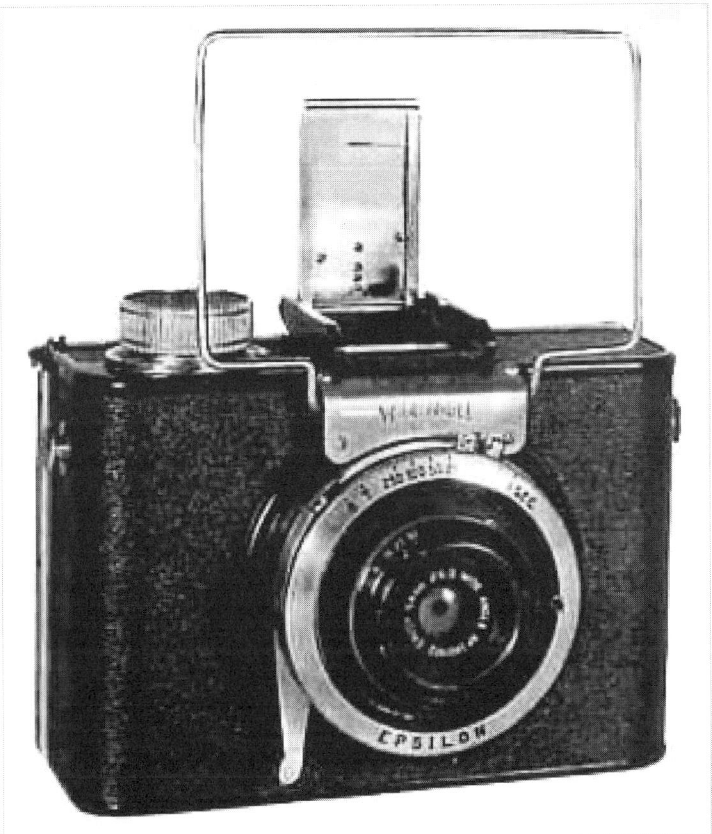

This Envoy Wide Angle shows the Epsilon shutter fitted.

In May 1960 the Ilford Photographic Materials, Professional Catalogue still listed the Envoy Wide Angle Camera Outfit, ten years after it first appeared. This, I believe, was the longest running camera, which Ilford marketed that remained unchanged throughout its life.

P.I.M. 4 x 5 in. Monorail - 1953

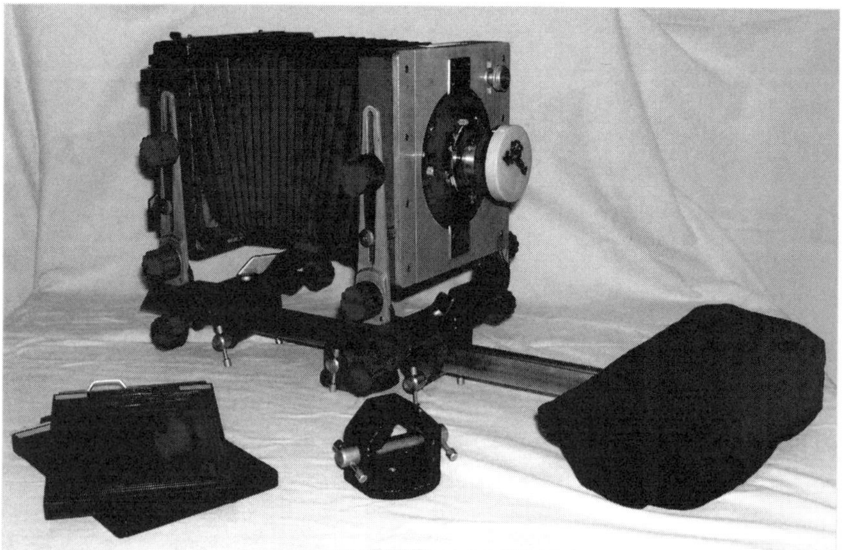

I am grateful to Doug McKee for this photograph and information about the camera.

This camera was marketed by Ilford under the maker's name. It was a general-purpose technical camera for commercial, industrial, medical and scientific use, made by P.I.M. Photographic Instrument Manufacturers.

The design of the PIM Monorail is attributed to a Mr. Wood. During the War he worked for MPP as their chief designer. Towards the end of the war he was asked to design some products for civilian use. He designed the Tripod 1, the 6x6 enlarger and slide and filmstrip printers. By the 1950's he had designed some cameras but was not happy with the direction that the company was going, presumably with the Microcord project. The result was that Mr. Wood and Mr. Cook, the firm's Works Manager, left MPP and set up P.I.M - Photographic Instrument Makers. This company like MPP was also in Kingston-on-Thames. This was Mr. Wood's last camera design as he died soon after its launch.

The PIM Monorail appeared as a new item in the British Journal Almanac of 1954 p221-222 so was probably launched in 1953. It sold for £53.

The camera was advertised in 1954, 1955 and 1956 but then seems to disappear. There was competition for this market coming from Criterion Trixale (£68) and DeVere (£60) and others from aboard; Sinar, Linhof SuperTechna and Plaubel Peco.

During this short production time some variations have been observed. Black and then shiny lens panels, metal side knobs and plastic ones. Different tripod bosses with and without a locking tommy bar.

MPP presumably did not react favourably to their designer and works manager leaving and creating this camera. They responded with their own design albeit some 5 to 10 years later using a much more sophisticated design with far more machining, better finish and specialized parts. Some have considered it an over engineered over reaction to the PIM.

The PIM did have a few technical and operational shortcomings but was a light weight and relatively easy to use monorail and remained a good choice for tabletop and indoor work.

It was made of aluminium alloy with a lens panel and control knobs in Bakelite. The square leather bellows permitted a maximum extension of 19 inches. The front and back carriages had every movement necessary for technical photography, moving smoothly on a rigid, triangular section monorail. The monorail was attached to a tripod head by a sliding bracket, which could be locked in any position on the rail.

When focusing, the front and back carriages moved on the rail and could be focused independently. A half a turn on the locking level would lock the carriage rigidly in the required position on the monorail.

The camera was offered with a choice of lenses from Dallmeyer, Ross, Taylor-Thompson-Hobson or Wray with or without shutters.
It sold for £53. 0s. 0d net with Dark slides at £2. 10s. 0d.

Watson Premier Half-plate Camera

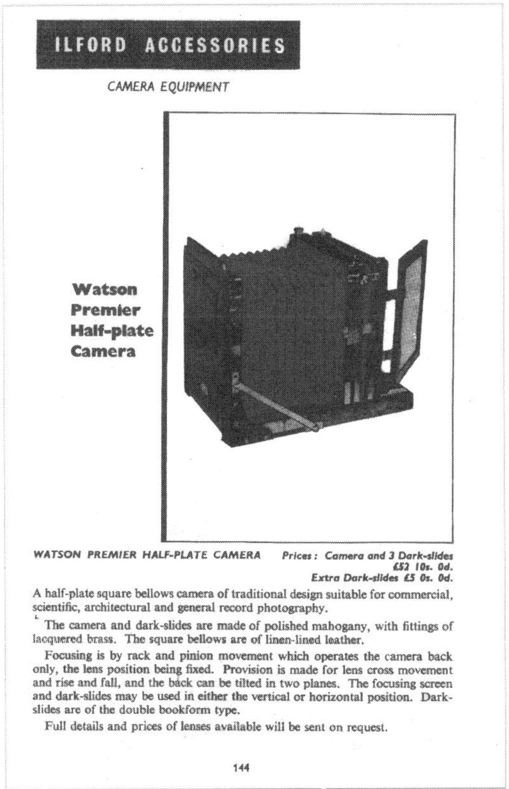
ILFORD ACCESSORIES

CAMERA EQUIPMENT

Watson Premier Half-plate Camera

WATSON PREMIER HALF-PLATE CAMERA — *Prices: Camera and 3 Dark-slides £52 10s. 0d. Extra Dark-slides £5 0s. 0d.*

A half-plate square bellows camera of traditional design suitable for commercial, scientific, architectural and general record photography.

The camera and dark-slides are made of polished mahogany, with fittings of lacquered brass. The square bellows are of linen-lined leather.

Focusing is by rack and pinion movement which operates the camera back only, the lens position being fixed. Provision is made for lens cross movement and rise and fall, and the back can be tilted in two planes. The focusing screen and dark-slides may be used in either the vertical or horizontal position. Dark-slides are of the double bookform type.

Full details and prices of lenses available will be sent on request.

144

The 1953 Ilford Photographic Materials, General Catalogue presented the Ilford Envoy Box camera, the Advocate Camera Series 2, the Envoy Wide Angle Camera Outfits, the 4 x 5 Monorail camera and the Watson Premier Half-plate camera. This was made of polished mahogany and lacquered brass. Interesting to note that these cameras were listed under, 'Ilford Accessories'.

PHASE 3 (1957-1963)

By this stage Ilford could no longer avoid the fact that German cameras were in the ascendancy and outclassed them in price, performance and popular appeal, and so James Mitchell started to look for an uncommitted German manufacturer with whom Ilford could work.

Most West German makers had already established agencies but not the Dacora company of Reutlingen in Wurtenberg.

Dacora had a presence in the U.K. with a range of cameras being stocked throughout the country. The range they produced at the time of Ilford's initial contact with them were the Dacora Standard, I, Ia, II, IIa and IIb. These cameras used Subita 5.6 and Ennar 4.5 and 3.5 coated lenses and the Vario, Pronto, Prontor S and Prontor SV shutters. All were synchronised for electronic flash at all speeds and flash bulbs at 1/25th. Their retail price was between £10 1s. 2d for the Standard and £21 3s. 4d. for the IIb which was a high price at the time.

The name Dacora came from DAnglemaier COmpany Reutlingen. The company had been started by Bernhard Dangelmaier in an attic after the end of the war. He personally made smuggling trips over the mountains to Switzerland and back, bringing with him springs, ball bearings, optical glass and whatever he could cram into his rucksack - real German enterprise.

My father was instrumental in setting up the Ilford/Dacora relationship. He made many visits to their factory and became a close personal friend of Heir Dangelmaier.

Dacora products were not of the highest quality in comparison with say Zeiss lkon but were well styled and well made catering for the middle market. He was willing to enter into collaboration with Ilford and an agreement was signed.

The Sportsman camera was born in late 1952/53 although it may not have come into full production until 1957. (A brief history of the Dacora company is shown on page 254)

The original Sportsman was based initially on the Dacora Dignette.

From an initial order of 1000 Sportsman cameras within a few years the orders were by the 10,000 and Ilford's yearly programme was for some 40-50,000 cameras.

The cameras were manufactured in West Germany and then shipped to Ilford for inspection and packaging. Cameras rejected on first inspection were repaired by one or more of Dangelmaier's employees, working in Ilford's warehouse. 100% inspection was carried out. It was anticipated that their lenses would give rise to a fairly high rejection rate and elaborate test methods were prepared in advance. This proved unnecessary which was an eye opener.

Dacora lenses had 3 elements, each element being separate and not cemented or edged up together optically. Two of the elements were air spaced by washers of which a variety of thicknesses were available. The lens elements had automatically been optically centred and edged so that the optical axis was maintained in the assembly tubes. The third lens was in a helical mount, which controlled the focusing of the assembly.

The choice of the 3rd element against the assembly of the other 2 ensured that the focal length could be kept within limits due to the variation of focal lengths of all the elements made. And so Dacora lenses gave a nearly equal performance to that of the Advocate for all practical purposes.

The success of the original model led to it's development and the introduction of models with more sophisticated shutters, rangefinders and the like and this in time led on to light meter exposure controls and then automatic exposure.

Ilford at one time held over 50% of the UK 35 mm market with Sportsman cameras and there was an assumption by the pro-camera lobby, within the company, that this had helped them to capture their preponderant share of the 35 mm film market. The anti-camera lobby held that this relationship was quite casual. Considering that the cost price of the original Sportsman in Germany was less than £3 (i.e. less than the cost in the UK of the Advocate lens alone!) and the purchase tax, which was then levied, these cameras represented very good value to the amateur photographer. The scale of sale was such that in one year it greatly exceeded the value of sales from the plate factory and kept Ilford's turnover up to an acceptable level when it had been threatened by the failure of a colour film project.

This phase also saw the introduction of 127 and 120 metal-bodied roll film cameras also made by Dacora under the name Sporti.

Kennedy Instruments by now had no standard Advocate production and were given leave to separately market the KI Monobar, which they had developed. The camera was also marketed under the Ilford name.

During this phase Ilford found that it did not have roll film sales commensurate with that of 35 mm and the total market in this other area exceeded the 35 mm market. The Sporti and Sporti 6 did not offer competition, mainly against Kodak, by reason of price and because of this it was determined to offer cheaper plastic based roll film cameras.

Dangelmaier produced the Sporti 4 to Ilford's requirements and against some opposition from him, Ilford took up with the firm of AGI (Aeronautical and General Instruments).

At the beginning of the war AGI made the ARL camera for the armed forces, which was based on the Reflex Korelle. They also had expertise in the field of aerial reconnaissance cameras. (They had in fact designed the camera for use in the abandoned TSR2 reconnaissance aircraft).

In 1946 AGI set up Agilux Ltd as a subsidiary company to manufacture cameras. The first camera was the Agiflex I, which was based on the ARL.

The Sprite 127 was the first camera made by Agilux to be marketed by Ilford. It was followed by the Pixie (127) and the Imp (127).

In this period Ilford had informal contact with Kodak who offered to supply their roll film cameras under the Ilford logo but Ilford decided not to proceed. My guess is that Kodak wished to un-load them with cameras soon to be outdated by their Instamatic system.

In 1951 a new company, Ilford Inc., was formed in the U.S.A. and ICI, who were interested in using its colour dyes in colour photography, made an offer for 35% of the issued share capital in Ilford. With ICI's support, a new colour negative film, "Ilfocolour", was introduced in 1960, which was very successful. A new colour slide film, "Ilfochrome", was launched in 1962.

Ilford moved into their new headquarters at Basildon in January 1960 with the intention of moving all of their smaller scattered sites onto a single site, near to Brentwood. My father, along with Jim Edwards, moved the Amateur Products division from their premises at Leyton and Ilford in the initial moves.

Jim Edwards remembers the day well. Having loaded up several wagons with all their belongings, he and others swept out the factory, leaving it as clean as a factory could be. They loaded the last items onto the lorry but could not get the dustbin and broom in, as it was completely full up. These items were the only items left behind, the doors were locked and on the Monday the lorries were unloaded at the new factory at Basildon.

Here they stayed until January 1970 when the Amateur Products division was finally closed down. The Ilford site (at Ilford) was eventually closed down in 1973 after 97 years occupation.

In May 1960 the Ilford Photographic Materials, Professional Catalogue listed the Sportsman Vario, Pronto, Prontor, Prontor SVS and Rangefinder with Pronto shutters. Additionally the Envoy Wide Angle Camera Outfit was still being marketed, ten years after it first appeared.

The Ilford Sportsman and Sportsmaster

Ilford Sportsman - (1953/7 – 1967+)

The Sportsman camera was the 'Ford Cortina' of the Company. It's life spanned more than ten years and, like the car, underwent many face-lifts and refinements, whilst retaining its basic design principles. Its objectives were certainly fulfilled; well made, long lasting, high quality and easily adaptable.

The first Sportsman was, like the rest of the series, manufactured by the Dacora Company in West Germany and based initially on the Dacora Dignette.

Once the partnership between Dacora and Ilford was established the design of cameras was undertaken jointly with Ilford taking the leading role. In most cases exactly the same cameras were marketed my Dacora but with their name in the logo and identification.

The original Sportsman prototype was created probably in 1953 but was not fully marketed until 1957. It continued in production up until 1970, when the Amateur Products division in the U.K. was closed down.

The range underwent continual development incorporating many technical achievements, which enhanced the camera in both appearance and technical ability. After the Amateur Products division was closed down, Sportsman cameras continued to be produced but were commissioned by CIBA-Ilford either from CIBA headquarters in Switzerland or from Ilford-France. However this statement is based on conjecture without any firm proof.

The Sportsman brand name was obviously a valuable asset in marketing terms and used on some cameras which were dissimilar and not from the standard 35mm. stable. Notably a range of previously named, ‘Sportina Rapid’ cameras were re-labelled and re-marketed as ‘Sportsman Rapid’. Additionally, Ilford at some time marketed a slide projector with the Sportsman name as shown below. This had the name, P36 in red on the side of the case and made in Italy on the projector itself.

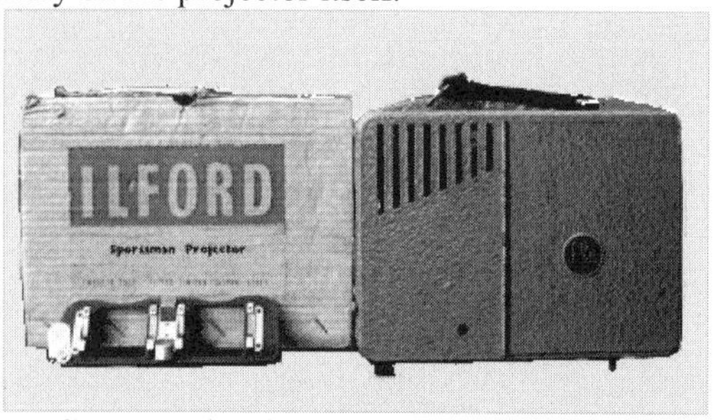

Cameras that bore the name Sportsman progressed and evolved through a variety of styles as detailed in the following summaries.

Viewfinder Changes

Sportsman cameras started with a very basic optical viewfinder with a small round eye aperture and a small square front window.

The second style enlarged both apertures and had a square eyepiece. This type I have called the Clearview.

The third transformation came when the Zeiss patents for the parallax viewfinder ran out and Ilford used the brightline principle with a gold image enhancement.

The next had a viewfinder, which was similar, but had a blue mirrored viewing enhancement. Another variation had the blue-mirrored viewfinder on the right of the camera body instead of the central location held for many years.

Logo Changes

The original Sportsman had two logo plates. Ilford was fitted to the lower left of the camera with Sportsman fitted to the upper right. These were then replaced by embossed wording to the top plate. After this and for a much longer time the front of the camera had a plastic trim with Ilford Sportsman in the upper right box. Then the top plates had a recessed area on the upper left into which was fitted a nameplate. Finally a very small logo strip with black writing on a silver background was placed above the light meter collector.

Shutter Changes

The shutters for the Sportsman progressed, with several types being available to the public at the same time. Most were made by AGC - Alfred Gauthier, Calmbach.

The Gauthier company was founded in 1902 and started building shutters from 1904. Carl Zeiss took over the company in 1932. In 1957 over 3,000 workers produced up to 10,000 shutters daily.

Ilford's use of Gauthier shutters went hand in hand with Gauthier releasing new models. When one model stopped being produced Ilford adopted the next one available.

Shutter mechanisms were initially mechanical devices as shown in this picture of a (Prontor-SVS):

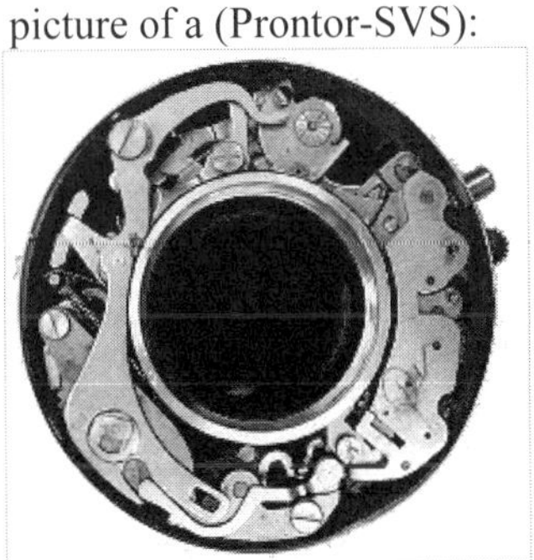

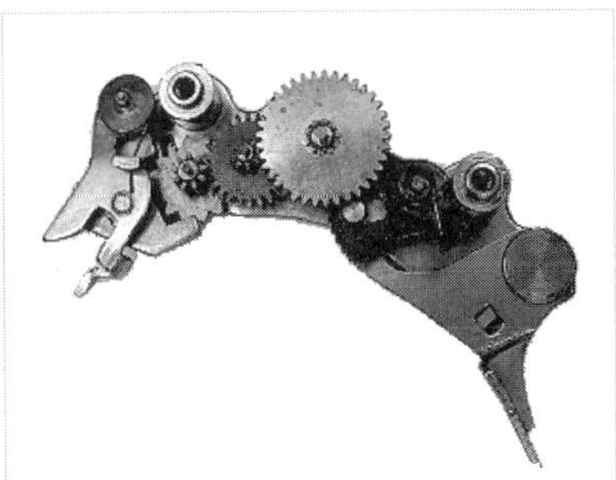

Mechanical shutters are made of many parts, screws and springs together with gear trains.

Most AGC shutters are designed to run dry with little or no lubrication. Over long periods of time the components will not function correctly and need to be stripped down and carefully cleaned. Not a job to be undertaken lightly.

Electronic shutters were created around 1965 and had fewer and smaller mechanical components as shown in the Prontor 300:

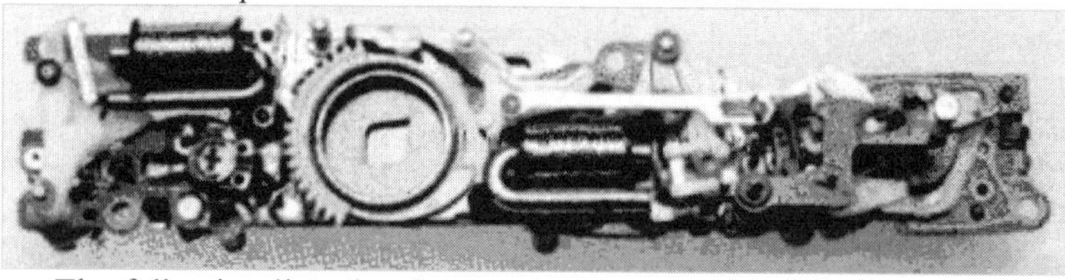

The following lists the shutters that were used in Ilford cameras constructed by Dacora. Some are mechanically the same but have a different logo.

Pronto	Pronto Lux	Prontor
Prontor 125	Prontor 250	Prontor 250 LK
Prontor 250 S	Prontor 300	Prontor 300 Electronic
Prontor 300 L	Prontor 300 L-E	Prontor 300 LK
Prontor 300 S	Prontor 300 S-E	Prontor 500 LK
Prontor 500 S-E	Prontor LK	Prontor SVS (300 and 500)
Prontor-Lux	Prontor-Matic	Vario
X 300		

Lens Changes

The lenses provided were initially Dacora Dignar 45mm f/2.8. The earlier models had a 45mm f/3.5 lens. Later f/2.8 was the standard. In addition the following lenses were used.

Color Dignar	Color Subitar
Rodenstock Color Isconar	Rodenstock Color Trinon-Lanthan
Rodenstock Yearex	Steinheil Cassar

Exposure Meters

Basic models did not have an exposure meter. In these days most photographers would be familiar with and carry a light meter.

The first innovation was the fitting of Bertram selenium exposure meters, which were not coupled to the shutter. The meter had a light collector on the front of the camera and the control dial on the top plate. You would set the film speed on the inner part of a dial and then the light reading would be shown by a needle. Moving the outer part of the dial would move a red pointer which, when it was on top of the meter needle would then show the shutter speed settings against the apertures. You then manually set the required aperture and speed.

The Sportsman Auto series were semi-automatic. The front of the camera still had the light collector but the dials that were previously used were now removed with just the meter needle and red pointer showing through a slot in the top plate.

The light meter would control the meter needle but the shutter speed and aperture controls would move the red pointer. Whatever combination of speed or aperture you set would alter the red pointer. When they coincided the exposure was set.

Fully automatic exposure was provided in the Sportsmaster and Sportsmaster Manumatic range. Here the camera could be set to fully automatic or to manual. The viewfinder provided an indication of the aperture being used via a very difficult to read area in the viewfinder.

The Electric Sportsman cameras had CdS exposure meters. These had the exposure needle visible within the viewfinder. You were required to adjust the exposure settings until the needle was displayed midway between a + (over exposed) and – (under exposed) marker.

Colouring

Most Sportsman cameras had black leatherette applied to the bodies. Some had grey leatherette. Most of these grey bodies were sold outside of the U.K. I have been told that in some countries most of the cameras sold outside the cities were grey ones while within cities buyers preferred the black. Very few if any grey coverings were sold in the U.K. The Ferrania company had developed the IBIS camera in around 1948. This was a very simple camera but had a grey covering. It sold very well in Europe. Its good sales were put down largely to the modern colour, which was more acceptable to progressive European customers. The idea was therefore copied to a certain level of success. (Some Dacora variants of the Sportsman range were sold with green leatherette covering.)

Shutter Release

For many years the shutter release was a round button that you pressed in towards the body of the camera. The button also incorporated threading for a shutter release cable. In later years these were replaced by a black and silver plastic slide that you pressed down. The cable release thread was now underneath the button.

Film Rewind Changes

The rewind mechanism underwent several changes. Some have solid metal cranks, others had cranks that fold back flush into the top and others had simple circular plastic rewind knobs.

Rear Cover Opening Changes

The catch to open the back was redesigned several times.

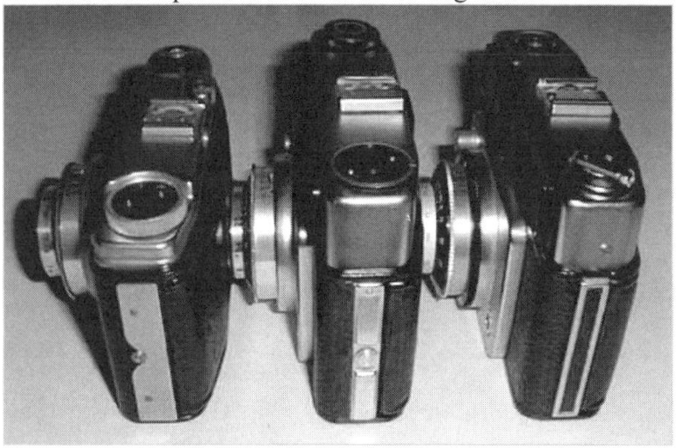

Initially it had a very awkward press-button (left hand picture) this was replaced by an improved sliding button catch (shown in the centre).

By 1963 the back release had become a rather more conventional arrangement, involving using the thumbnail to lift up the latch at the top of the side release. Finally the door release was in the shoulder of the top plate as shown in this example of a Sportsman 300 LK:

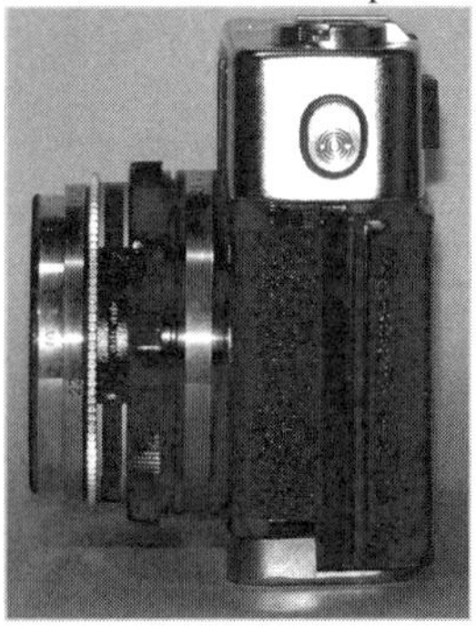

Top Plate Changes

With each change in viewfinder the top plate housing was re-styled. From a slim top with a surface mounted film advance lever and metal rewind knob to a deeper top with recessed film advance lever and with more clearly marked, sometimes plastic, film counter and rewind knobs.

All the models were made with pressed and chromium plated brass top plates and lens/shutter mounting plates.

Dacora took pride in this fact as against similar parts on the main competition at the time - the Agfa Silette, which was made of aluminium or of die-castings sprayed aluminium.

The shutter release was for most models on the top left of the front plate with the flash socket on the bottom right.

The bottom plate held the tripod bush and the rewind release button. Later models had the exposure counter located on the bottom plate as well.

These styles can be identified by the top part of the camera as shown in this montage:

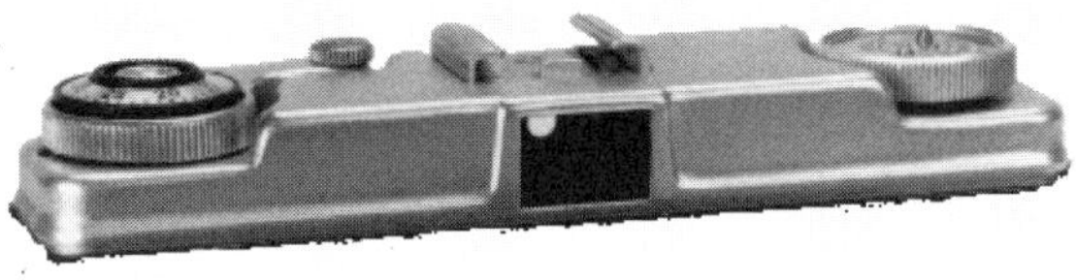

Style 1
1957

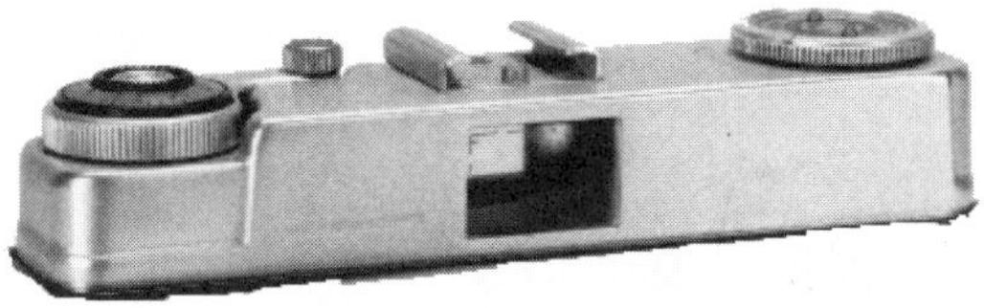

Style 2

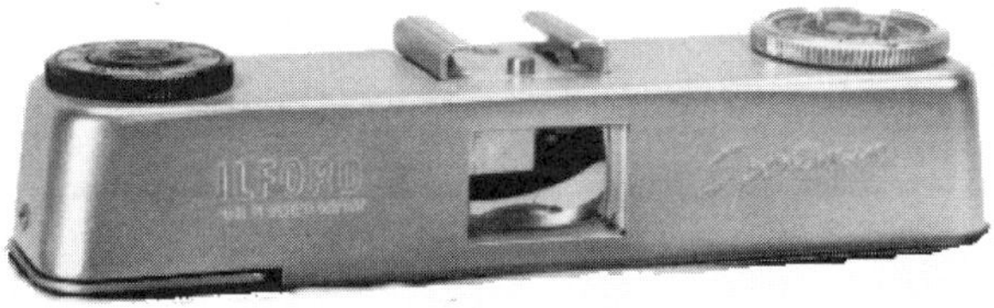

Style 3

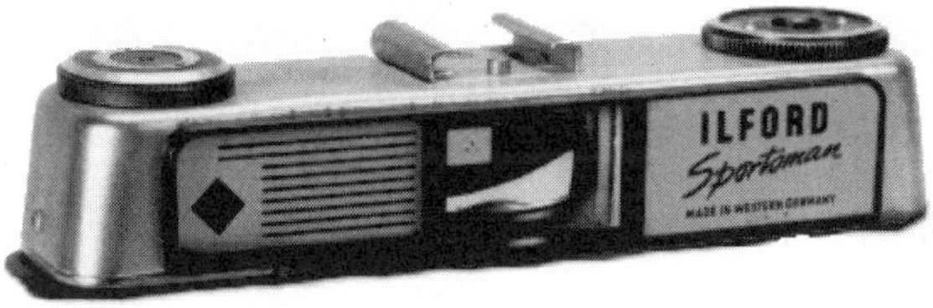

Style 4
1960

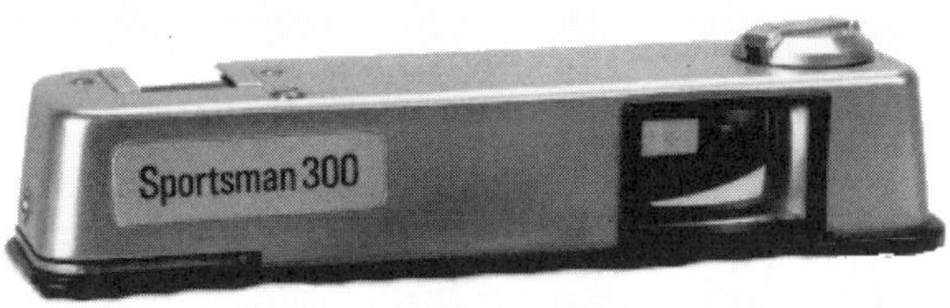

Style 5
1967

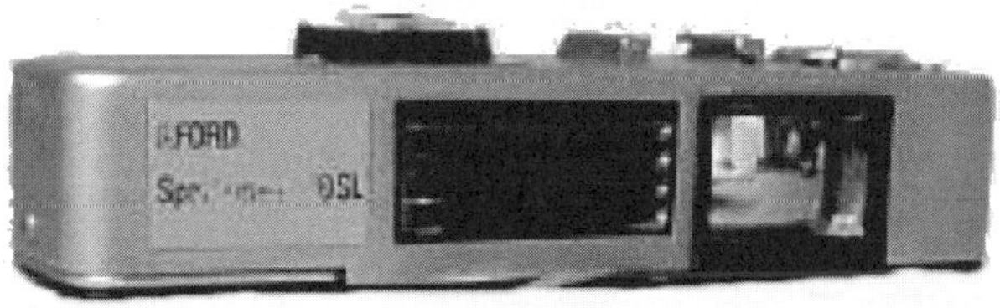

Style 6

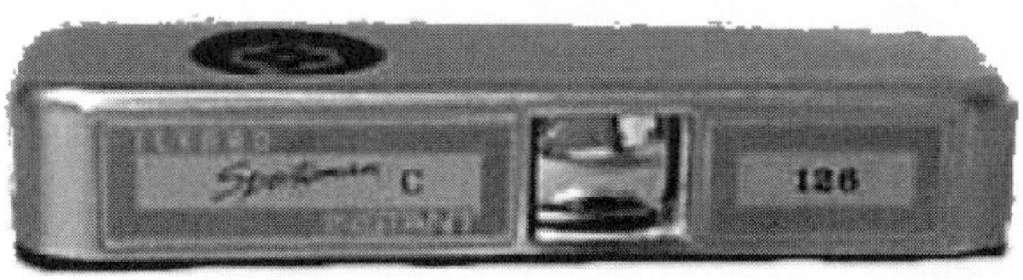

Style 7

Film Speed Reminders and Light Meter dials

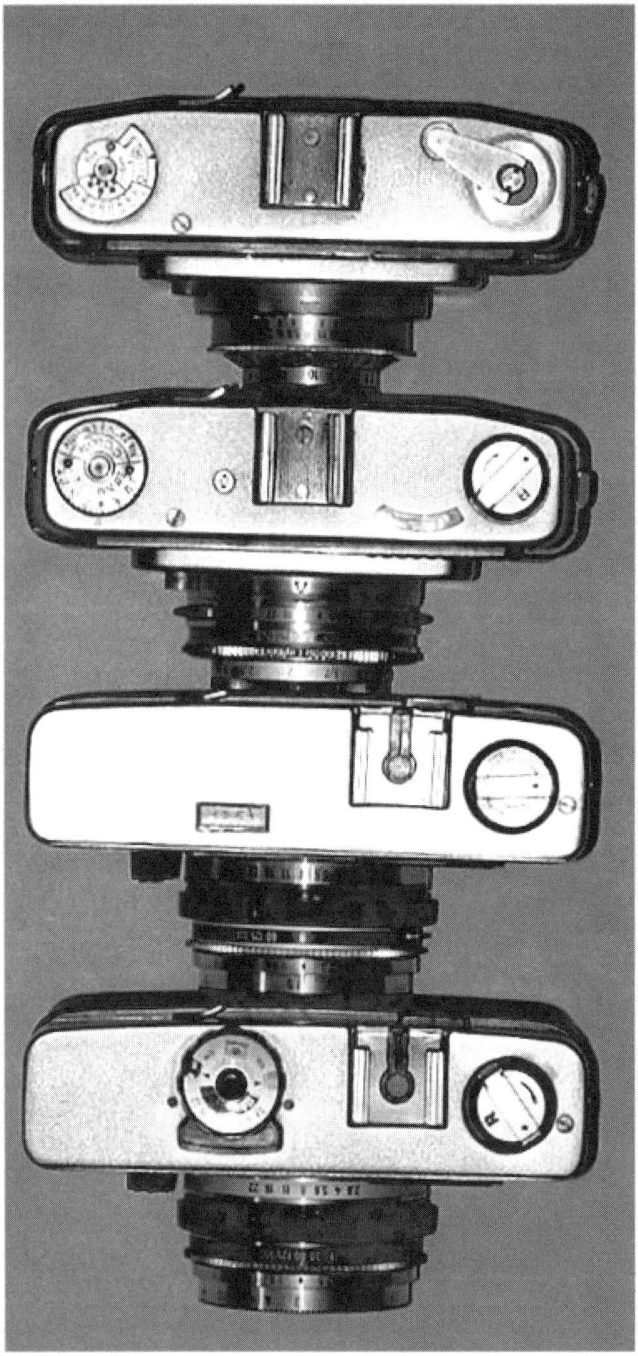

Quadrant film speed reminder.
Large film rewind crank.
(Sportsman Vario)

Round flush film speed reminder.
Inset rewind crank.
Meter needle seen through curved window.
(Sportsman Auto RF 500 LK)

Meter needle seen through rectangular window.
Inset rewind crank.
(Sportsman 300 LK)

Meter needle seen through shaped window.
Inset rewind crank.
(Sportsman 300 L)

Flash Shoes

All Sportsman cameras had a standard flash shoe up until 1967 when they were given hot shoe fittings. Most of the shutters had “X” type synchronisation so that either electronic flash units or expendable flashbulbs could be used. Electronic flash units could be used at any shutter speed although a speed of 1/500 second was recommended and the expendable flashbulbs at a shutter speed of 1/25 or 1/30 second. Earlier models had a coaxial flash contact on the lens mount panel. Finally some cameras had an internal power supply and socket to accept flashcubes. A few models took AG flash bulbs, which were placed directly into the top plate.

Flash Accessories

The early models had a range of flash units available including Ilford’s Sportslite and Ilfolux amongst others. As far as I am aware only the Sportsman F could take AG flash bulbs directly on the camera (Of course other flash guns which took the AG bulb could be used) See Page 141. When the Flashcube was created, Ilford cameras were changed to take the new fitting. Some models even had both a Flashcube and a flash shoe fitted. See Page 179.

Rangefinders

Some of the models had a rangefinder option, which employed a parallax mirror rangefinder. Two overlapping images are seen in the viewfinder. By rotating the focussing ring the two images are brought into coincidence and the camera is then focussed.

Accessories

Dangelmaier made a range of flashguns for Ilford some of which had considerable success.

Other accessories included a high quality leather case, lens hood, supplementary lens, colour filters, cable release and lens cap.

(€)

Some of the cameras listed have (€) in the title. These were either never marketed in the U.K. only being found in Europe or appeared in Holland and Europe some time after any U.K. distribution.

Dates

I should perhaps at this stage make a comment about any dates that I have used.

Dates are always difficult to apply retrospectively. A camera may have been first marketed in the U.K. and then distributed worldwide some years later. I know that Ilford used to test market the introduction of a new camera model to a discrete local area (see page 191). Feedback obtained from retailers might influence minor modifications or dictate a particular marketing 'strategy'. Whenever dates are quoted there will always be someone who believes that are either too early or too late. I can only document that which I am aware of and leave any comment to you, the reader.

Some dates can be deduced from the supporting documentation, marketing leaflets and instruction manuals. Luckily all Ilford instruction manuals (and most other publications will have a document identifier. This is often found on the back page. It takes the form of identifier/date/suffix.
Here are some examples:

IAC/C49/LH	IAC – Ilford, Advocate, Camera
	C49 - March 1949 A=January, B=February, etc
	LH - ?
ICC/G49/PLH	ICC – Ilford, Craftsman, Camera
	G49 – July, 1949
	PLH - ?
AC2/E53/S	AC2 - Advocate, Camera, Series 2
	May 1953
	S - ?
SCVPR/L60/E	SCVPR - Sportsman, Camera, Vario, Pronto, Rangefinder
	L = December, 1960
	E ?

Some manuals will have just the date coding:

A67/B	January, 1967	(On a Sportsman Electric manual)
	B - ?	
L66	December, 1966	(On a Monarch manual)

However, like most 'standards' there are examples where such deduction is not possible, as the standard has not been adhered to. So far I have not been able to 'crack' the code for the suffix shown in the above examples.

Ilford Sportsman Vario (Style 1) Advert from 1958

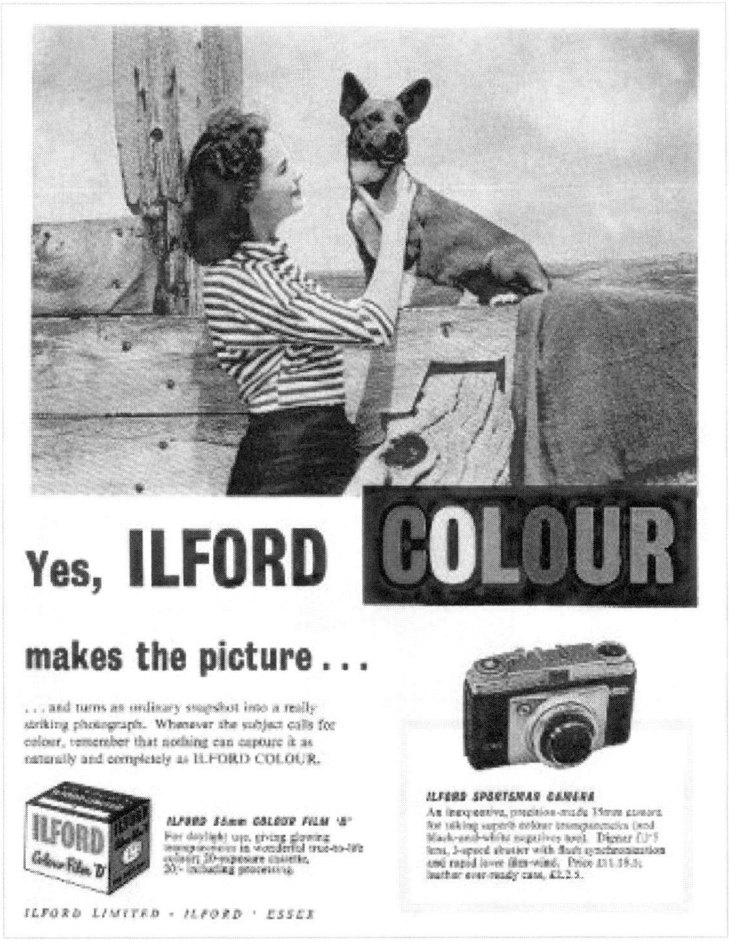

Ilford Sportsman Vario - 1st. Style

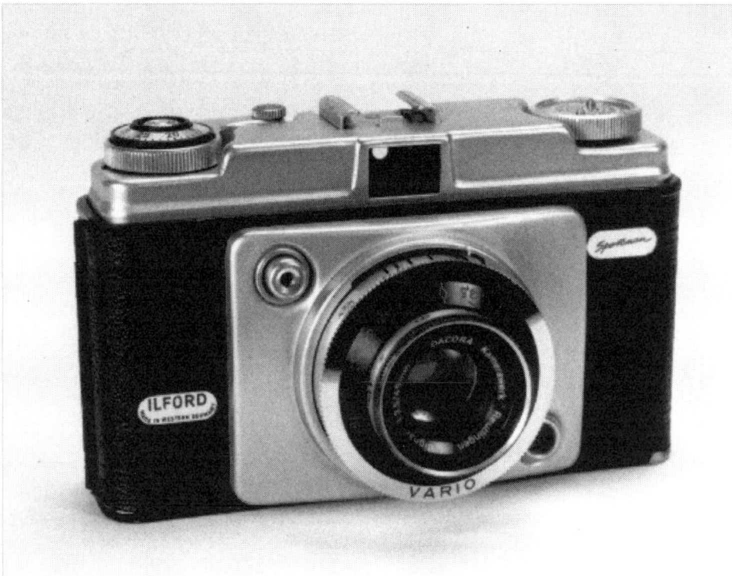

The Sportsman Vario was the basic model and was obviously identified by its Vario shutter providing speeds of B, 25, 50 and 200. It always had a three element coated Dacora Kamerawerk Dignar lens either as a 45mm f/3.5 or a 45mm f/2.8.

The shutter and exposure counting were interlocked with the film winding mechanism. Two of the versions had top plate wind on levers whilst the others had levers inset between the top plate and the body. The rewind knob, released by pressing a button on the bottom plate, carried a film reminder indicator. Minor variations included red lettering on the aperture ring instead of silver/white.

The Ilford logo was on lower front left and Sportsman on the upper right. This camera was based on the Dacora Dignette of the time. Thereafter, the Dacora Dignette range followed (rather than led) the Ilford versions of the cameras. Only on a few occasions did Dacora go their own way with a particular model. Such examples are noted in the text that follows.

Ilford Sportsman Vario (Style 2) Advert from 1959

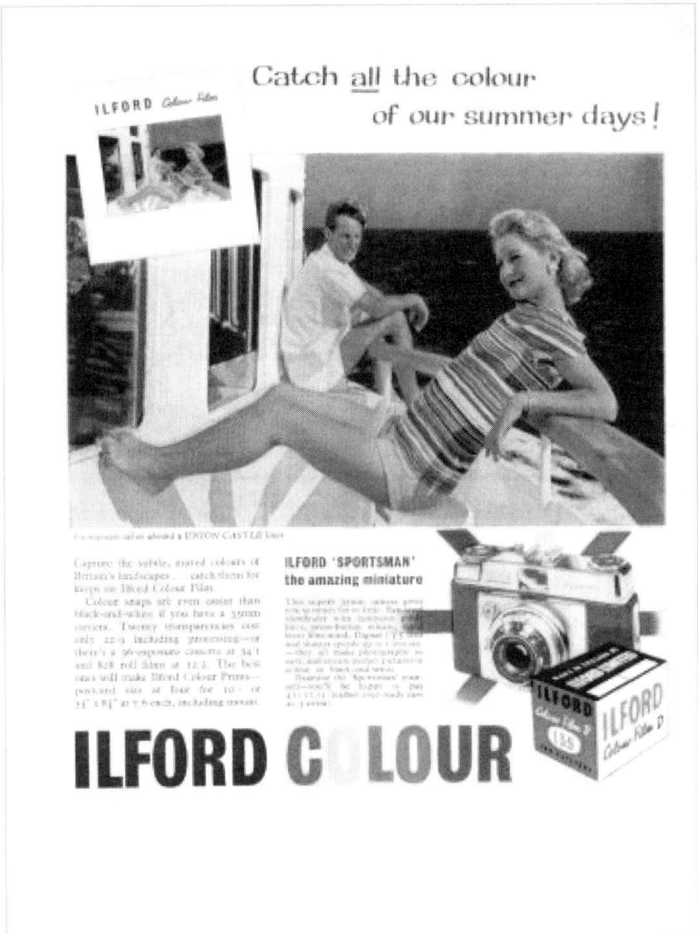

Ilford Sportsman Vario - 2nd. Style

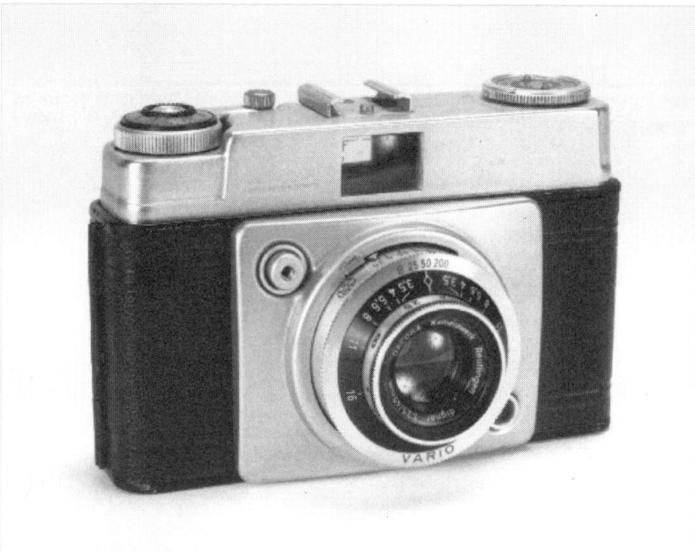

Black leatherette, Dacora Dignar 45mm lens, Vario shutter, metal rewind knob, speed reminder dial on top of film advance lever. Ilford and Sportsman logos embossed into the top plate.

Ilford Sportsman Pronto - 3rd. Style

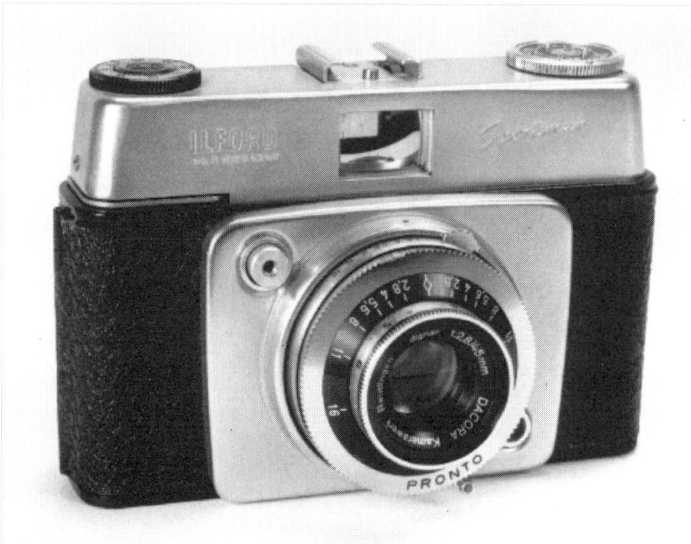

Black leatherette, Dacora Dignar 45mm lens, Pronto shutter, metal rewind knob, plastic film speed reminder dial, and self-timer.

Ilford Sportsman Vario - 4th. Style

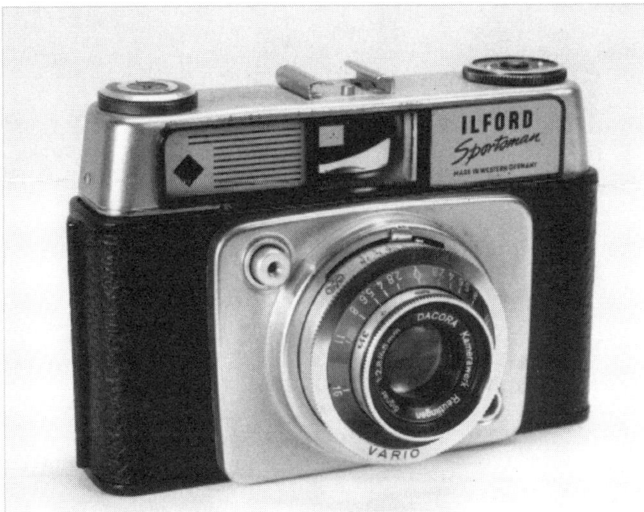

The diamond in the left (facing) segment was just a transfer to match stylistically the active window on the Rangefinder models. If the segment has a black square, it indicates that it is a Rangefinder variant as shown below.
Ilford and Sportsman logos in upper right plastic trim.

Ilford Sportsman Vario Rangefinder

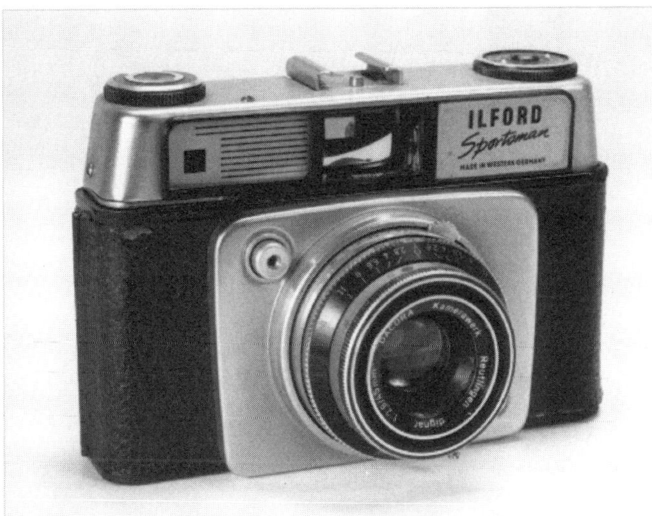

Black leatherette, Dacora Dignar 45mm lens, Vario shutter, plastic rewind knob, plastic film speed reminder dial, and self-timer.

Ilford Sportsman Vario Rangefinder (€)

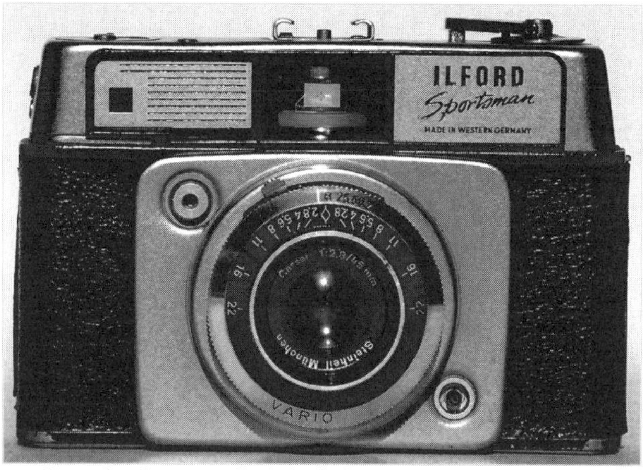

Grey leatherette, Steinheil Cassar 45mm lens, Vario shutter, Large rewind crank, and Quadrant film speed reminder dial.

Ilford Sportsman Prontor-SVS

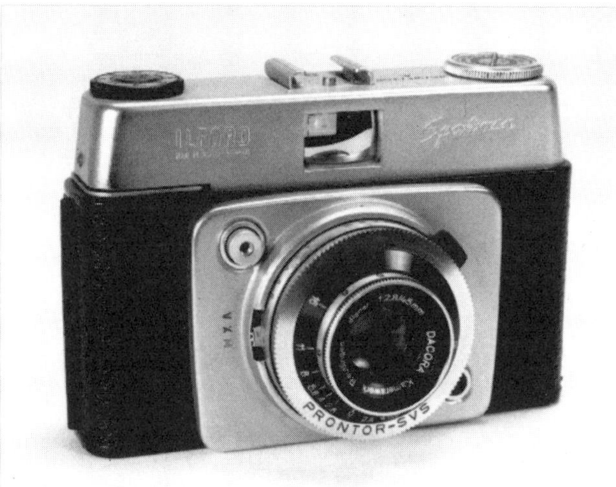

This example has the Prontor SVS shutter (B, 1/1, 1/2, 1/5, 1/15, 1/30,1/60, 1/125 and 1/300 sec.) with V X and M synchronisation (M for Flash bulbs firing just before the shutter opens to enable the bulb to reach optimum brightness, X for electronic flash firing when the shutter is fully open and V for Delayed firing.)

Black leatherette, Dacora Dignar 45mm lens, metal rewind knob, plastic film speed reminder dial.

The Prontor-SVS maximum shutter speed was up-rated from $1/300^{th}$ to $1/500^{th}$, sometime during or after 1956.

Ilford Sportsman Prontor 125

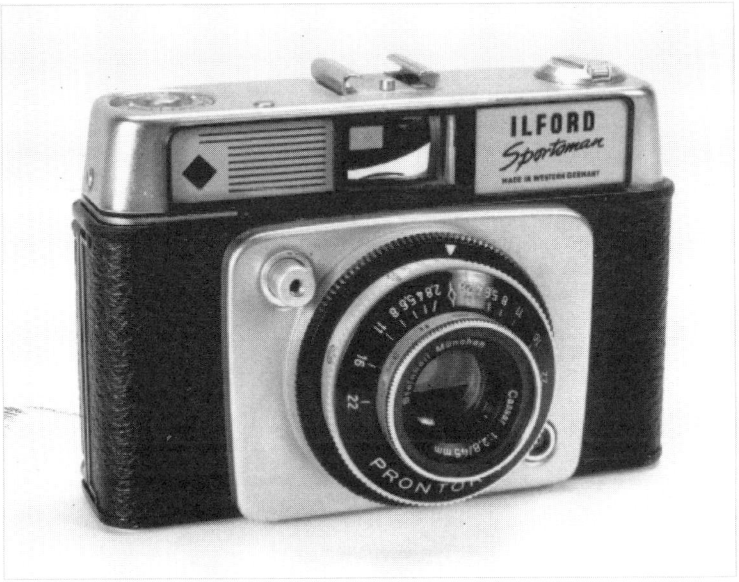

Black leatherette, Steinheil Cassar 45mm lens, Prontor 125 shutter, flush inset rewind crank, inset film speed reminder dial.

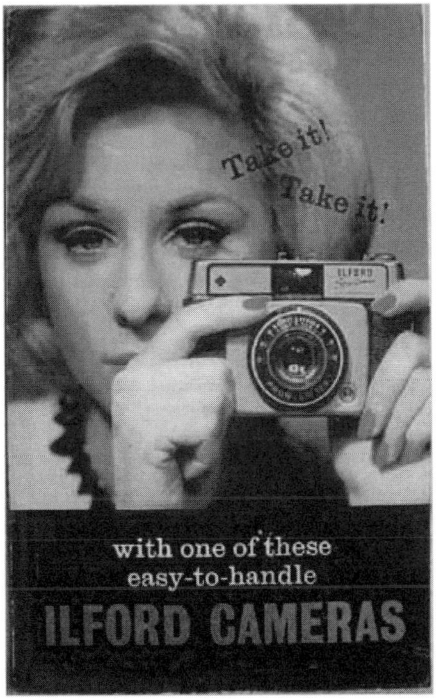

Here is an advert for the new Sportsman 125. “This versatile new camera is the successor to the outstandingly successful Sportsman Vario”.

Ilford Sportsman F (€)

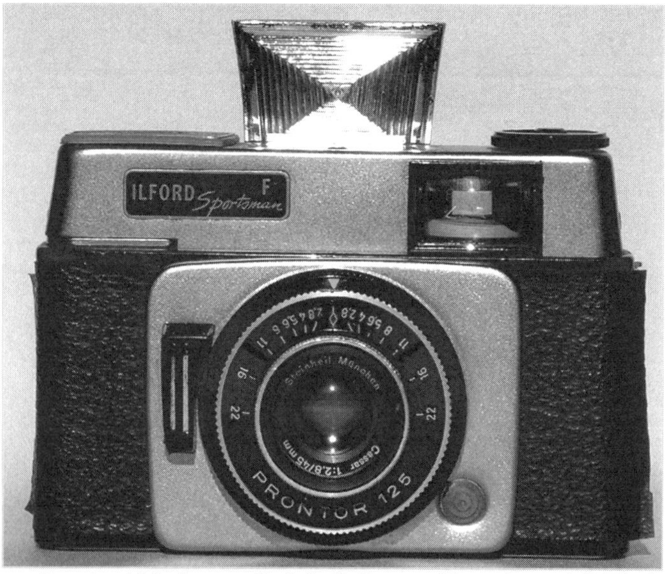

Prontor 125 shutter, Steinheil Cassar 45mm lens, AG Flash bulb socket and flip-up reflector, Down shutter release button, battery compartment on top plate under plastic slide cover (labelled 'open' and 'offnen'), film rewind knob. Film speed reminder on top right knob (labelled with Negativ and Positiv).

Ilford Sportsman Prontor

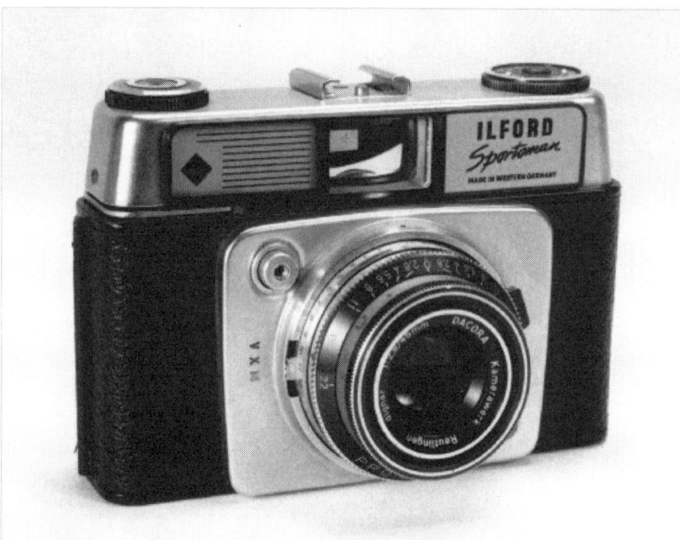

Black leatherette, Steinheil Cassar 45mm lens, Prontor 250 shutter, plastic rewind knob, and Plastic film speed reminder dial. V X M flash synchronisation.

Ilford Sportsman Prontor 250 (€)

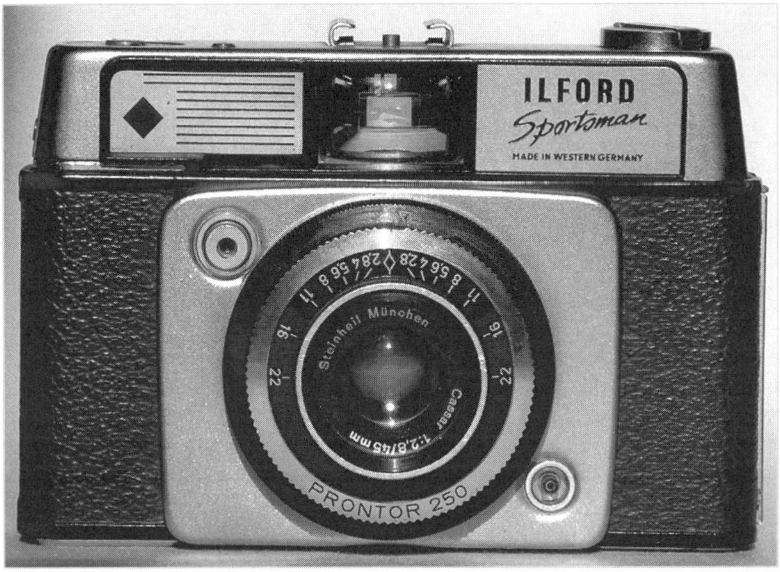

Grey leatherette, Steinheil Cassar 45mm lens, Inset rewind crank, Flush film speed reminder dial.

Ilford Sportsman Prontor 250 - ISCO (€)

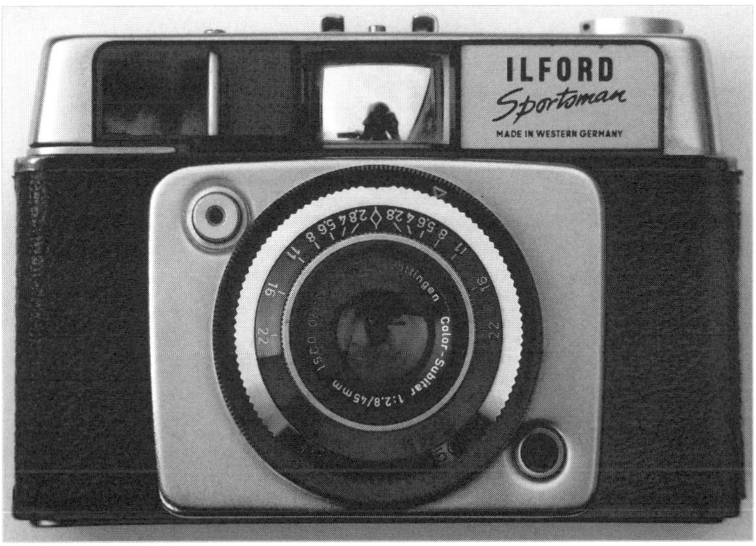

This camera is identical to the previous except that it is fitted with an ISCO Optische Werke Gottingen Color – Subitar 1:2.8/45mm lens. Interesting to note that is has black leatherette instead of the usual European grey.

Ilford Sportsman Prontor 250 S (€)

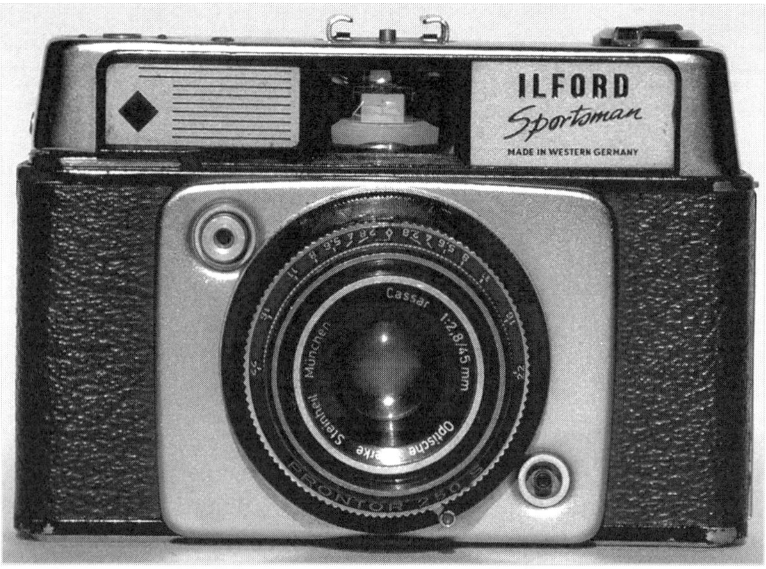

The Prontor 250S had a self-timer and a plastic shutter identification logo. Grey leatherette, Steinheil Cassar 45mm lens, Inset rewind crank, Flush film speed reminder dial.

Ilford Sportsman Prontor 300 S (€)

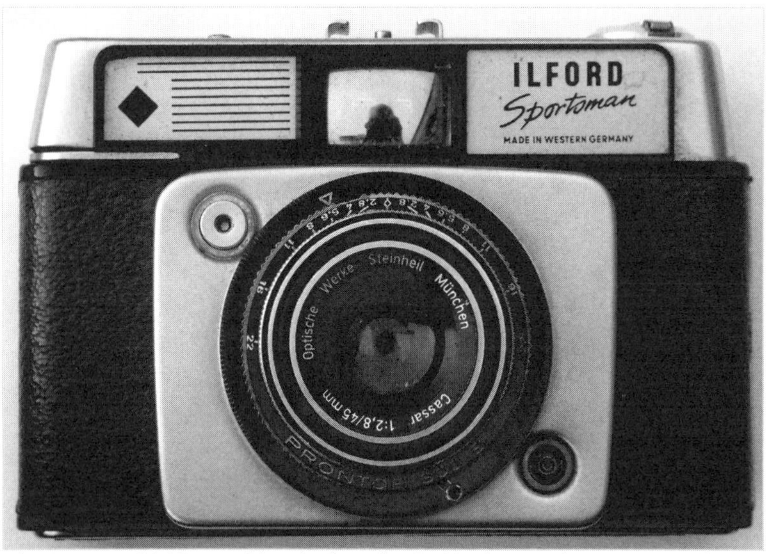

The Prontor 300S was identical to the 250S shown above except for the faster shutter.

Ilford Sportsman Rangefinder - 1958

The Sportsman Rangefinder started life in late 1958 (but may not have come to market till 1960) and lasted for several years undergoing some minor changes. It had a Gauthier Pronto shutter giving four speeds of B, 1/30, 1/60, 1/125 and 1/250 second. The shutter also had a delayed action release and 'X' type synchronisation for either electronic flash at all speeds or expendable flashbulbs at 1/30 second only.

The Rangefinder was coupled directly to the lens and was of the coincidence type. Turning the lens mount brought the yellow image square in the centre of the viewfinder into co-incidence with the full frame.
It had a Dacora Dignar lens with a 45mm focal length and aperture of f/2.8.

This version like the rest of the Sportsman range was well balanced and comfortable to hold, the bevelled back and rough grained leather-cloth affording a good grip. The shutter release button located on the front panel on an axis parallel to that of the lens was easy to locate and use.

It sold for £19. 19s. 11d and had the standard Ilford range of accessories available to it.

Ilford Sportsman Pronto - Rangefinder

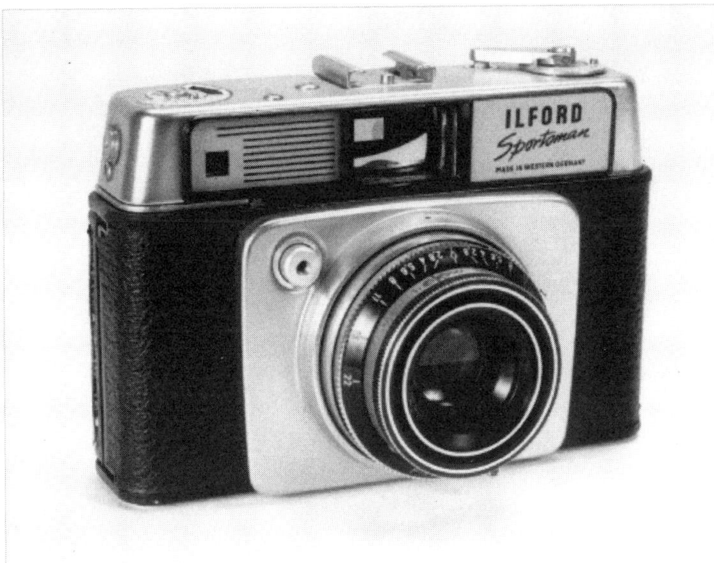

Black leatherette, Steinheil Cassar 45mm lens, Pronto shutter, large rewind crank, quadrant film speed reminder dial, and self-timer.

Ilford Sportsman Prontor 125 Rangefinder (€)

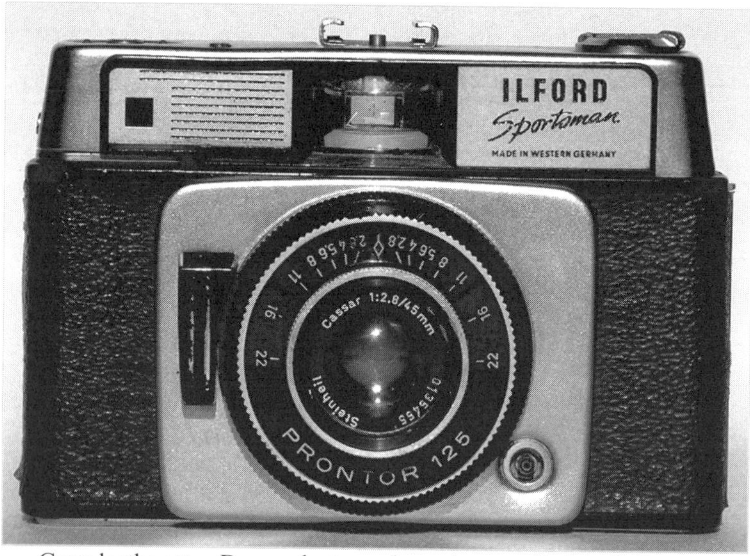

Grey leatherette, Down shutter release button, Steinheil Cassar 45mm lens, Prontor 125 shutter, Inset rewind crank, Flush film speed reminder dial.

Ilford Sportsman Printers Block

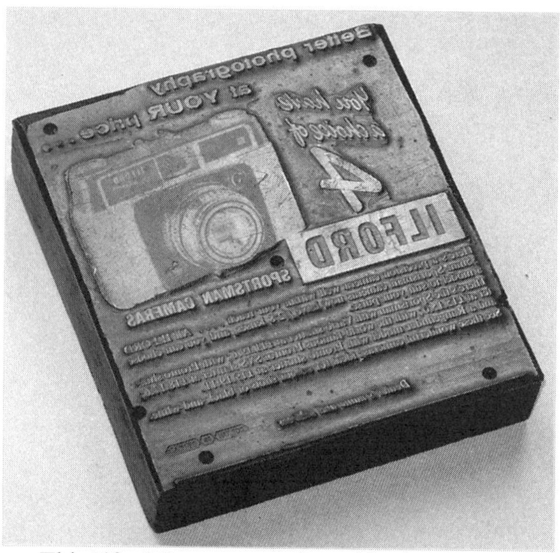

This Ilford Sportsman printer block (Zinco) is a reminder as to how printing was performed at the time. It says, "Better photography at YOUR price...You have a choice of 4 Ilford Sportsman Cameras.

Ilford Sportsman Automatic

The Sportsman Automatic and the Sportsman Automatic Rangefinder were largely identical cameras incorporating a built-in semi automatic exposure control and following the same basic design of the Sportsmaster and Sportsmaster Manumatic with lever rewinding, a new styled exposure counter and film reminder disc. The first samples of Sportsman cameras fitted with exposure meters arrived in approximately 1958.

The Automatic Rangefinder incorporated a built-in coupled, parallax mirror rangefinder.

The exposure control consisted of a photoelectric cell (not requiring a battery) and two moving pointers. The pointers could be seen through two windows, one on top of the camera and the other through the viewfinder. One pointer, the white one, was actuated by the photoelectric cell, moving automatically according to the strength of the prevailing light. The other needle coloured red, was moved by turning the lens aperture ring. When the two needles coincided the lens aperture was set for the correct exposure. Before the exposure control could be operated, the film speed scale had first to be set according to the film in the camera.

The shutter speed was then selected. The shutter speed and aperture ring could be locked together so that equivalent exposures were secured whether the aperture or the speed was the prime consideration.

The camera had a three element, f/2.8 Steinheil Cassar, coated lens with a focal length of 45mm. Aperture ranges were from f/2.8 to f/22.

It had a six-speed Pronto-LK shutter giving speeds of B, 1/15, 1/30, 1/60, 1/125, 1/250 and 1/500 second.

This camera was a natural bridge between the manual Sportsman and the fully automatic Sportsmaster. It sold for £27. 19s. 6d and £32. 5s. 0d for the Auto Rangefinder.

Ilford Sportsman Pronto Automatic

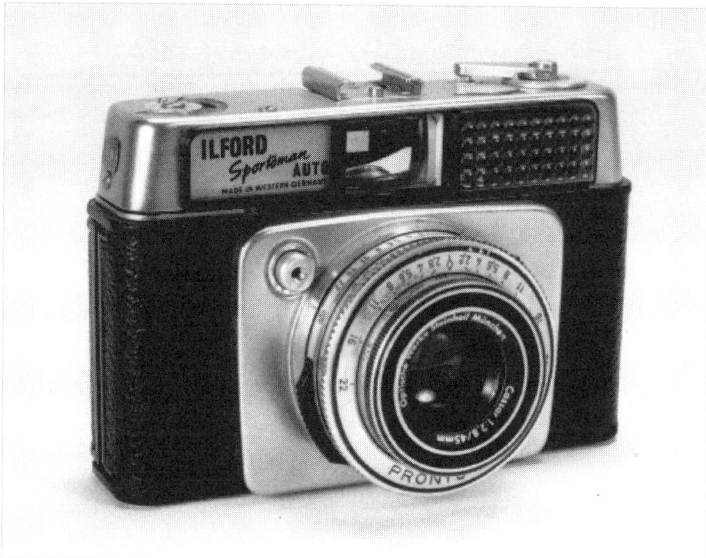

Black leatherette, Prontor shutter, Steinheil Cassar 45mm lens, large rewind crank, Inset co-incidence light meter needle, quadrant film speed reminder dial.

Ilford Sportsman Prontor 250 LK Automatic (€)

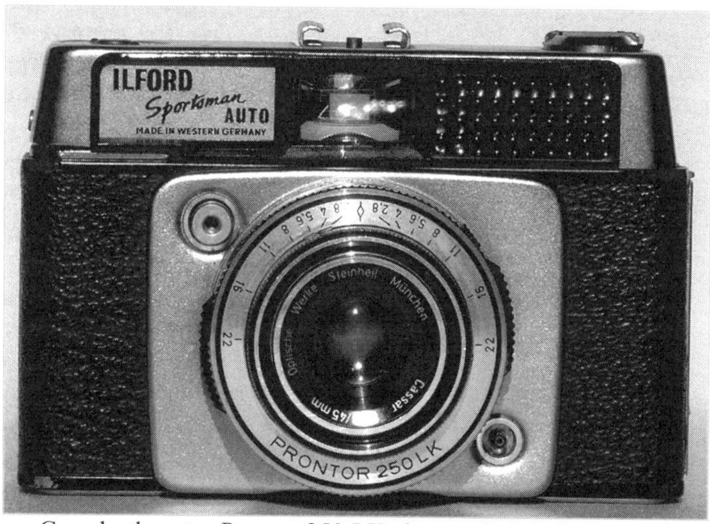

Grey leatherette, Prontor 250 LK shutter, Steinheil Cassar 45mm lens, inset rewind crank, Inset co-incidence light meter needle, flush film speed reminder dial.

Ilford Sportsman Prontor 300 LK Automatic (€)

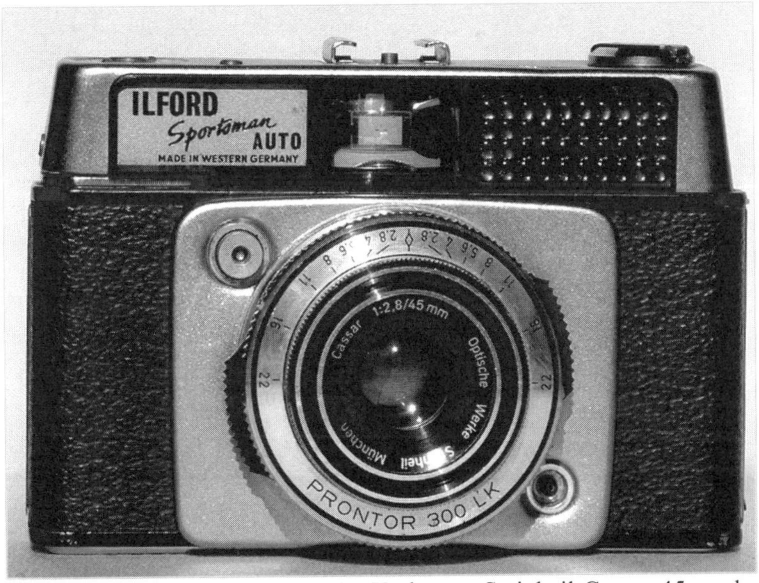

Grey leatherette, Prontor 300 LK shutter, Steinheil Cassar 45mm lens, inset rewind crank, Inset co-incidence light meter needle.

Ilford Sportsman Prontor 500 LK Automatic (€)

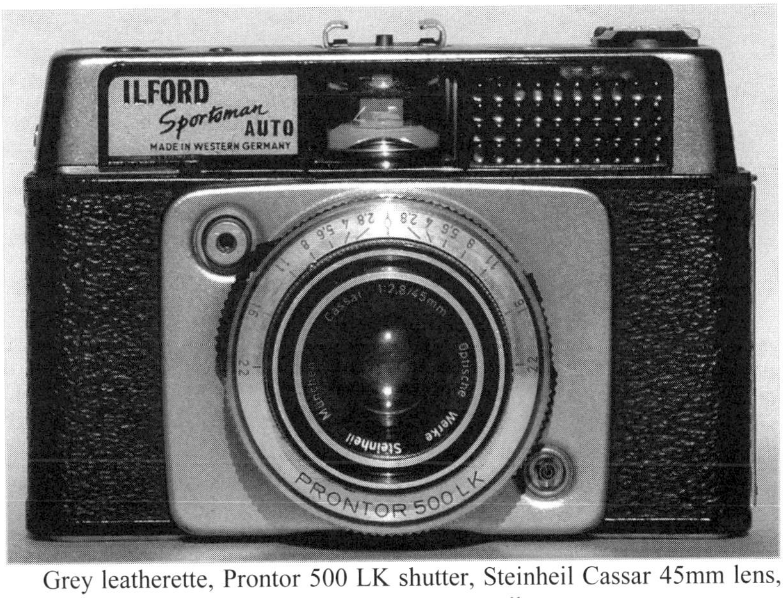

Grey leatherette, Prontor 500 LK shutter, Steinheil Cassar 45mm lens, inset rewind crank, Inset co-incidence light meter needle.

Ilford Sportsman Pronto Automatic Rangefinder

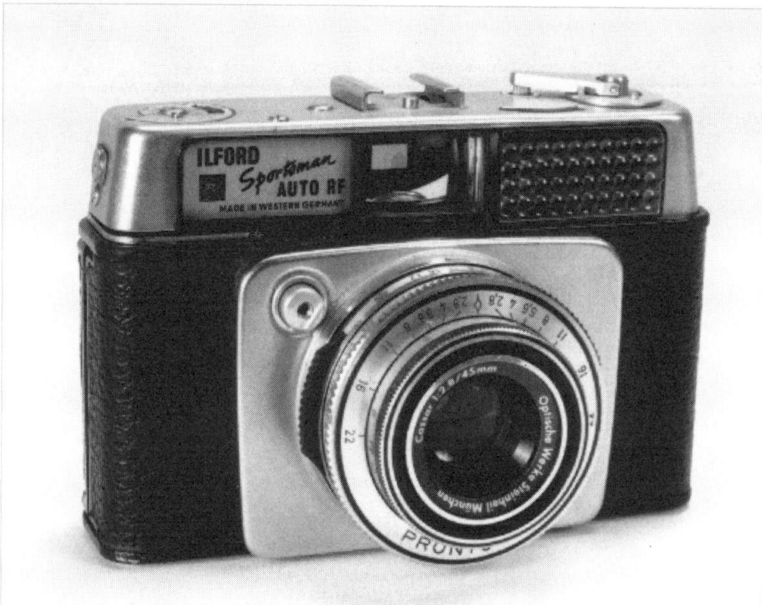

Black leatherette, Prontor shutter, Steinheil Cassar 45mm lens, large rewind crank, Inset co-incidence light meter needle, quadrant film speed reminder dial.

Ilford Sportsman Prontor Automatic Rangefinder (€)

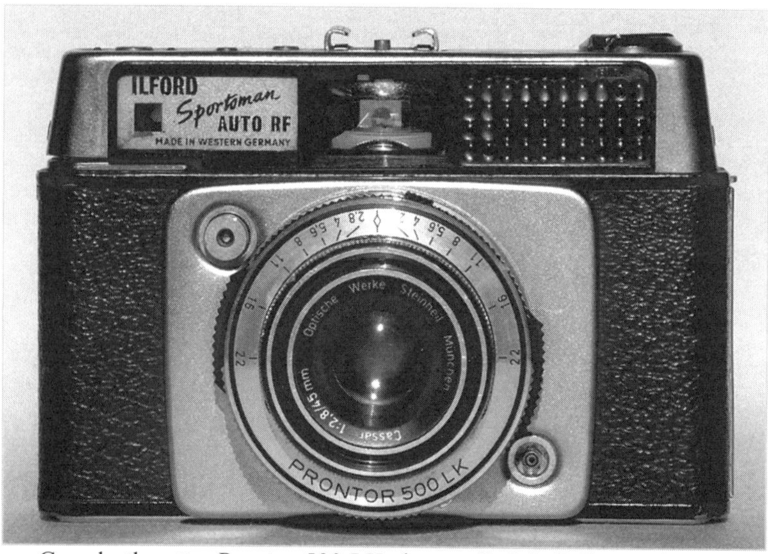

Grey leatherette, Prontor 500 LK shutter, Steinheil Cassar 45mm lens, inset rewind crank, Inset co-incidence light meter needle, quadrant film speed reminder dial.

Ilford Sportsmaster Automatic

The Sportsmaster Automatic was an automatic push button camera. Like all the other cameras in the Sportsman range it was a precision made 35mm camera of sturdy construction.

The shutter of the Sportsmaster was the Pronto-LUX, which was coupled to the automatic exposure control. It could be used in either fully automatic mode or manually controlled aperture settings. When set to Automatic a signal would show in the viewfinder; red for under-exposure, green for correct exposure.

The most distinct and unique feature of the Sportsmaster was the focusing arrangements. It had 4 shutter release buttons, related to the distance of the subject. From top to bottom these were used for scenes, groups, people, faces or Infinity, 13 feet, 8 feet and 5 feet. On pressing one of the buttons the lens would rotate in or out to the required focusing position, set the aperture to the computed opening and finally fire the shutter.

The shutter speed was governed by the speed rating of the film used in the camera. The speeds ranged from 1/30 second on 10 ASA to 1/500 second on 200 ASA. Films with intermediate speeds needed intermediate settings. To adjust the film speed on the camera, a small locking catch on the left hand side of the lens mount was depressed and the milled outer ring turned to link up a small red marking dot to correspond with either the ASA or DIN film speed markings.

The camera normally employed the standard Sportsman lens the Dacora 45mm f/2.8. Some later models had a Steinheil Cassar lens.
As well as this change it also underwent several other cosmetic changes.
The eyepiece of the viewfinder was increased in size by nearly 100%.

The film number indicator was moved from the bottom plate to the more familiar top right dial.
Longer and slightly deeper film advance levers were fitted.

The round rewind knob was replaced by a metal crank and finally this was updated by another design similar to the one shown on the Sportsmaster Manumatic overleaf.

At a basic price of £24. 10s. 0d plus £3. 19s. 8d tax this camera was a masterpiece of German workmanship and innovative English design.

Ilford Sportsmaster Automatic - # 1

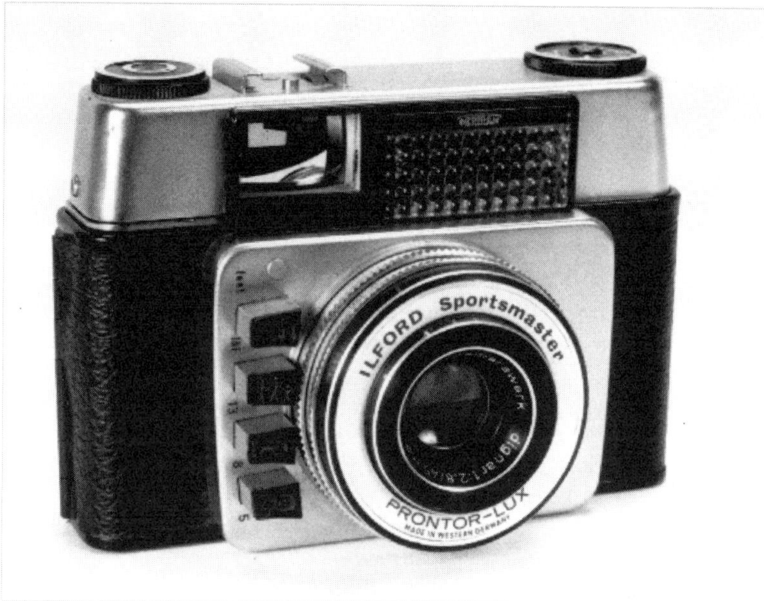

Prontor-LUX shutter, Dacora Dignar 45mm f/2.8 lens, distance in feet, plastic rewind knob.

Ilford Sportsmaster Automatic - # 2 (€)

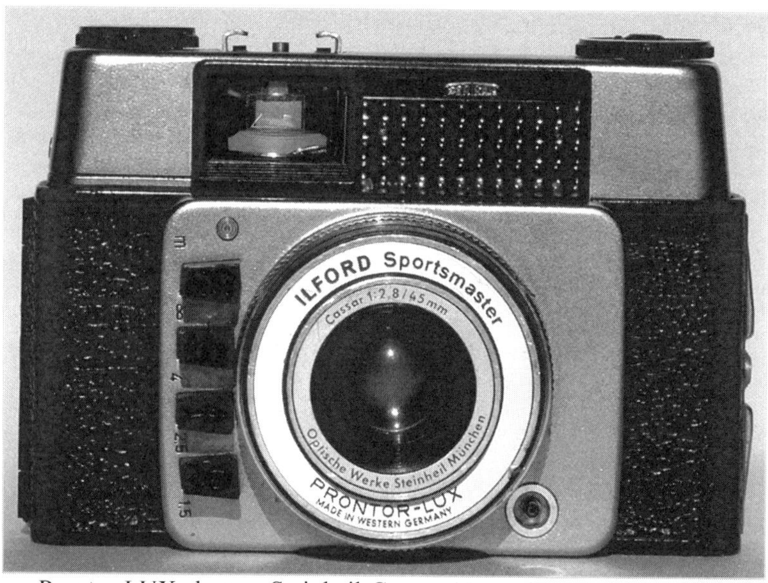

Prontor-LUX shutter, Steinheil Cassar 45mm f/2.8 lens, distance in meters, plastic rewind knob.

Ilford Sportsmaster Automatic - # 3

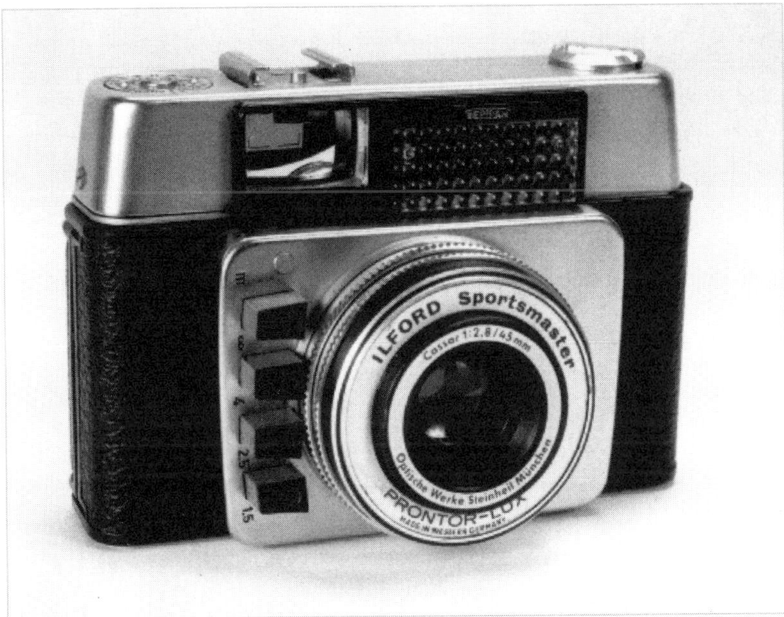

Prontor-Lux shutter, Steinheil Cassar 45mm f/2.8 lens, distance in meters, metal inset rewind crank.

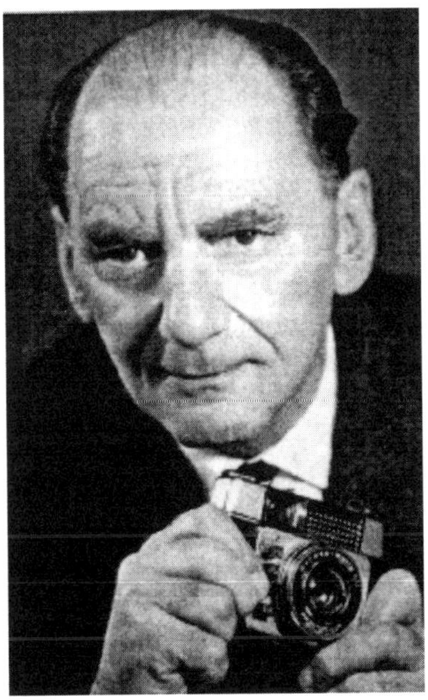

Here is a photograph of Bernhard Dangelmaier holding a Dacora version of the Sportsmaster camera. This picture appeared in a German photography magazine in 2003 which retrospectively reviewed the camera.

The picture had the following caption, “Bernhard Dangelmeier, one the most important entrepreneur personalities of the German camera industry after the Second World War.”

Ilford Sportsmaster Manumatic - 1962

The Sportsmaster Manumatic was made in 1962 and could be used either as an automatic or as a manual camera. When set to Auto an exposure control automatically adjusted the lens aperture to give correct exposure with the shutter speed selected. A moving green and red optical signal incorporated in the viewfinder would come to rest opposite a fixed under mark. If the green signal was opposite the marker there was enough light, if the red signal was there, there was not enough light. The approximate F-number to which the iris would be automatically adjusted was also shown on the green part of the indicator. If the signal was red then by setting the shutter speed lower the signal could be shifted to green. In manual, although the control exposure would be disengaged it still controlled the light meter.

It was fitted with either a Steinheil Cassar 45mm f/2.8 lens or with a four element, f/2.8 Rodenstock Yearex, coated lens with a focal length of 45mm. Aperture ranges were from f/2.8 to f/22.

The camera used a five speed Prontor-Matic shutter giving, B, 1/30, 1/60, 1/125, 1/250 and 1/500 second.
The lens was focused in the normal manner by rotating the front cell mount.

The finish of this camera was excellent; its die cast metal body was covered in hardwearing black leatherette and had parts finished in black enamel, satin chrome and bright chrome. It sold for £44. 19s. 6d. and was arguably the finest camera the company made during this and later phases.

Ilford Sportsmaster Manumatic - Style 1

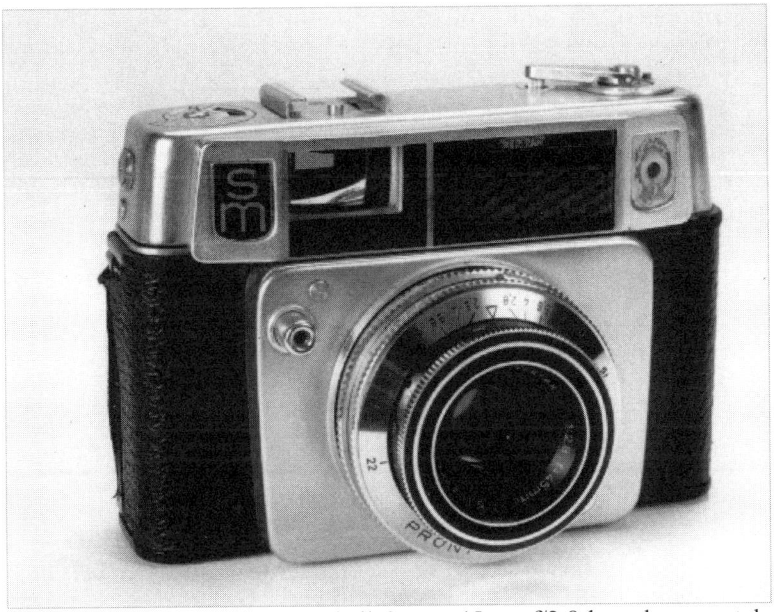

Prontor-Matic shutter, Steinheil Cassar 45mm f/2.8 lens, large metal rewind crank, quadrant film speed reminder dial.

For the keen collector/observer, some models of the Manumatic had the Ilford badge and the SM logos reversed as shown below. Whether this was a deliberate change or just an indication that the cameras were all finished by hand, I do not know.

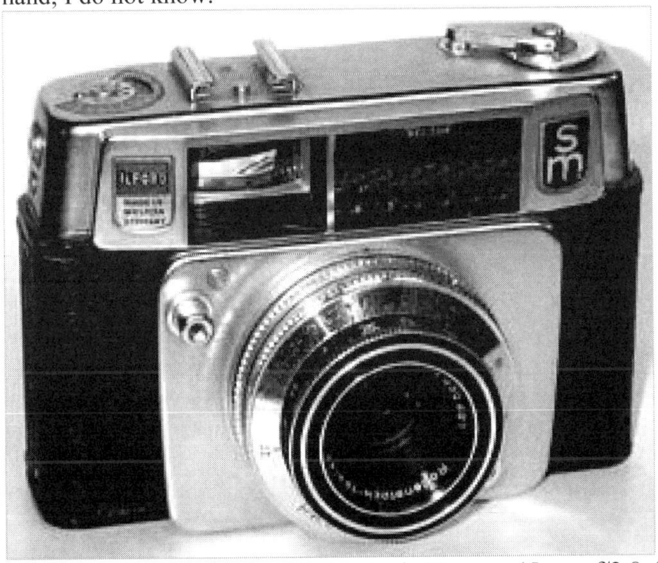

Prontor-Matic shutter, Rodenstock Yearex 45mm f/2.8 lens, large metal rewind crank, quadrant film speed reminder dial.

Ilford Sportsmaster Manumatic - (€)

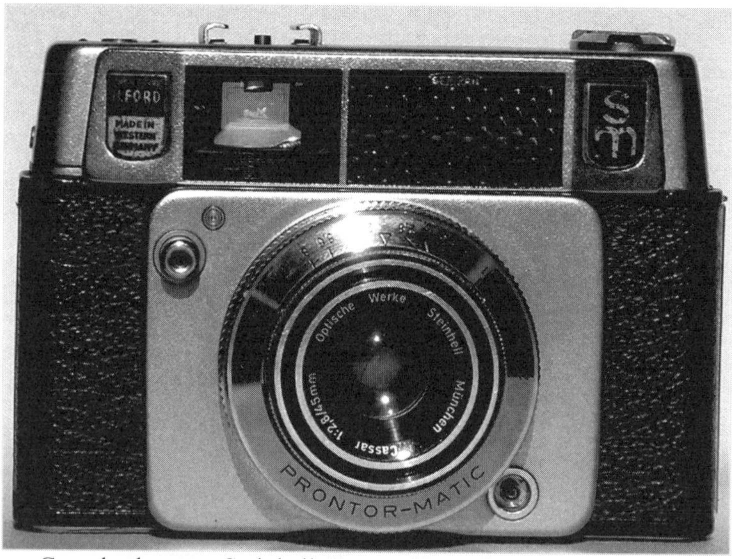

Grey leatherette, Steinheil Cassar 45mm lens, Prontor-Matic shutter, Inset rewind crank, flat surface fitting film type reminder.

Ilford Sportsman L (€)

These three Sportsman models were based on the 'standard' Sportsman styling and also have a similarity to the slightly deeper Sportsmaster Manumatic top plate. Most notable is the change in logo being a small name strip applied above the light collector.

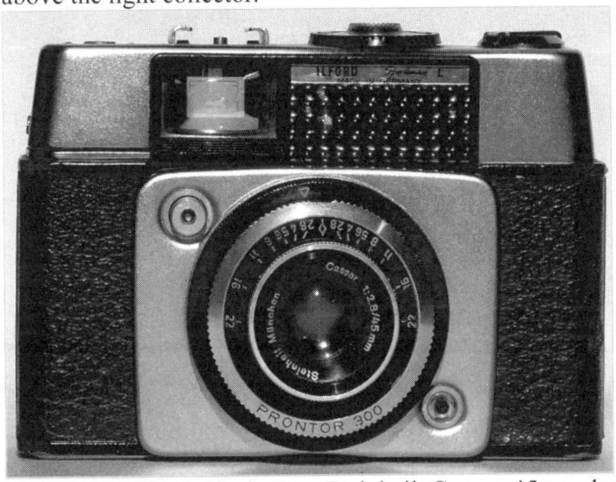

Prontor 300 L-E shutter, Steinheil Cassar 45mm lens, Light meter, Film speed and Exposure meter on top, recessed rewind crank, flush film speed reminder dial. Small logos above the light meter collector. Grey leatherette. Logo also says, 'Made in Germany', not Western Germany.

Ilford Sportsman S-L 300 (€)

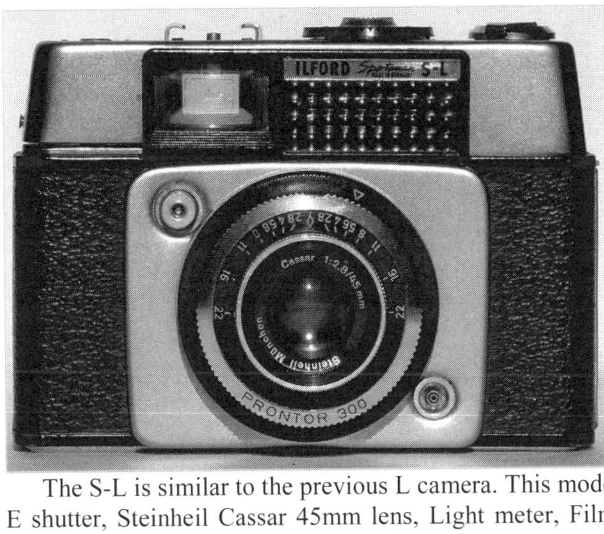

The S-L is similar to the previous L camera. This model has a Prontor 300 S-E shutter, Steinheil Cassar 45mm lens, Light meter, Film speed and Exposure meter on top, recessed rewind crank, flush film speed reminder dial. Small logos above the light meter collector. Logo also says, Made in Germany, not Western Germany. Black leatherette.

Ilford Sportsman S-L Prontor 250-S(€)

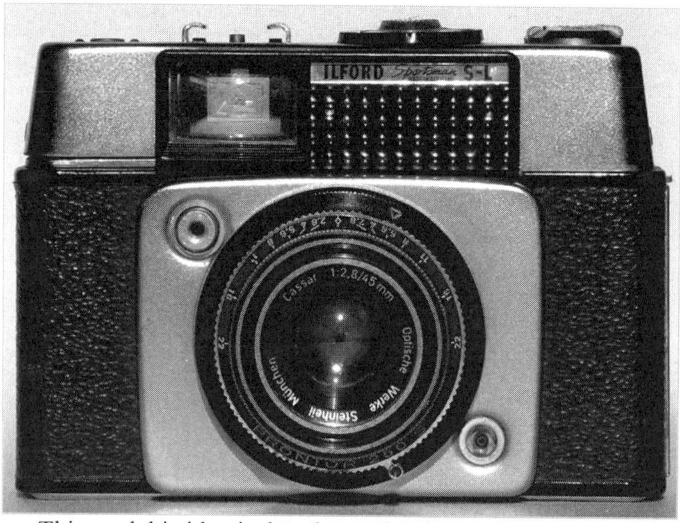

This model is identical to the model shown above except it has a Prontor 250 S shutter. As such it has shutter speeds of B, 30, 60, 125 and 250 with a self-timer. This model is also fitted with grey leatherette covering.

Ilford Sportsman 125 – 5th Style

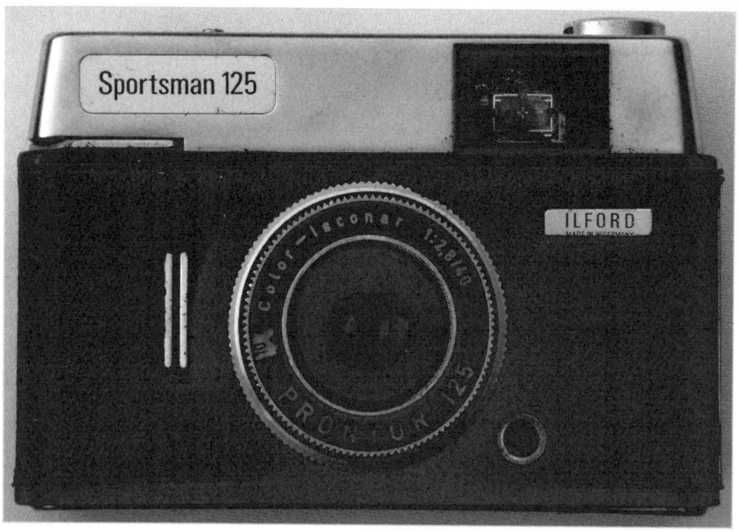

Ilford Sportsman 300 – 5th Style

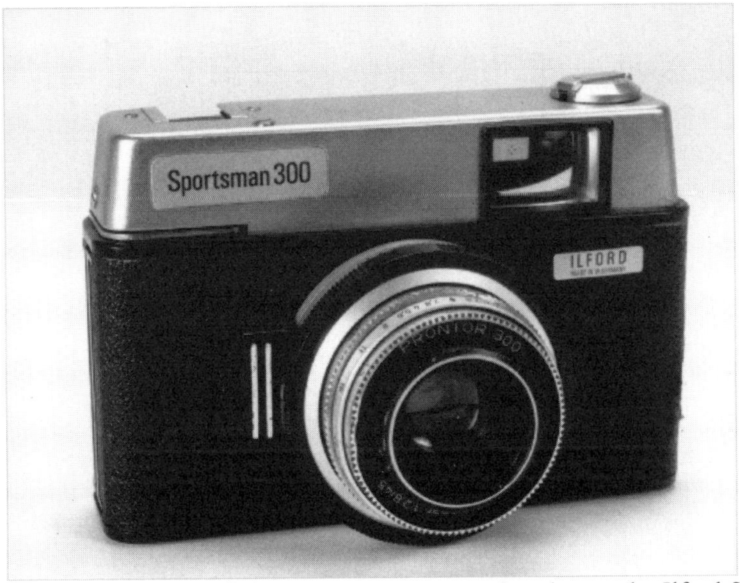

The last 'standard' Sportsman cameras produced were the Ilford Sportsman 125 and the Ilford Sportsman 300.

The '125' had a Prontor 125 shutter and shared the same lens as the 300.

The '300' had a Color-Isconar 2.8 f/4.5 lens and Prontor 300 shutter. The body styling had been considerably tidied up with a large brightline viewfinder on the right (facing) front of the camera.

The centre contact flash shoe was fitted on the left where the original film counter was positioned. This was moved to the bottom plate. The shutter release button was replaced by a plastic vertically operated slide button.

The rest of this section shows Sportsman models that were available in Europe but not in the U.K.

Dacora 300 L (Black Body)

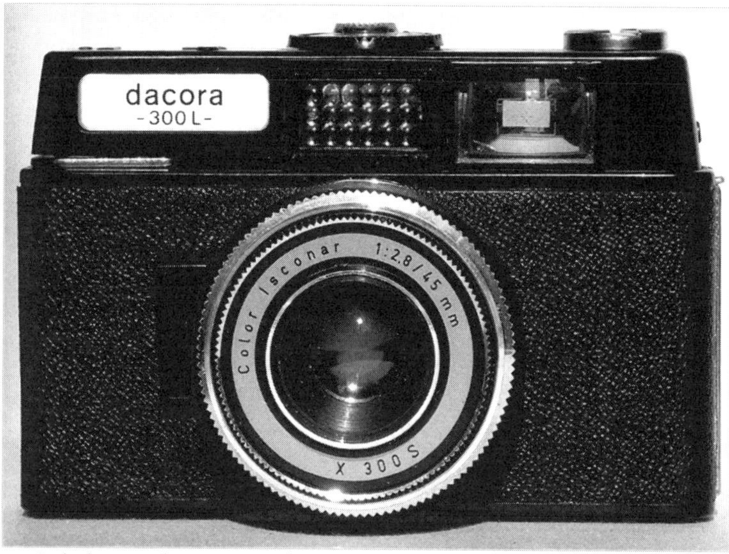

It is interesting to note that Dacora made some variations of their own to the joint venture cameras that they made for Ilford. This model shows a 300L with all black paintwork. Fitted with a Color Isconar 45mm lens and an X 300S shutter. Maybe they thought this would be more acceptable in Europe whilst Ilford continued with the chrome finish. I have however only seen one of this type and so this might be a one-off or a progression, which was overtaken by other events.

Ilford Sportsman 300 L (€)

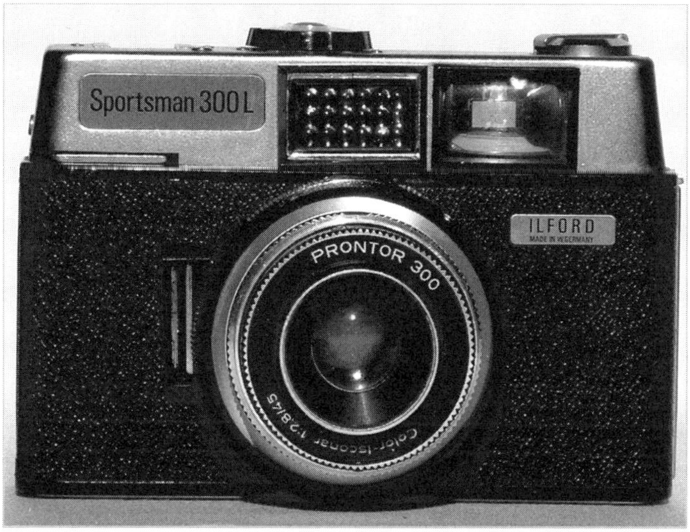

This model is based on the Sportsman 300 shown previously but as far as I am aware was not marketed in the UK. It shared all of the features of the basic 300 but had the addition of an exposure meter fitted to the top plate with a rectangular light collector on the front of the camera.

Ilford Sportsman 300 (€) – 6th Style

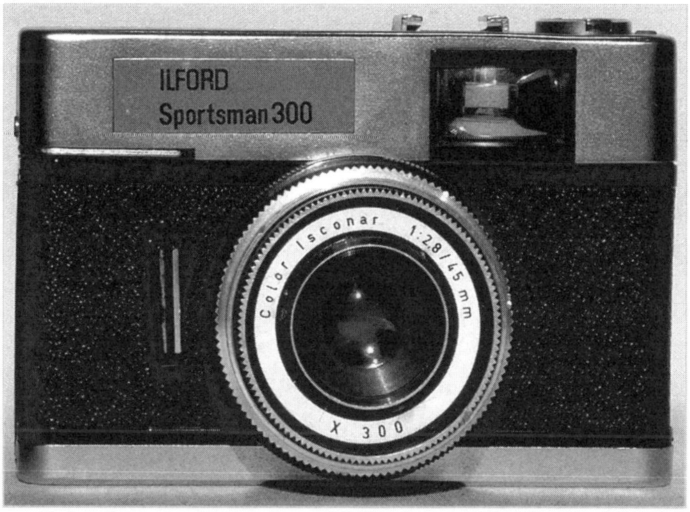

Color Isconar 45mm lens, X300 shutter (B, 30, 60, 125, 300), Flash shoe over viewfinder on the right, recessed rewind crank. The bottom plate has the exposure counter.

Ilford Sportsman 300 S (€)

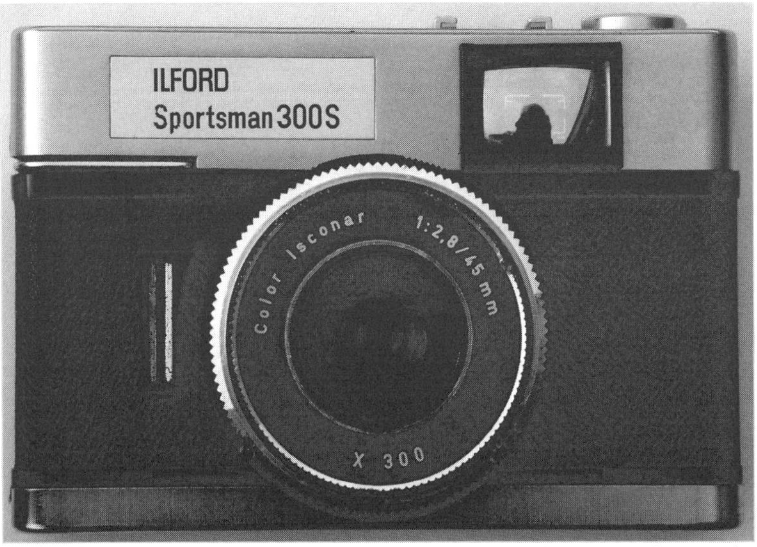

This model is identical to the Sportsman 300 shown on the previous page except that it has a self timer fitted and has white lettering on a black background around the lens plate.

Ilford Sportsman 300 L (€)

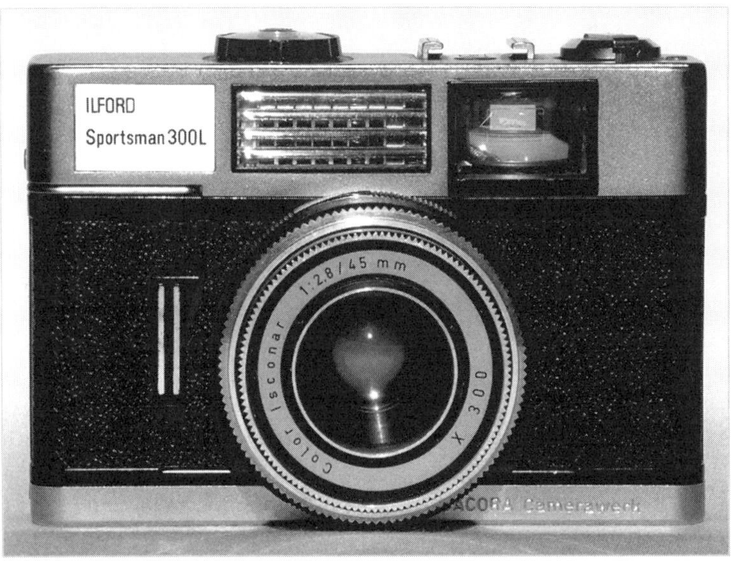

X 300 shutter, Color-Isconar 45mm lens, Light meter, Film speed and Exposure meter on top. Logo in top left of top plate. Some models have white lettering on a black background on the lens/shutter plate instead of the reverse as shown here.

Ilford Sportsman 300 LK (€)

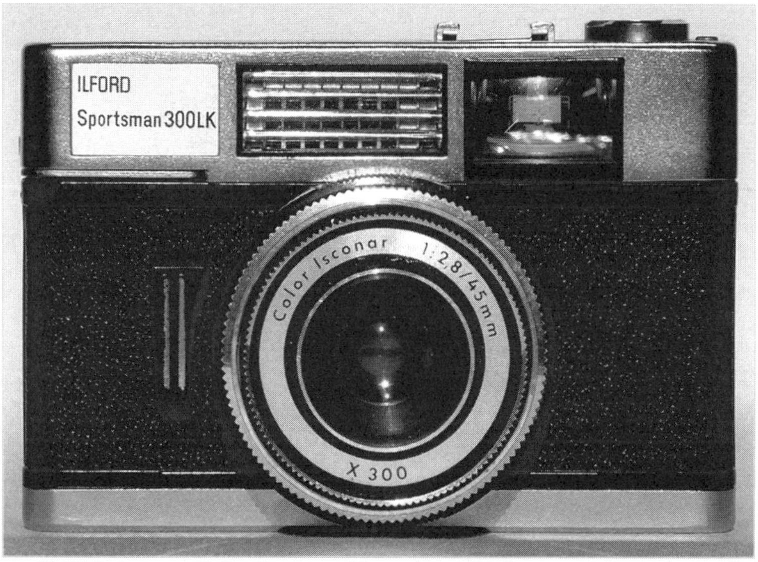

X 300 shutter, Color-Isconar 45mm lens, Light meter, Logo in top left of top plate. recessed rewind crank, coupled exposure meter, light meter with needle -><+ area on top plate.

Ilford Sportsman 300 SL (€)

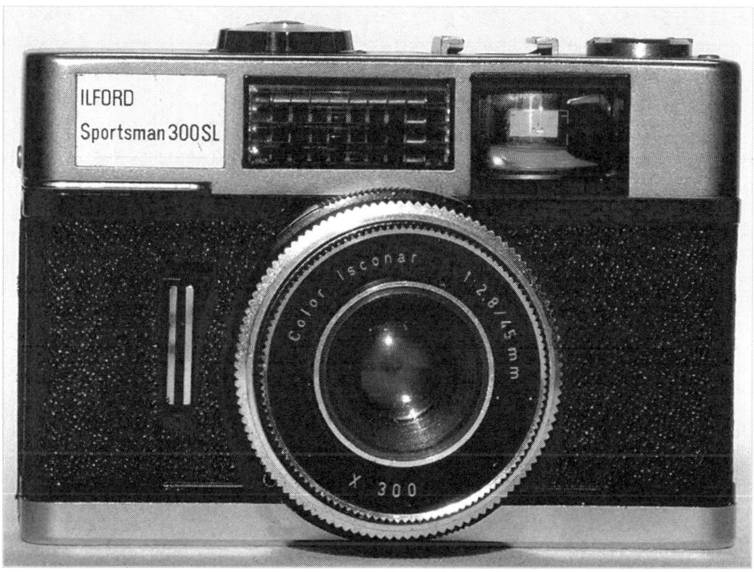

X 300 shutter, Color-Isconar 45mm lens, Light meter, Film speed and non-coupled Exposure meter on top. Logo in top left of top plate, recessed rewind crank.

Ilford Sportsman 300 EB

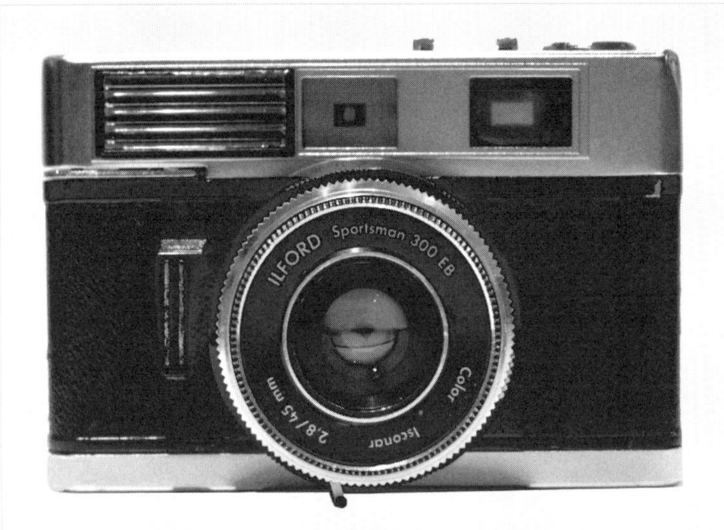

Image courtesy of the National Museum of Film and Photography.

The Sportsman 300 EB was similar to the others in this range except it had the light collector on the left (facing) side instead of being central. It had a Color Isconar f/2.8 45mm lens and a 300 EB shutter with self-timer. It had a light meter with a needle visible in the viewfinder and a rangefinder.

Ilford Sportsman Instant - 1963

The Sportsman Instant models are included here as they all have the 'Sportsman' model name but chronologically should strictly appear under Phase 5. They used the Kodak 126 Instamatic cartridge.

Ilford Sportsman C Instant – 7th Style

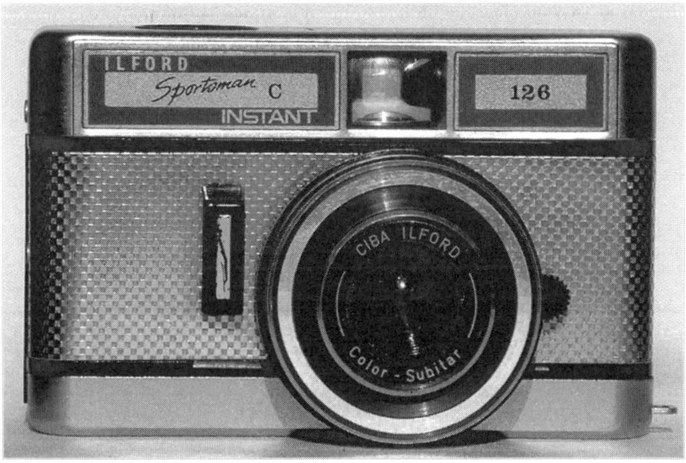

The Sportsman C Instant had a Color-Subitar anastigmat lens and two shutter speeds, 1/90 and 1/30 sec, and marked 'Sunny' and 'Cloudy'.

Ilford Sportsman R Instant

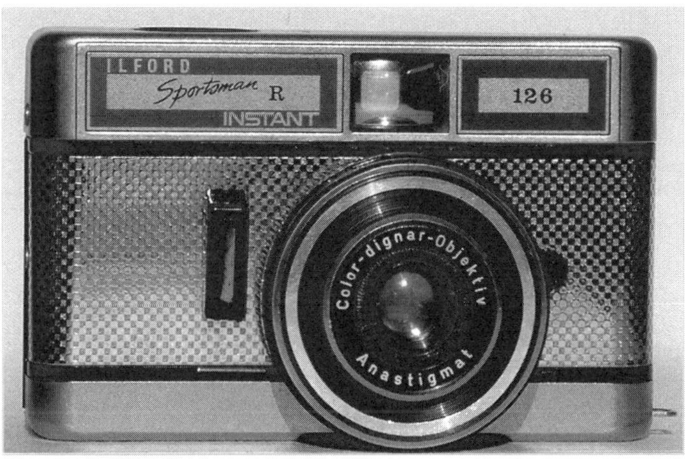

The Sportsman R Instant had a Color-Dignar lens without distance indicators and with four exposure setting symbols, Sun, Sun and Cloud, Cloud and Flash. See also the Instacora R version 2 on page 209.

Ilford Sportsman E Instant (€)

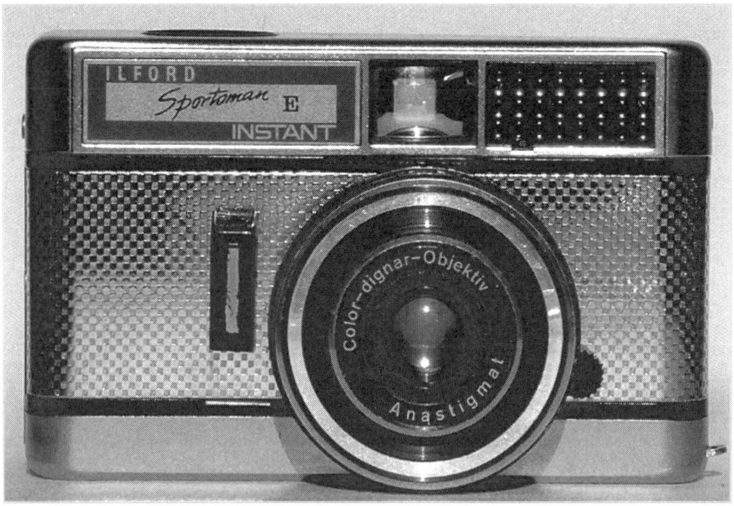

The Sportsman E Instant has a Color-Dignar anastigmat lens, a built-in selenium exposure meter and has a fitting for flashcubes. The body styling is related to the Sportina Rapid and may have only been marketed in Europe.

Beck Diamax Photomicrography Camera

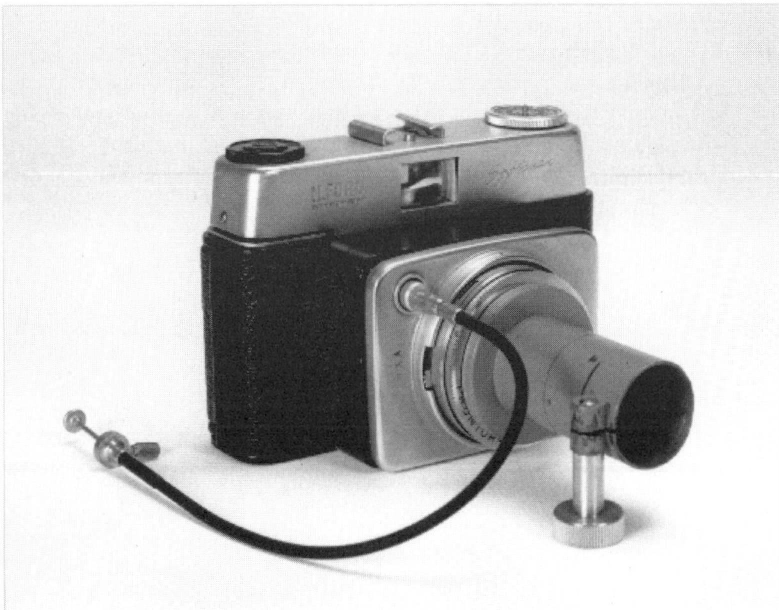

R and J Beck Limited used the Sportsman as the basis for a photomicrography camera. Primarily intended for application with the Beck Diamax microscope the camera could be used with other microscopes where the 25 mm adapter tube was suitable.

The adapter contained a projection lens system producing x 4 magnification. The camera was supplied with a X10 viewing ocular with film frame graticule.

The basic Sportsman Prontor-SVS camera was modified by both the replacement of the standard optics and by the inclusion of a spacing block between the camera body and the lens/shutter assembly.

Using the Beck Diamax microscope the user could view and photograph the specimens simultaneously using the Tetravar unit. This used a beam - splitting mirror to direct the light either to the camera and the viewing body simultaneously or to a Microsix exposure meter.

The R. & J. Beck company was established in 1865. R. & J. Beck came from a family of notable medical people. J. J. Lister was co-inventor of the compound microscope. His son was a famous surgeon. His nephews were Richard Beck (1827-1866) and Joseph Beck (1828-1891).

Richard and Joseph Beck worked in partnership with a leading instrument maker, James Smith (d. 1870). The name of the company was originally, Smith, Beck & Beck. This was changed to R & J Beck after the retirement of Smith in 1865.

In the early years, R & J Beck introduced a number of inexpensive microscope models, which helped popularise the use of the microscope.

Among the items that they produced were; microscopes, optical dissecting platforms, camera lenses including wide-angle lenses, falling plate box cameras and other related equipment.

Their lenses found their way onto diverse cameras as listed here:
1896 - Henry Clay Regular Camera
1905 - R. & J. Beck, 'Dai Cornex' Camera
1920 - Hills Cloud Camera
1937 - Purma Camera.

With their involvement with microscopes and lenses it was not surprising that they also made photomicrography cameras. I understand, but have not been able to confirm that they were taken over by the Ealing Optical company.

Ilford Sporti

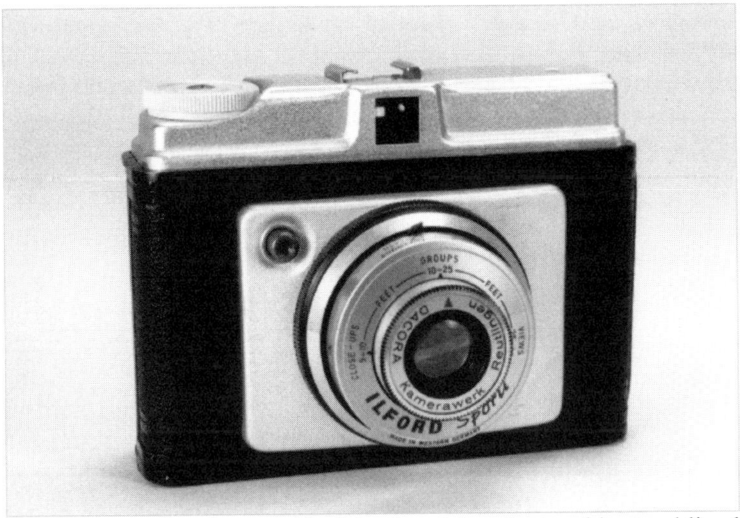

Ilford sales brochures said of the Sporti that the two big stumbling blocks for the beginner, focusing and the correct exposure, are extremely simplified, and anyone who has never used a camera before will be able to take pictures right from the start.

The Sporti and the Super Sporti took 12, 2 ¼ in. square pictures on standard 120 size roll film and like all the West German Ilford cameras was made by the Dacora Company.

They had smart eye-catching styling, which gave them all the handling advantages of the more expensive Sportsman range and were made in metal with tough black leatherette and satin chrome trim.

They had a built-in direct-vision optical viewfinder and the shutter release was threaded to accept a cable release. It also had an accessory shoe fitted above the viewfinder to take any suitable flashgun and was synchronised for flash using a co-axial outlet.

The Sporti was fitted with a two-position exposure control; 'Sunny' and 'Cloudy'. Three focusing settings were available; 'close-ups' 'groups' and 'views'. Focusing zones in feet are also marked on the lens mount.

The camera was originally offered to Ilford with a pull out/push in lens mount similar to the Envoy. This was soon replaced in favour of the conventional rotary lens adjustment.

The Sporti was sold for £3. 19s. 9d

Ilford Sporti (€)

Most European Sporti's have grey leatherette but are otherwise identical to the U.K. version. They had a Dignar 75mm f/4,5 lens and Vario shutter. A few had an Isco Westar 75mm f/2.9 lens, Pronto shutter and self-timer. I do not believe that these were made available in the U.K.

Ilford Super Sporti - 1960

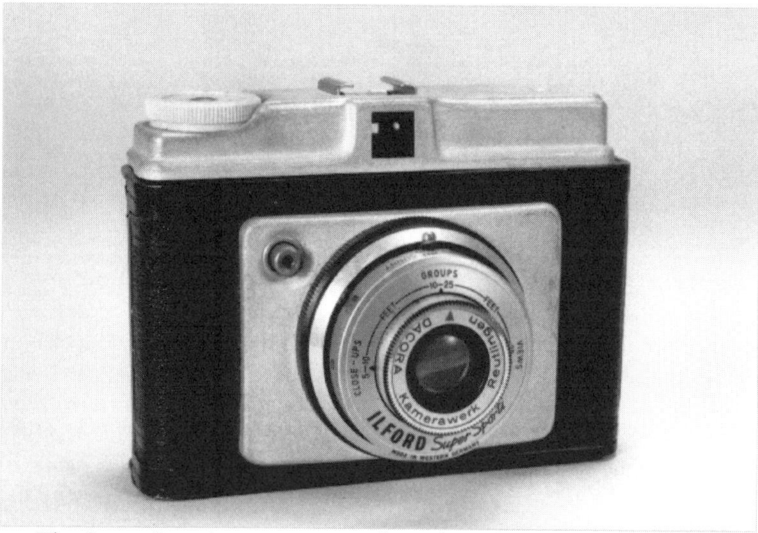

The Super Sporti was an up rated version of the Sporti. Its construction and appearance was exactly the same except for the following enhancements; the lens aperture could be set to 'sunny', 'light cloud' or 'dull'. The Super Sporti also had double exposure prevention and an extra setting for brief time exposures.

The lens and shutter speed settings were interlocked and although three exposure settings were marked, the lens actually was set to either of two apertures, f/11 or f/9. The third exposure setting was achieved by simultaneously changing to a slower shutter speed on the cloudy-dull setting.

The Super Sporti was sold for £4. 16s. 9d.

Ilford Sporti 4

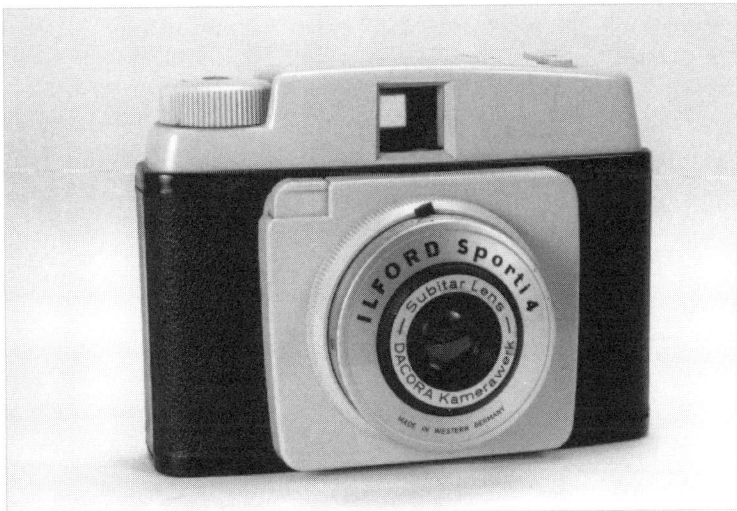

The Sporti 4 was made in 1961 and was a very well made plastic camera taking 12 pictures 1 5/8 inches square on 127 size roll film. The camera had one adjustment for 'sunny' or 'cloudy' depending on the weather conditions. The camera was fitted with a fixed focus Subitar meniscus lens that was in focus between 6 feet and infinity. Its large optical eye level viewfinder gave a clear subject view. The large shutter release was built into the top right hand corner of the lens panel. It was made in black-grey plastic with a built in tripod bush and covered in black leatherette.

It was synchronised for flash using a standard 3mm co-axial socket mounted on the bottom of the shutter housing.

This camera was designed for use by the youngster wishing to emulate the antics of his father. Not a toy, it was made by Dacora Kamerawerk in Western Germany and gave excellent results within its limitations. It sold for 34s 11d.

This was one of several cameras designed by my father in the garage alongside our house. The original visualisation mock-up was made of balsa wood and pieces of plastic, painted and decorated to a highly authentic standard.

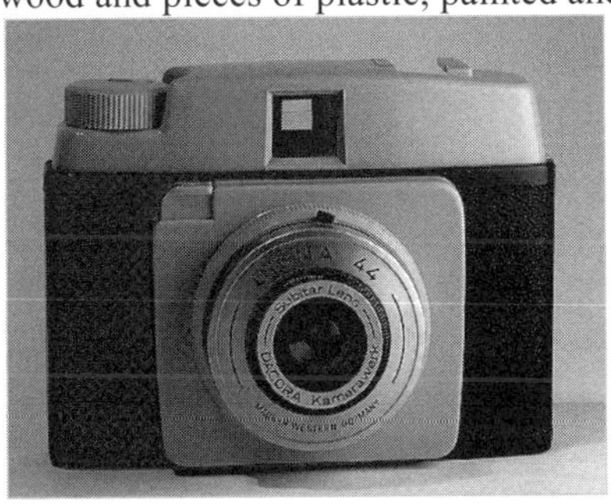

The Sporti was, like many of the Ilford cameras also marketed by Dacora under their own name. The Sporti 4 was for example identical (except for the labelling) as the Dacora Digna 44.

Sporti 4 Printers Block

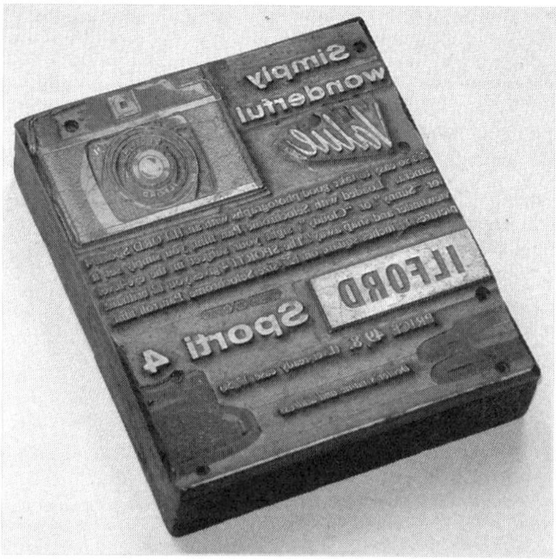

This printers block (Zinco) for a Sporti 4 advert proclaims, "Simply wonderful Value"

The price of the camera, is 49s 8d. and Ever-ready case for 17s. 5d.

Ilford Sporti 6 - 1962

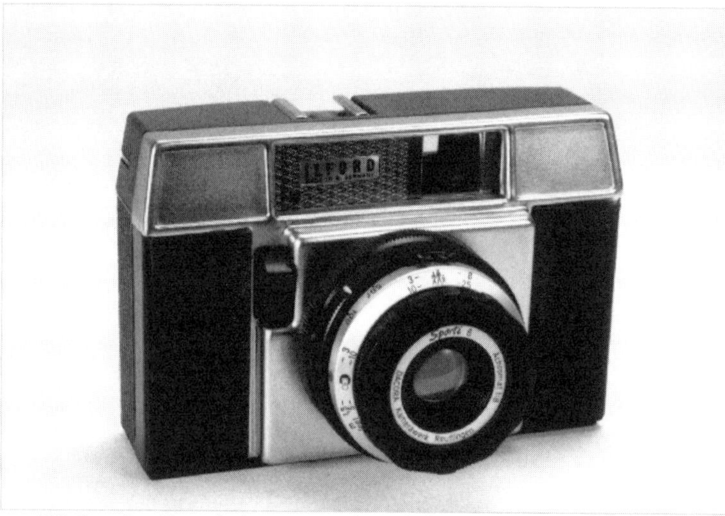

Whilst the Sporti 4 was produced for the 127 market, the Sporti 6 was produced for 120 roll film.

It was constructed from black plastic with aluminium trim. The lens mount and top cover housed the optical viewfinder. It had an f/8 Achromat lens with three apertures of f/8, f/11 and f/16. The lens was focused with symbol settings - faces people and places. When the shutter was cocked a double exposure prevention signal showed in the viewfinder. It was synchronised for flash with the accessory shoe mounted on the top. The shutter had two speeds 1/50 and 1/100 second and double exposure prevention. It sold for £4. 12s. 6d.

Ilford Sprite 127 - 1962

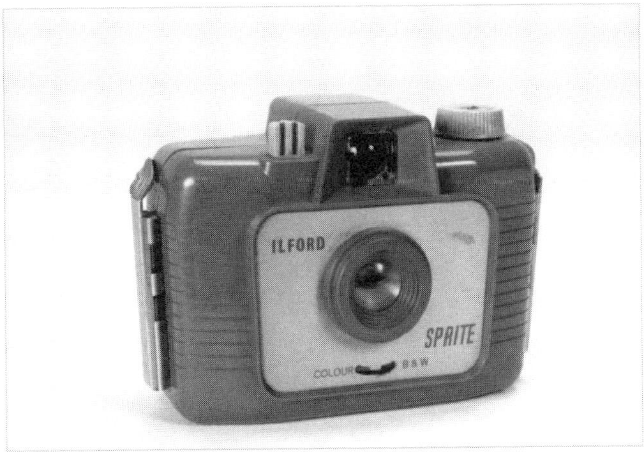

The Sprite 127 was made in England by the Agilux company. The body made of plastic, light grey in colour and ribbed for easier holding. Inside construction was simple and effective. The 127 film slid over rounded plastic edge guides.

It had a single speed shutter (1/40th) and two apertures, one for colour and a smaller one for black and white.

The lens was a single element made of plastic and of a fixed focus.

Wind-on was by a knob, on the top left of the camera with film numbers showing in the red window at the back.

The viewfinder gave a clear image, a little less than half natural size.

At 23s. 6d. it represented first class value for anyone starting on photography.

At the time that this camera was produced, people going on holiday brought a camera at a seaside resort. They would take one or two rolls of film and probably not use a camera again until next year's holiday, by which time they would probably buy another camera.

The type of market that this camera was aimed at gave rise to many amusing true stories. For example a person came back into a photographers shop and said, 'This film has not been processed correctly, I took half my photos in black and white and half in colour'. Thinking that the black and white - colour switch on the front of the camera could change the print produced!

These cameras were sold by the thousand in cases of 250 predominately for the holiday market.

Ilford Imp

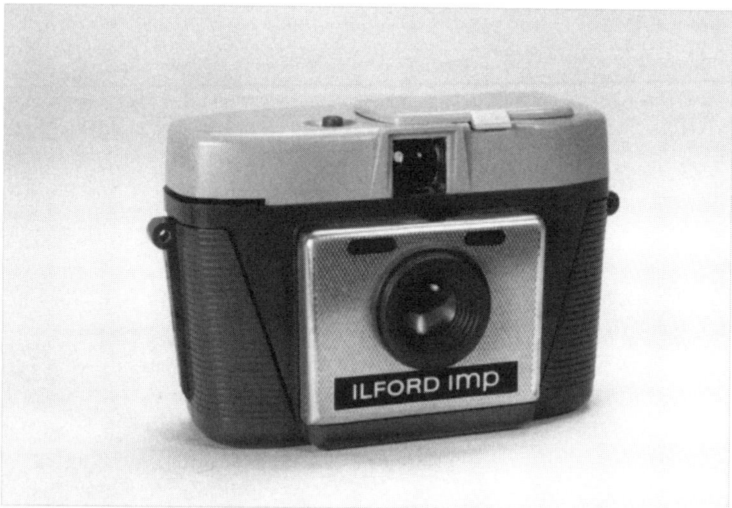

The Imp made in 1964 by Agilux and was a very simple camera with a single setting. This was a shutter lever, which was moved to a position corresponding to the type of film in the camera Colour or Black and White. Picture taking was equally simple after dark or indoors because a flash unit was provided as a built in feature of the camera.

The Imp took 127 film, had an eye level, optical viewfinder with a built-in-pop-over signal, which is visible after each picture is taken. This served as a reminder that the film must be wound on, and the shutter release would not work until the film had been wound on.

The built-in-flash unit was of the battery-capacitor type and was powered by a 22 ½ volt battery. A flap on the camera top concealed the flash reflector and bulb holder. Lifting the flap raised the reflector into position allowing the flash bulbs to be inserted. PF 1 type capless bulbs were used.

Ilford Pixie - 1966

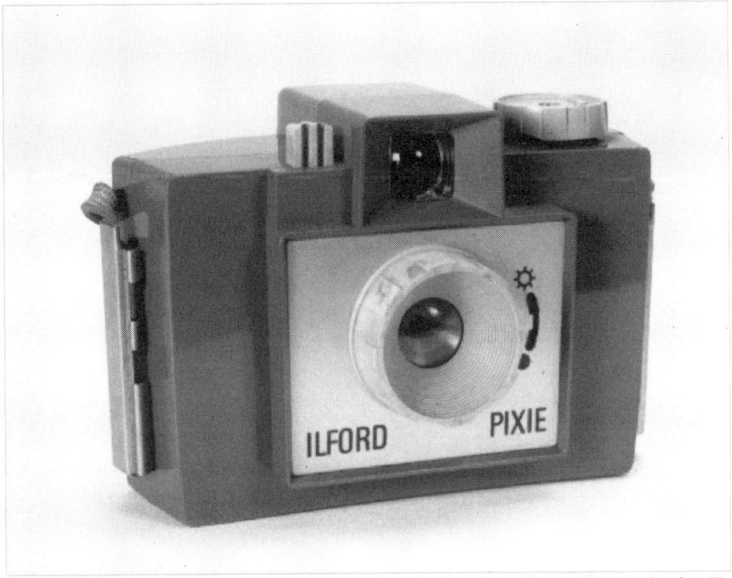

The Ilford Pixie camera was simplicity itself, well made in England, by Agilux and attractively designed. it had a body made from impact resistant polystyrene and used 127 film.

The lens was a fixed-focus type with two apertures, one for sunny and one for dull. The setting for these was via a small lever on the front plate. The rounded back and the positive shutter release made the camera feel very comfortable to adult and child hands alike.

At £1. 4s. 6d. this little camera was very good value.

Some of the promotional material, which I have found, shows the Pixie with fluted front panels as an aid for holding the camera. However I believe that this idea was not adopted in production and the camera had smooth front panels as shown in the photograph above.

PHASE 4 (1964-1965)

Kodak shattered the photographic world with the introduction of the 126 cartridge system (Instamatic). They sold some 15 million cameras in 18 months! By 1970 their sales increased to some 50 million. To support these incredible sales they needed many kilometres of Kodacolor film and many miles of printing paper in addition to tons of developing and fixing chemicals.

The members of the Photographic dovecot into which this cat had been projected attended a meeting at the Agfa works at Leverkusen.

Agfa proposed to counter Kodak by updating the Agfa Karat system. This was renamed the 'Rapid System'. It had been developed in 1936 and abandoned years before and all were invited to join the club.

Agfa would withhold nothing but of course they would be set for a flying start. Everyone swore loyalty to the new legion and death to Kodak. Each then got busy with their designers to create new cameras following the stages in which Agfa released details. Ilford got busy with Dangelmaier and Agilux.

Of course Kodak would have allowed anyone to make cameras to their patents but for a price. Kodak were not interested in putting the Kodacolor film into the Rapid cartridge, and why should they? Non-Kodak manufacturers had to pay 25 cents per camera for the rights to use their Instamatic system in their own camera design and another 25 cents for the rights to use the flashcube system. Eventually all, including Agfa, reneged on the deal and joined in, however belatedly. The outcome from the Ilford side was:

Sportina Rapid	Dangelmaier
Sprite Rapid Flash	Agilux

To cover its bet, Ilford and Agilux thought up the Sprite 35 a 35 mm camera of exceptional low cost.

Sad to relate the possible advantages of the Rapid System were not realised due mainly to the delays, which enabled Kodak to indoctrinate the market to their way of thinking. Also the Germans thought of the Rapid system in the idiom of the high-class, black leather and chrome production of a photographic industry devoted to 'fine mekanicks'. Kodak thought of Instamatic in a different way - use as much plastic as possible, make sure its attractive and 100% reliable and above all very cheap.

The German industry was now showing a stick-in-the mud attitude, which had already begun to yield benefits to the Japanese competitors. At this time Ilford began to investigate a possible collaboration on 35 mm cameras with Smiths of Cricklewood (Smiths English Clocks) and visualisations were produced. Strange to relate, one variety was a banana shaped camera, where the wings of the banana pointed back, not forward. This idea was abandoned and the model was never produced.

Eventually the Rapid system collapsed due to the absence of Kodacolor film.

In 1963 Ilford had agreed to an exchange of research ideas with CIBA AG of Switzerland. CIBA were interested in using their dyes for a new silver dye-bleaching process they were developing. Three years later "Cilchrome" was introduced which was later named "Cibachrome".

In 1965 colour film was not selling as well as Ilford had hoped and eventually Ilford discontinued selling Ilford branded colour film and paper and eventually all colour film materials, except Cibachrome, were discontinued in 1970.

In 1970 CIBA merged with J.R. Geigy. Ilford continued developing its black and white and Cibachrome products.

In the rest of this section I will continue with the Sportsman development first before returning to the chronological order of events.

Ilford Sportsman Electric and Sportsman 35

Ilford Sportsman Electric - 1967

In 1967, three new Sportsman models joined the stable. These were the Electric range, which were fitted with CdS non-coupled light meters.

The Electric models did not have the Sportsman logo on the camera itself but were identified as such in marketing material and the owner's manuals as shown here.

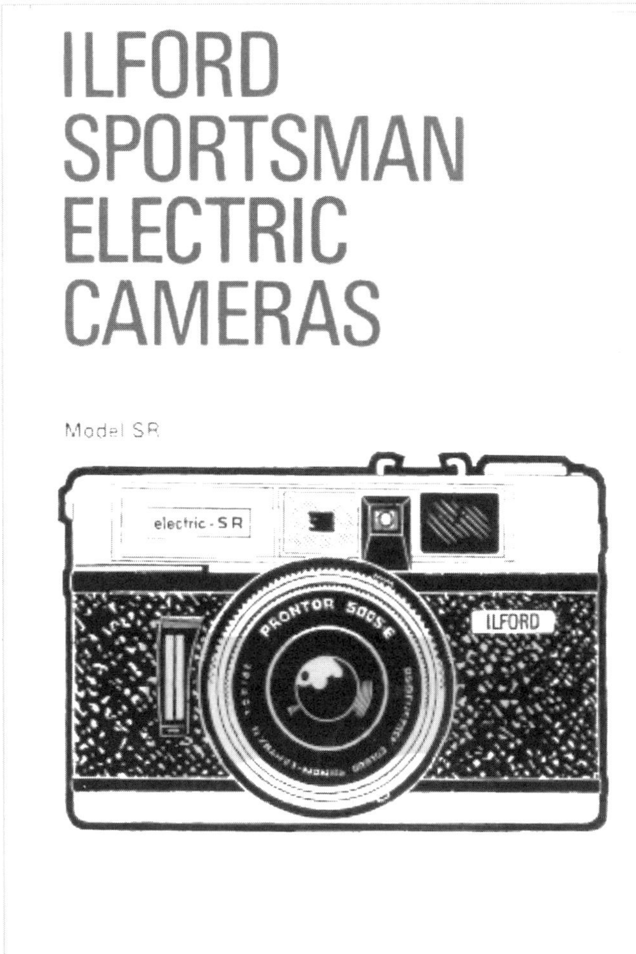

There were four models, the Electric-CR, Electric-SR and the Electric-L. The Electric-S was presumably a later addition (at least, it was not mentioned in the manual which covered the other models).

Ilford Electric-CR

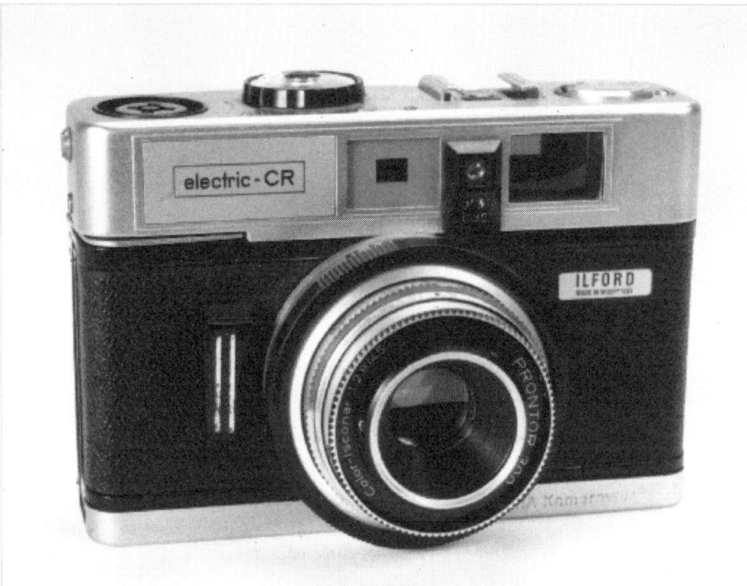

The 'CR' had a CdS (Cadmium Sulphide) exposure meter from Bertram, which was not coupled to the iris diaphragm. The exposure monitored was read from the top plate mounted light meter and manually the speed and aperture values were set.

It had a Rodenstock Colour-Isconar aperture coated lens of 45 mm focal length with a maximum aperture of f/2.8. It used a Prontor 300 shutter giving speeds of 1/30, 1/60, 1/125, and 1/300 second and B.

It was produced during the time the flashcube was first released and conveniently provided both a hot shoe centre contact flash holder as well as a flashcube socket. The power for the light meter was a PX-13 battery, which was housed in the centre of the top plate next to the eyepiece. The battery for the flashcube was two 825 batteries mounted in the base of the camera.

Like the Sportsman 125 and 300 a plastic vertically operated shutter release button was used and the exposure counter was located on the base plate.
It sold for £26 10s. 0d. in 1967.

Ilford Electric-S

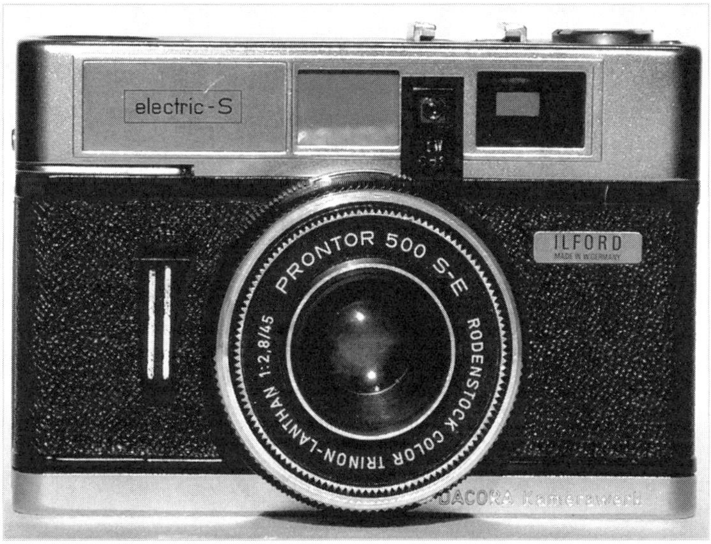

The Electric S had a Prontor 500 S-E shutter with a self-timer. Rodenstock Color Trinon-Lanthan 45mm lens.

Ilford Electric-SR

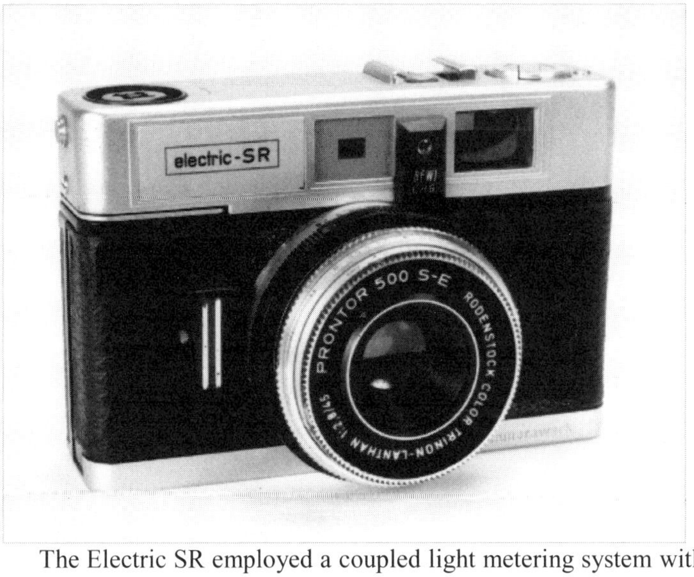

The Electric SR employed a coupled light metering system with an exposure needle shown within the viewfinder area. It had a Rodenstock Colour Trinon-Lathan lens of 45 mm and aperture f/2.8. The shutter was a Prontor 500 S-E giving speeds of 1/30, 1/60, 1/125, 1/250, 1/500. (Some models had a Prontor 500-E shutter). In all other respects the SR was the same as the CR, except that it had a coupled rangefinder as well.

Ilford Electric-L

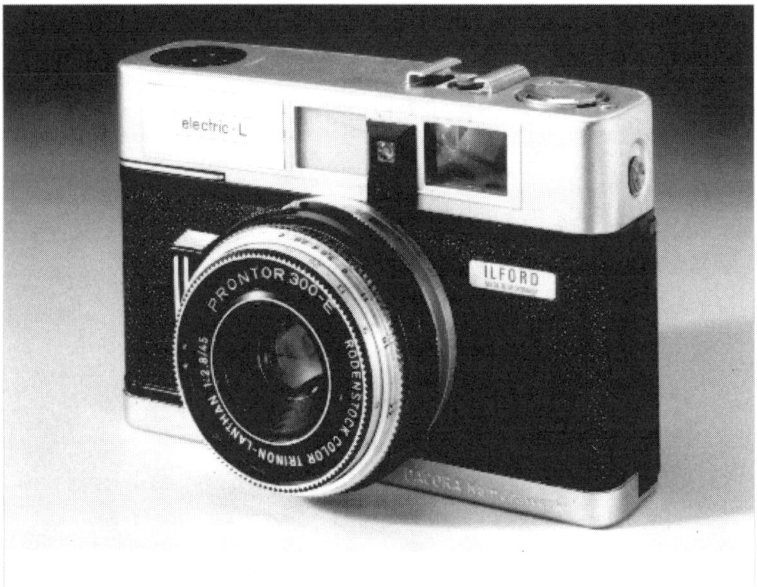

The Electric 'L' model was fitted with a Prontor 300-E shutter and a Rodenstock Color Trinon-Lathan lens. This models light metering system was of the needle matching type similar to the CR with the meter needle seen in the viewfinder.

The Electric models arrived with the advent of microelectronics. Built-in light meters were only just being produced and once again Ilford's designers showed that they could keep abreast of related developments.

Ilford 35 Sportsman – 8th Style

This model of Sportsman is very different. It looks and feels like none of the previous models. It is however similar to the Cilmatic 300 CC (See Page 222). The '35' series were the last Sportsman models and appeared in 1972 (in Europe). Very soon after these cameras were made, the Dacora/Ilford partnership ended.

The 35 R marked the end of camera production for Dacora in Reutlingen although some cameras continued to be made at the Munich factory.

In 1966 Rollei introduced their Rollei 35 camera with tremendous applaud and very high sales. It was the smallest full frame 35mm camera on the market, complete with a Carl Zeiss lens. During this time the camera business in Germany became very difficult. Competition from Japan and the Far East caused many companies to close (with the notable exception of Balda).
The Dacora 35 could not cope with such competition and neither could Dacora.

Ilford Sportsman 35 CL (€) - 1972

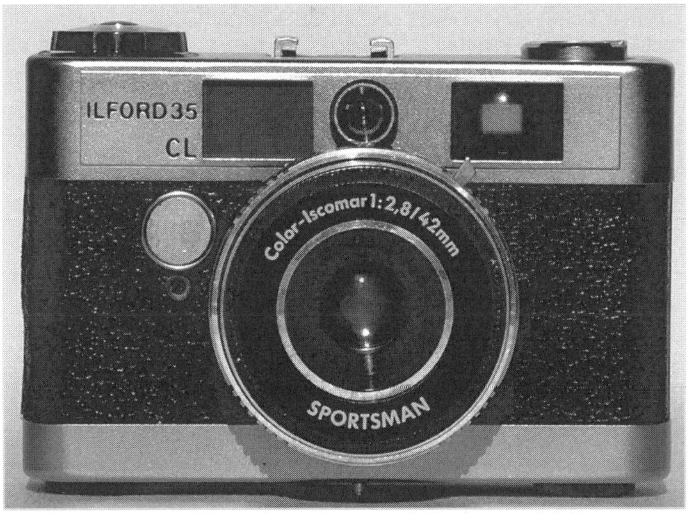

Color-Isconar 42mm lens, Prontor 300 shutter, Light meter controls top left CdS not coupled, Light collector on front above lens, recessed rewind crank, Self timer, Press in exposure button on front, Synchronised flash shoe, Bottom plate holds Exposure counter, battery compartment, tripod bush and plastic film advance crank.

Made in W. Germany embossed on the bottom plate. 'Sportsman' on lens plate. A lanyard attachment was supplied which screwed into the tripod bush.

Ilford Sportsman 35 C (€) - 1972

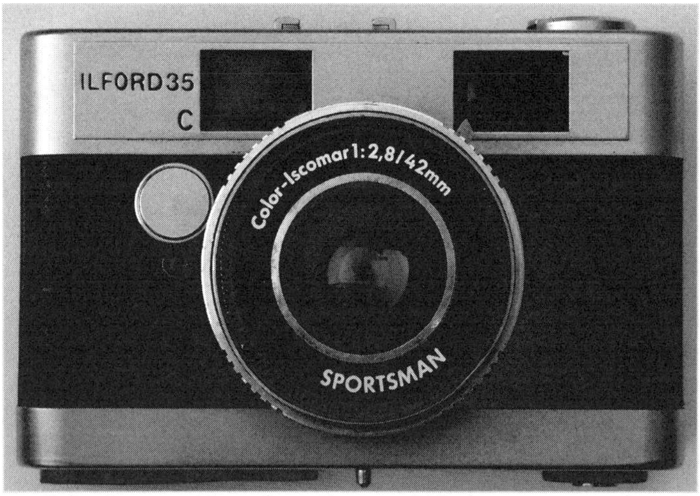

Color-Isconar 42mm lens, Prontor 300 shutter, recessed rewind crank, Self timer, Press in exposure button on front, Synchronised flash shoe, Bottom plate holds Exposure counter, battery compartment, tripod bush and plastic film advance crank.

Made in W. Germany embossed on the bottom plate. 'Sportsman' on lens plate. A lanyard attachment was supplied which screwed into the tripod bush.

Ilford Sportsman 35 L (€)

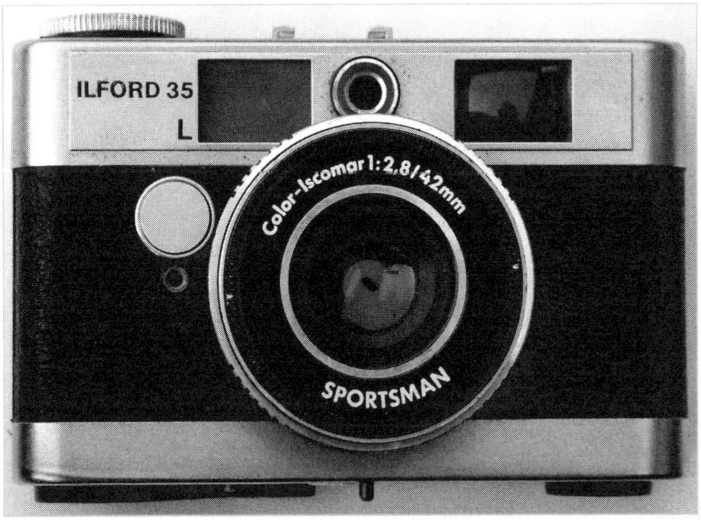

Color-Isconar 42mm lens, Prontor 300 shutter, recessed rewind crank, Press in exposure button on front, Synchronised flash shoe, Bottom plate holds Exposure counter, battery compartment, tripod bush and plastic film advance crank.

Made in W. Germany embossed on the bottom plate. 'Sportsman' on lens plate. The model above has a metal exposure meter dial instead of the plastic fitting as seen below.

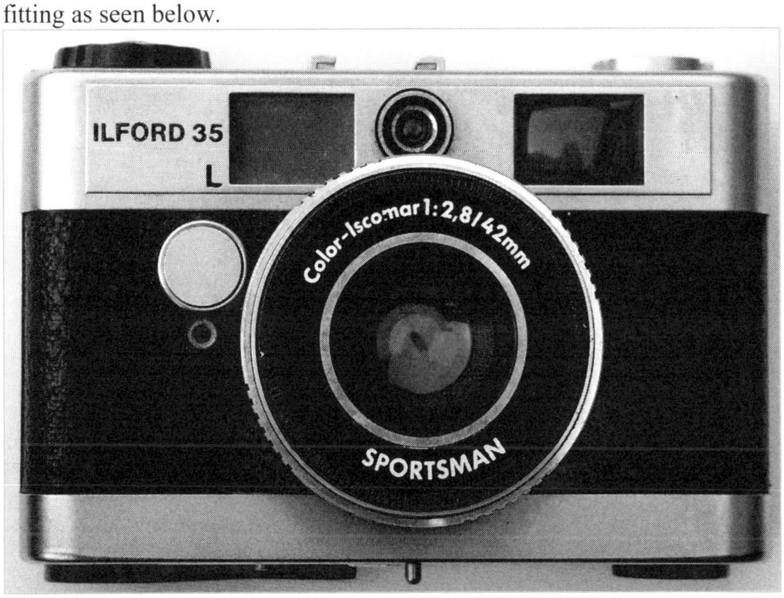

Ilford Sportsman 35 R (€)

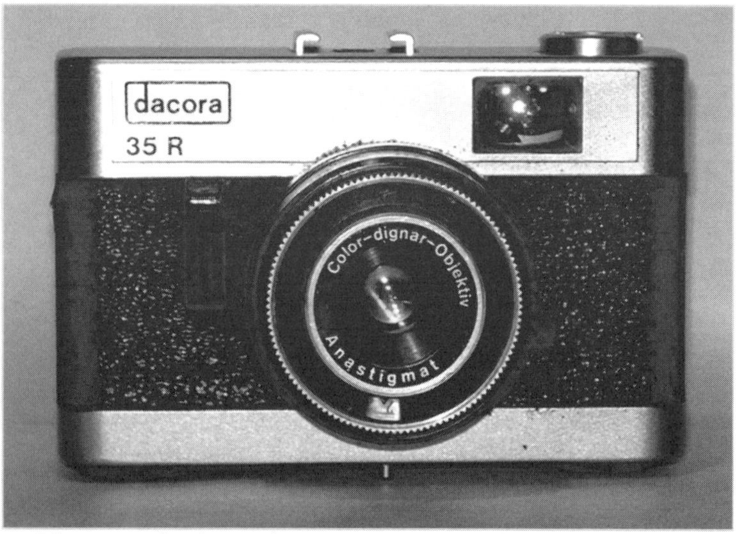

The example shown is a Dacora 35 R. The Ilford version was identical except for the nameplate. It has a Color-Dignar lens, four weather symbols (sunny, overcast, cloudy and flash), Symbols for Faces, People and Places with the distance setting showing in the window under the lens.

Ilford Sportsman 35 RL (€)

Same as the 35R but with a non-coupled selium exposure meter.

Ilford Sportsman 35 CC - 1972

This model (probably only a prototype) was the top of the '35' range including all (?) of the lower model features and was also fitted with a rangefinder.

Ilford Sportina Rapid and Sportina Ilfomatic - 1964

The Ilford Sportina Rapid cameras employed an old idea of Agfa's using a Karat film cassette. These obviated the need for the photographer to thread the film onto the take up spool. It could also set the film speed automatically via a key on the cassette body, the length of the key set the ASA rating of the film.

The Rapid pack cassette was placed in the camera and the back was closed. The film wind-on lever was operated until it automatically stopped. The film being fed into another identical but empty Rapid cassette. The metal cassettes were of tear-shaped section with a light-tight, velvet-lined slot. The shutter could not be operated until the film was in position.

Winding on to the first frame also cocked the shutter. The camera had a plastic body with satin chrome parts and leatherette covering.

The lens aperture was automatically set according to the film speed by the insertion of the Rapid pack, which had a key on the outside, which set the camera. With black and white film the aperture was approximately f 12.5, with Colorslide and Colorprint films the aperture was set to f 6.3. The cameras could take the full range of films (speeds 25 to 100 ASA) for which the rapid system was designed.

The cameras had a 'weather' setting to adjust the shutter speed. The 'sunny' symbol gave 1/125 second, the 'overcast' symbol gave 1/60 second the 'flash' symbol gave 1/30 second.

The lens (3 element, bloomed, 46 mm, Dacora Dignar and on some models a Subitar) was focused by rotating the lens ring. The standard 'faces and people and places' symbols were engraved on the fixed part. It also showed the distance setting through a small window beside the lens.

The exposure counter displayed the number of exposures remaining on the film. On reaching the end an 'E' was displayed. The back could then be opened and the take-up cassette removed. The original but now empty rapid cassette could be moved to the left side and a new pack inserted in the right. The film moved in the un-conventional direction of right to left.

The camera had a hot flash shoe above the large plain direct vision optical viewfinder.

The camera was slightly modified during its life. Later models had the flash shoe flush mounted to the top of the camera body and positioned centrally over the lens axis. The wind-on lever was also re-styled.

Ilford Sportina Rapid - Style 1

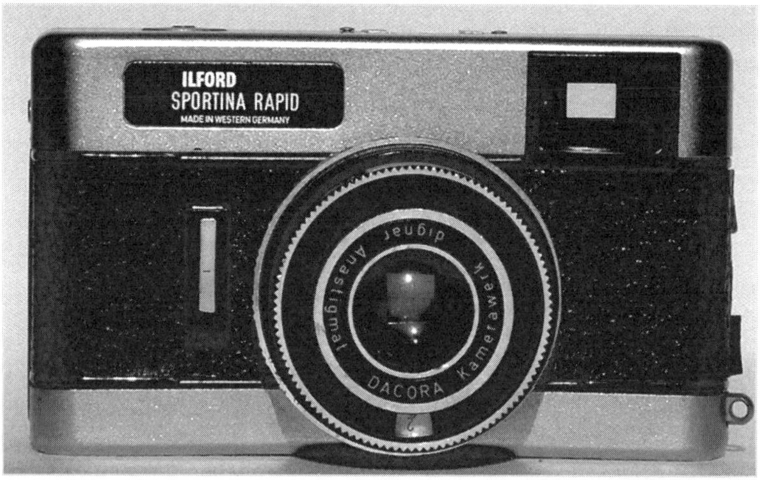

This version has a Dignar anastigmat lens.

Ilford Sportina Rapid - Style 1B

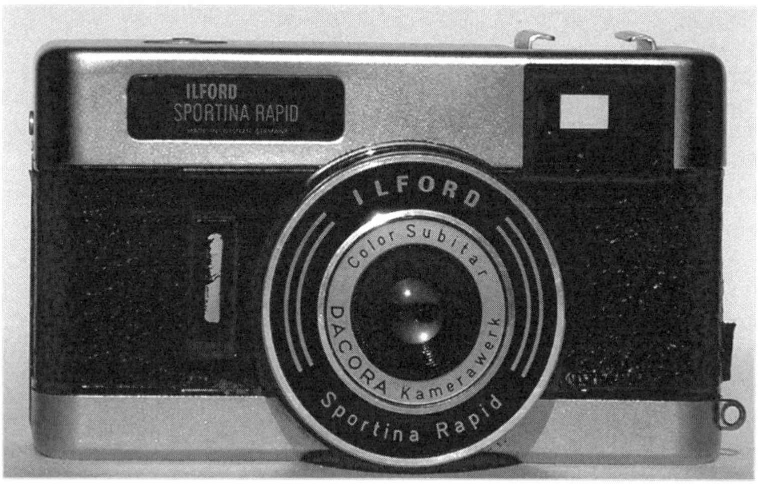

This variation has a prominent Dacora logo and does not have the distance-setting window on the front face unlike the model shown above. It has a Subitar lens.

Ilford Sportina Rapid - Style 1C

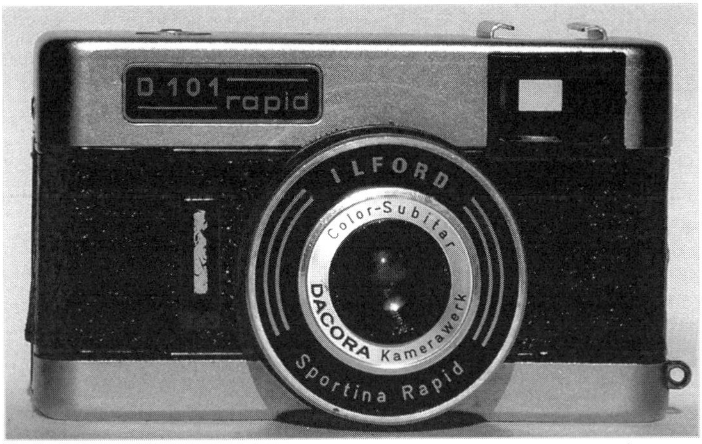

When looking at the above and the previous two examples you can see how Ilford and Dacora would ring the changes.

- Ilford Sportina Rapid (previous page) – pure Ilford
- Ilford Sportina Rapid with Dacora on the shutter plate (previous page)
- D101 Rapid with Ilford on the shutter plate (above)

Ilford Sportina Rapid - Style 2

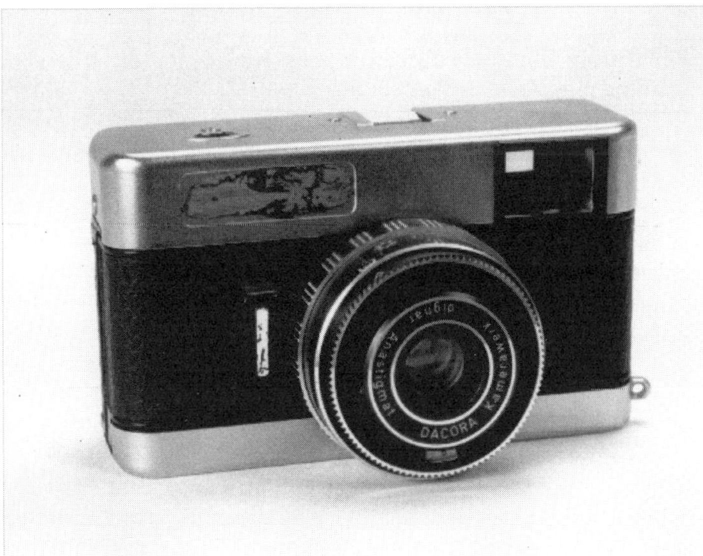

In this example the flash shoe has been repositioned above the lens rather than above the viewfinder and is inset into the top plate.

Ilford Sportina Rapid III

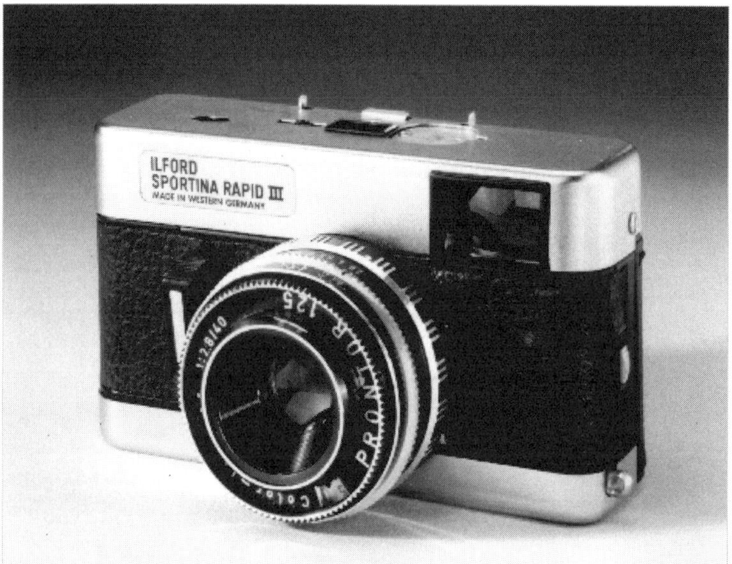

The Sportina Rapid III was a precision camera, adjustable but simple to use, designed around the Rapid easy-loading system.

It used a 40 mm f/2.8 Color Isconar lens with apertures from f/2.8 to f/22.

The Prontor 125 shutter was fitted giving shutter speeds of 1/30, 1/60, 1/125 second plus B. Focusing from 3 ½ feet to infinity by rotating the lens with distances marked both in feet and by the focusing symbols.

It had a built-in capacitor flashgun, which took the small AG bulbs. This was located on the top of the camera, the reflector, a simple curved metal film, could be flipped-up when required. (The design of the flip up mirror was poor and often came adrift from the camera body, as shown in the picture above)

It was made in West Germany by the Dacora company of satin chrome on brass with black leatherette on the plastic body and sold for £14. 19s. 6d.

It took built-in AG flash bulbs and had a Prontor 125 shutter and Color-Isconar 40mm f/2.8 lens.

Ilford Sportsman Rapid III (€)

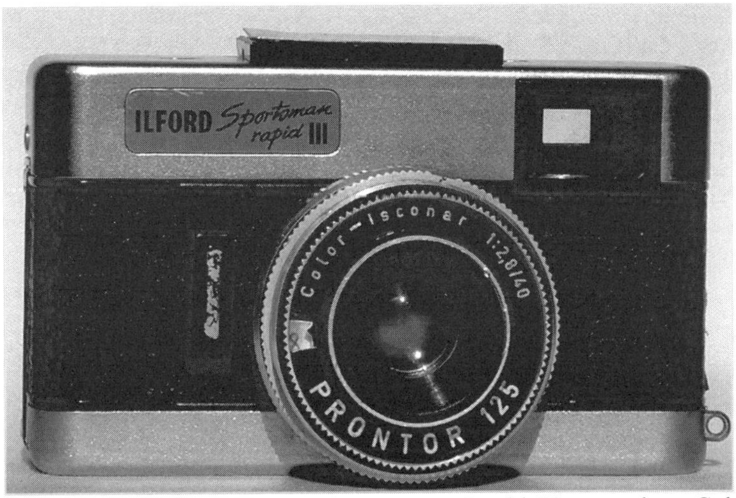

This example has the Ilford Sportsman Rapid III nameplate. Color-Isconar 40mm lens, built-in flash bulb holder for AG bulbs and flip up mirror, Prontor 125 shutter.

Ilford Test Marketing from 1966

New Products for the Rapid System

Two new Ilford Rapid Cameras - the Ilford Sportina Rapid III and the Ilford Auto Rapid - will be test marketed in the South West distribution area this year.

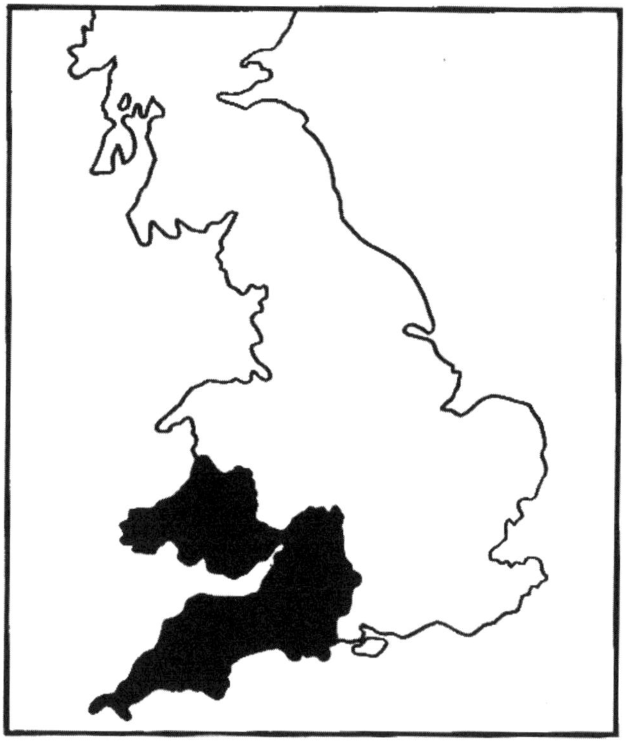

15

Ilford test marketed most of their cameras in specific regions before they went on 'general release'. Their salesmen would visit retailers in the selected region and present the new models. They would report back comments made as to the price, ease of use and predicted sales and a marketing strategy would be developed.

The image above was taken from a brochure given to their marketing team during this period.

My father developed a deep suspicion about salesmen when they gave him a prediction of the number of cameras that they could sell. My father took a less optimistic (and as it turned out, realistic) view but was often overruled and had to stock the warehouse with too many cameras which they then had to off-load at reduced prices. Stock taking at the Basildon factory was never an enjoyable time, especially when they had to report the vast sums of money tied up in unsold stock waiting to be sold.

Ilford Sportina Rapid IV / Ilford Sportsman Rapid IV (€) Dignar

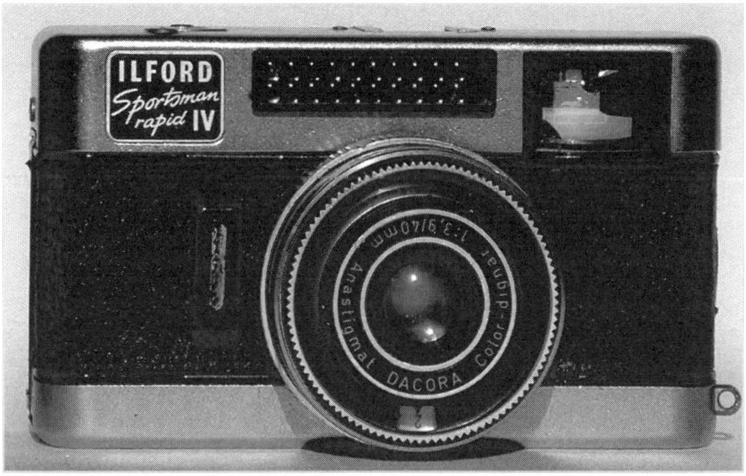

Color Dignar lens 40mm, f/3.9 lens, fully automatic, Flash shoe.

Ilford Sportina Rapid IV / Ilford Sportsman Rapid IV (€) Subitar

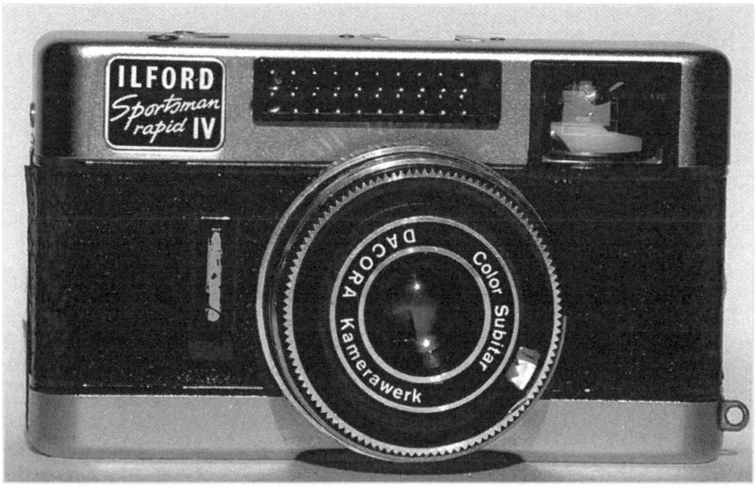

The same as previous but with a Color Subitar 40mm, f/3.9 lens, fully automatic, Flash shoe.

Ilford Sportina Auto-Rapid / Sportsman Rapid IV - 1966

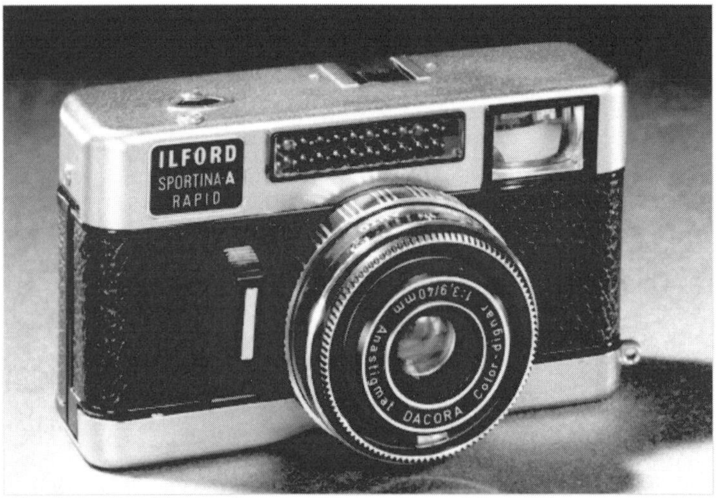

The Auto-Rapid was the top of the range rapid model.

Some variants had the name, 'Sportina Auto Rapid' on the faceplate whilst others had the name, 'Sportina-A Rapid'.

It had only two settings, one for flash/auto and the other for focusing.

It used a Color-Dignar Anastigmat f/3.9 40 mm focal length lens. The aperture was controlled by the built in automatic exposure meter and the Rapid pack ASA key.

It provided two speeds, 1/40th for flash and 1/100th for automatic exposure set by the 'auto' and 'flash' symbols.

It had an optical bright-line viewfinder with an automatic signal showing whether the light conditions were sufficient. If the red indicator showed the user would have to use a hot-shoe flashgun mounted on the top of the camera.

It sold for £18. 19s. 6d and provided an excellent camera producing good results with minimal controls.

Ilford Sportina Ilfomatic

The Sportina Ilfomatic was made by the Dacora company and was a straightforward adaptation of the Sportina Rapid models. Indeed it was the belated answer to the Kodak Instamatic. This camera was the same size as the Sportina Rapid except it was slightly taller to accommodate the Instamatic cartridge, which was dropped into the camera in the standard manner.

Ilford Sportina Ilfomatic Style 1

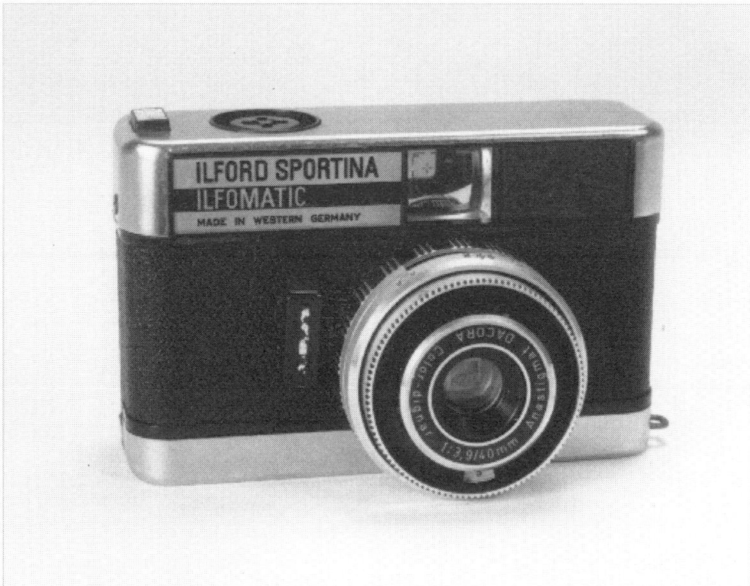

It used a three-element Color-Dignar f/3.9 anastigmat lens of 40 mm focal length. The lens aperture, a simple two-part leaf forming a square had 4 settings indicated by coloured symbols for; very cloudy, cloudy, cloudy but bright and sunny.

Focusing used the faces, people and places symbols on the lens ring with distances appearing in a window next to the lens itself.

It could use flashcubes, which were accumulated on the top plate, powered by a 15 volt battery located in the base of the camera, and would be fired when the aperture was set to the 'lightning flash' symbol.

The shutter was coupled to the aperture setting giving the following speeds;

Sunny	1/90 second f/16
Cloudy-but bright	1/90 second f/11
Cloudy	1/90 second f/8
Very cloudy	1/90 second f/5.6
Flash	1/40 second f/8

Ilford Sportina Ilfomatic Style 2

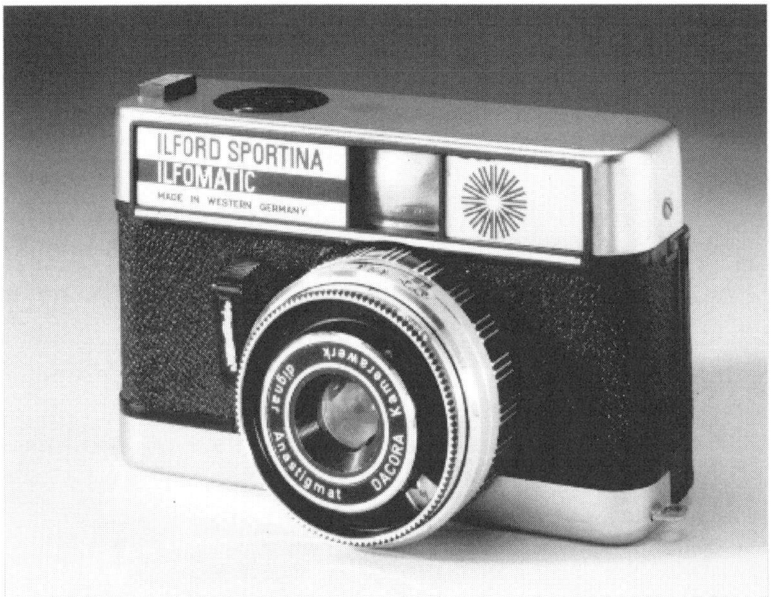

As previous picture but with Dacora Dignar Anastigmat lens.

Ilford Sprite Rapid Flash

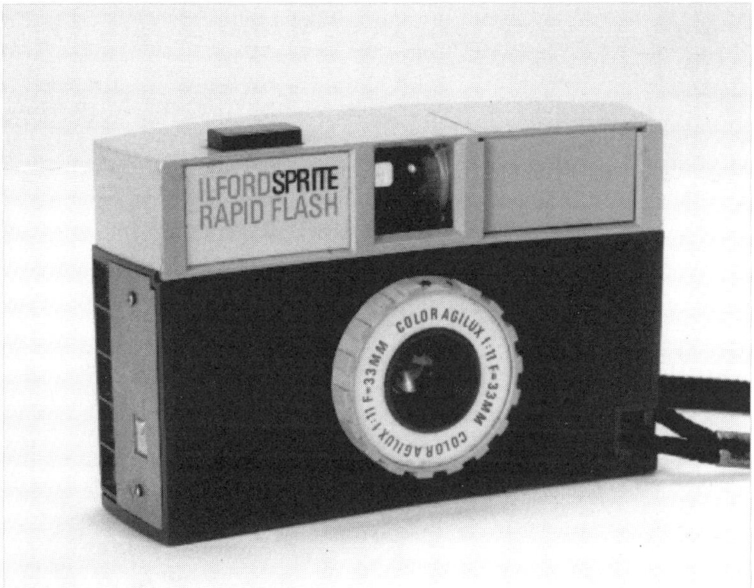

Another camera which employed the Ilford Rapid pack system was the Ilford Sprite Rapid Flash. This was another simple to operate camera where the Rapid system enhanced its ease of use further.

The camera was made of two-tone grey plastic with a built in flip up flash reflector taking AG type bulbs.

The lens was a meniscus type, made of plastic with a focal length of 33mm and a fixed aperture of f 11. The shutter had two speeds. The faster, marked with a sun symbol was about 1/90 second and the other, indicated by a conventional flash symbol was about 1/45 second.

To power the flash two AAA cells were fitted via a swing back cover plate in the bottom plate of the camera.

The viewfinder was an optical type giving an image about 5/8th format size.

Winding on was performed by a flush-mounted thumb wheel.

The camera felt very good to hold because of its banana shape the back being curved allowing for the users thumbs to be out of the way of ones nose when looking through the finder.

It was made for Ilford by Agilux Limited and sold for £2. 17s. 6d.

Ilford Sprite 35

The Sprite 35 was the cheapest 35 mm camera on the market at the time. It was made of two-tone grey plastic with a green-grey plastic trim on the front face.

The 40mm meniscus lens had three aperture settings; f/8, f/11, f/16 set by a side lever on the front face.

It used a single speed shutter timed at 1/45 sec. It had a self-setting film counter, double exposure prevention and lever-wind film transport.

It did not have the conventional sprockets and film advance mechanism but simply one fat take-up spindle at the end. This meant that the spacing between frames became wider and wider as the film went through the camera, as the take-up spindle diameter increased.

It was synchronised for flash without the need for plugs or leads by having its own flashgun, which made the contact when fitted to the top of the camera. As a lightweight, robust and extremely easy to use camera it was intended to make an ideal starting point for 35mm photography.

Ilford Sprite 35 - Style 1

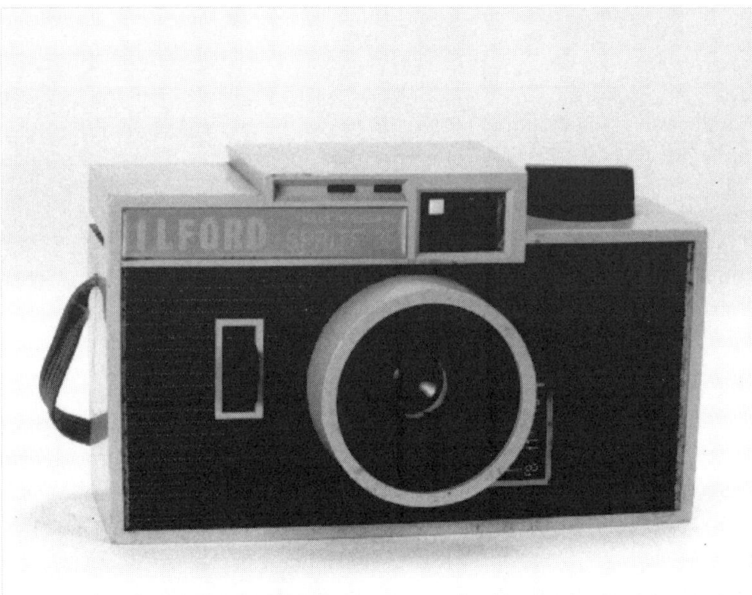

Ilford Sprite 35 - Style 2

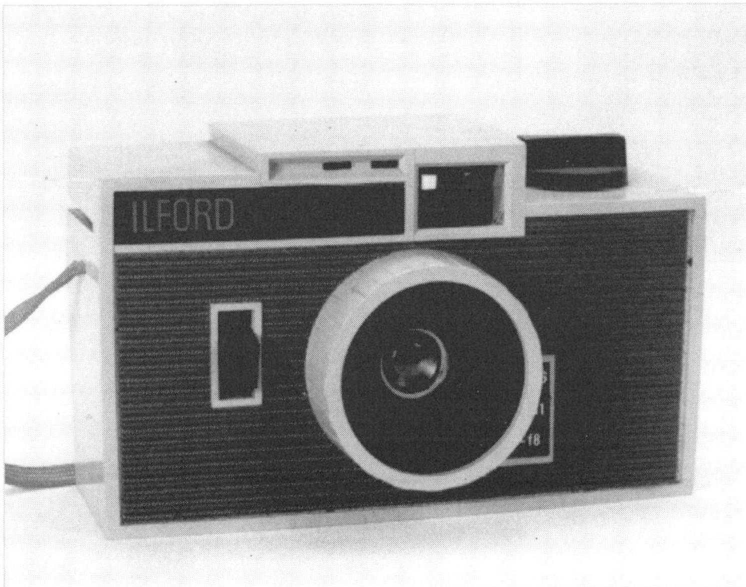

The camera had one facelift. The outside of the plastic lens hood changed from being smooth to knurled and the letter colouring and background colour of the logo plate was changed. The lettering for the aperture settings also changed from a horizontal to a vertical alignment.

Ilford Sprite 35 - Style 3

Yet again, another variant has come to light (2004). This version is similar to the Style 1, with a darker green plastic facia (the Style 2 shown previously has a green/grey facia) and with the Ilford logo in green rather than the light blue. The lens surround is grey as opposed to the previous black colour.

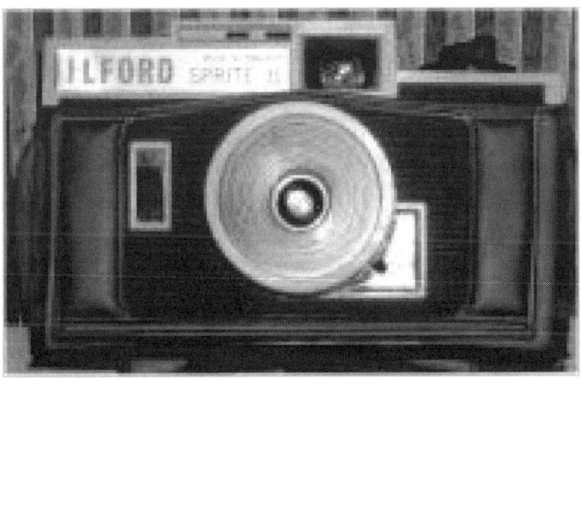

Sprite 35 Flash Gun

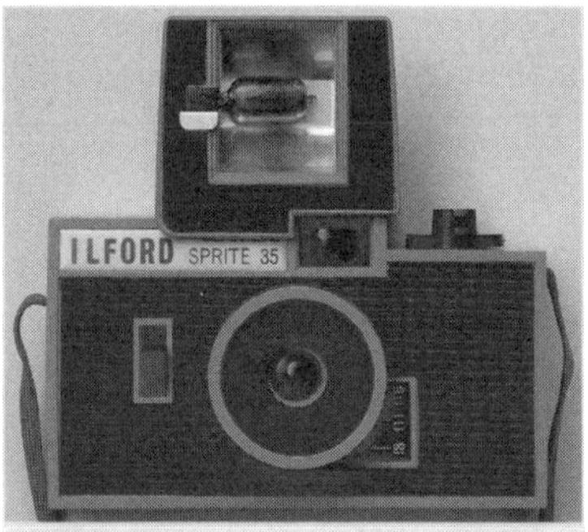

The Sprite 35 has a unique flashgun. Unique because it cannot be fitted onto any other camera and also unique in its design.

The front of the flashgun has the same green trim as the body of the camera.

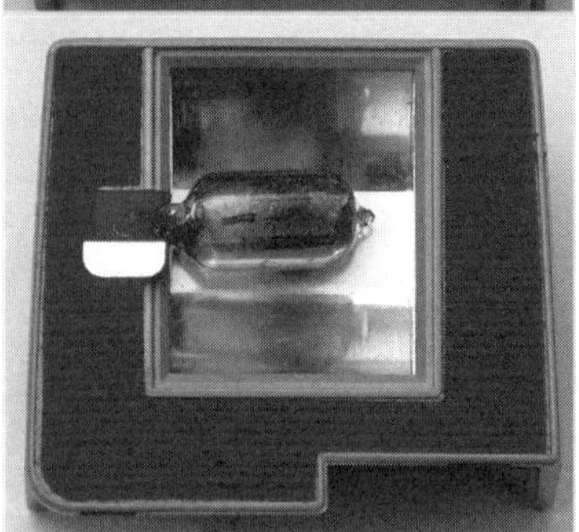

On the front of the camera, next to the viewfinder there are 2 contact slots for the flashgun.

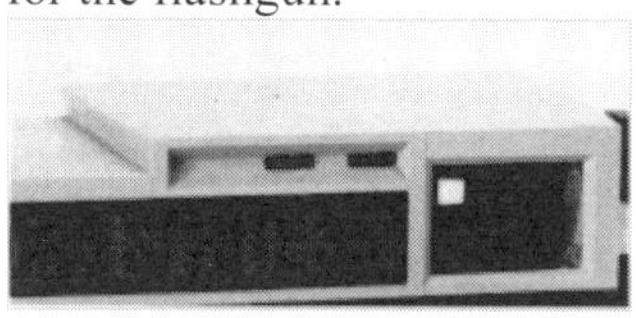

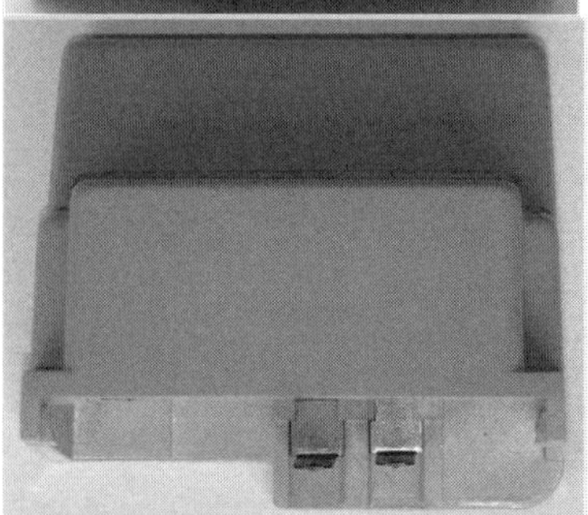

The edge of the plastic on the top, on both the viewfinder side and the opposite side, is angled (like a dovetail joint) to allow the flash head to slide onto the top with the contacts being made and the flashgun held securely in place.

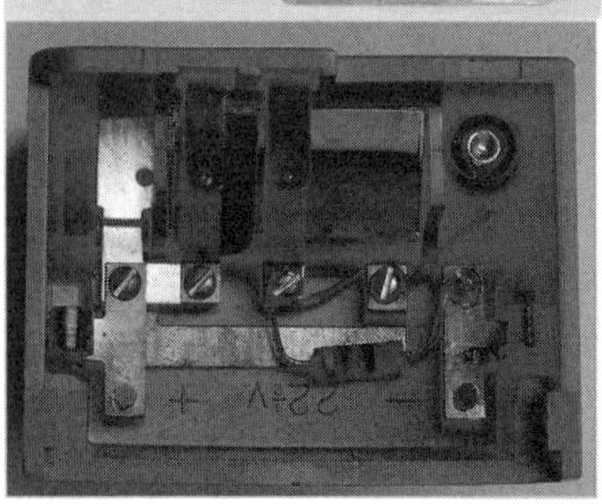

The underneath of the flashgun does not have a cover so you have immediate access to the battery compartment, which takes a 22 ½ volt battery, when you take the unit off the camera.

PHASE 5 (1966-1969)

The comparative failure of the Rapid System and reducing sales of Sportsman and Sporti models made it necessary to take a new look for competitive suppliers.

Ilford visited Japan and secured the agency for the Elmo cine cameras to be sold under the joint Ilford-Elmo logo. They were able to do this because their agent had made an arrangement to supply John Bloom in breach of their agents understanding with Elmo.

The Japanese still camera manufacturers all had existing agencies, which they could not drop, and there were obstacles imposed by MITI (Japanese Board of Trade) on the supply of private label cameras.

I have been told that Ilford turned down the offer of the Nikon agency because their products were not in the price bracket required.

They had also decided not to go ahead with the offer to take on the Rolleiflex agency from Germany. At this time Ilford saw the Haking Wong Halina camera factory in Hong Kong but were not impressed. However not much later, Ilford was split up into divisions, one being that of 'Amateur Products'.

A further visit to Hong Kong resulted in an agreement with Haking to take his Instamatic cameras, which he made under patent license. Haking had first been the largest maker of toothbrushes in the world, then he switched to gumboots and became their largest manufacturer and now with Miss Pauline Chan as their technical 'man' were determined to become the largest camera manufacturer in the East - and they succeeded.

A range of cameras was produced in short time. Unfortunately the new Amateur Products Division was set to pioneer new marketing methods in the U.K. Black and White was out and Colour was in.

Color prints had a margin, which would support colour film, and cameras, which could be sold or nearly given away (possibly with one or more films) to ensure a continued business via the 'silent salesman'.

This business was to be direct to the public and not through dealers. Then it was counter-decided that this was not in Ilford's best image and would affect dealer sales adversely. The cameras ordered for this new market were to be sold through normal dealer channels to which they were not ideally switched. None the less sales to dealers were particularly good and the Amateur Photographer commented on the particularly good marketing methods.

At this stage other suppliers were also involved and the following cameras resulted.

Ilfoflex 127	unknown
Ilford Pixie 127	AGI
Ilford Monarch	Minolta
Ilford Ilfomatic	Dacora

The arrangement with Minolta was a gem of Eastern diplomacy. Minolta had UK agents and also agents in all European countries and so Ilford could not become their agent. But Minolta was entitled by MITI Rules to have a main European agent wholesaling to all European countries. Ilford could be made this main agent, because their UK agent did not take the Autopak camera and Ilford agreed not to exploit their position.

Shortly after starting with Haking, Ilford decided to use the more sophisticated system of sample testing and thereafter only 10% of their intake was fully tested.

To dispose of any surplus cameras Ilford successfully entered the premium market. Vast numbers of cameras were sold in this way. In this phase something of the order of 500,000 cameras passed from Ilford to the trade.

Ilford Ilfomatic

The Ilfomatic range were plastic, 126 cartridge loading, cameras produced during 1967 to 1969 and manufactured in Hong Kong, by the Haking Wong Company. (The Sportina Ilfomatic was produced by Dacora in West Germany). They all had a rectangular body with very simple minimal controls.

Ilford Ilfomatic Universal Flash

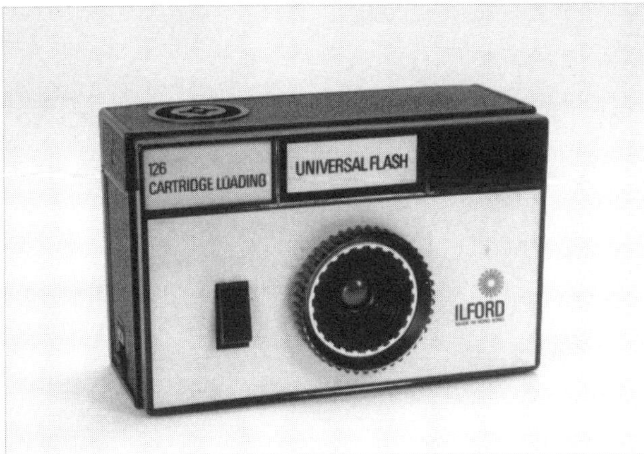

The Universal Flash was the smallest camera in this series, and was produced in 1967. Again using a fixed focus lens with a fixed shutter speed.

The shutter was released by pressing a flush mounted push-in release button as opposed to the push-down style utilised on the other models. It had double exposure prevention and a thumb wheel film advance. The film advance would also wind the flashcube onto the next bulb. It cost £4. 2s. 0d.

Ilford Ilfomatic Super 100

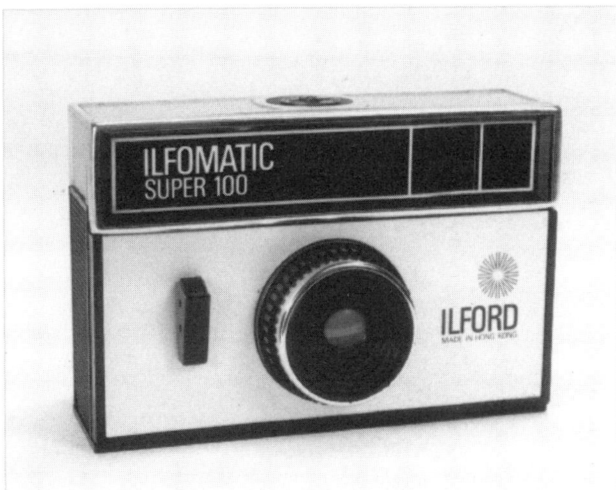

The Super 100 was the physically largest of these 126 cameras. It had a fixed focus lens and a fixed shutter speed. To power the flashcube two AAA batteries, which were fitted into the side of the camera.

This camera was never initially sold direct to the public, as it was a promotional camera obtained by collecting cereal packet tops and the like. It started life in 1966.

Ilford Ilfomatic Universal 50

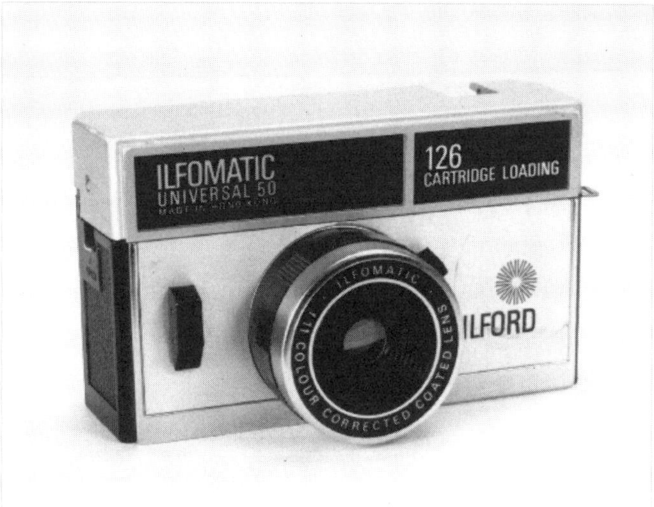

The Universal 50 and the 50C were identical except that the 50 accepted a flash shoe. It had settings for bright sun or cloudy/flash and used a two-element 49mm f/11 fixed-focus lens. It had a centre-contact accessory shoe, eye-level finder and thumb-wheel film advance. It was finished in black and silver grey. It sold for £2. 3s. 6d complete with wrist strap and lens cap.

Ilford Ilfomatic Universal 50C

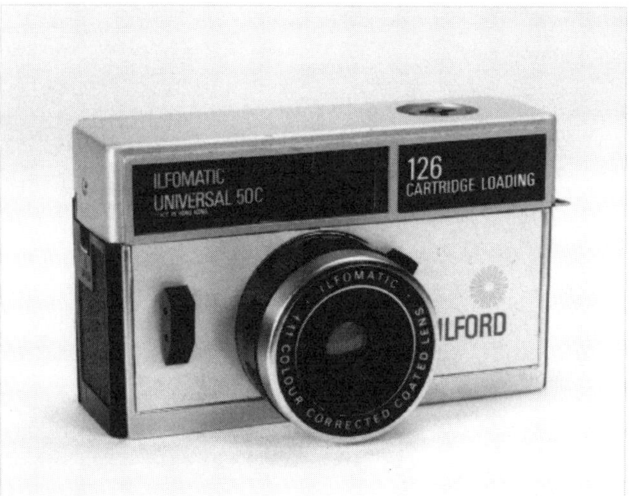

The Universal 50C had the following refinements: The accessory shoe was replaced by a flashcube socket, and the power was provided by two AA cells which fitted into the base of the camera. This model was originally sold for £4 19s. 8d and then, as Ilford disposed of its stocks before their camera marketing division closed down, it was discounted to £2 19s. 7d in 1968.

Ilford Super Universal

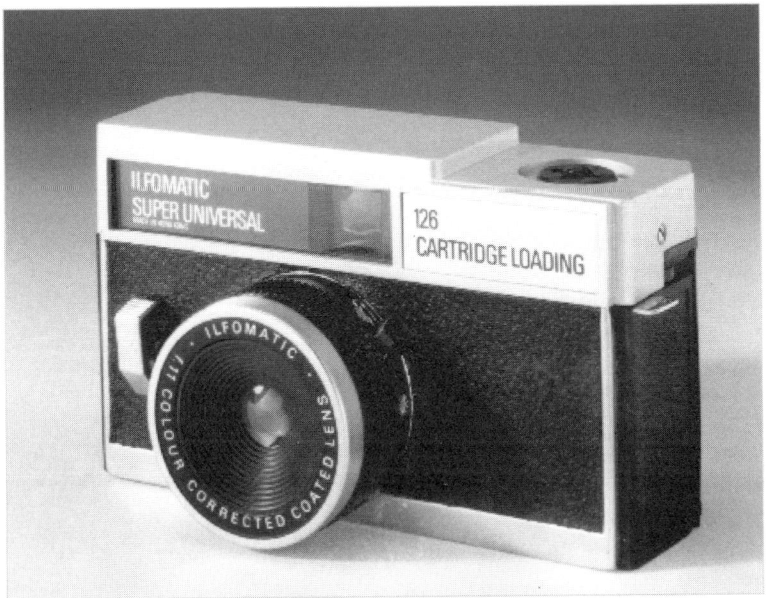

I have found no details about the Super Universal except for its photograph. As shown it is similar to the Universal 50C and would appear to be a better-finished model.

Ilford Ilfomatic Compact

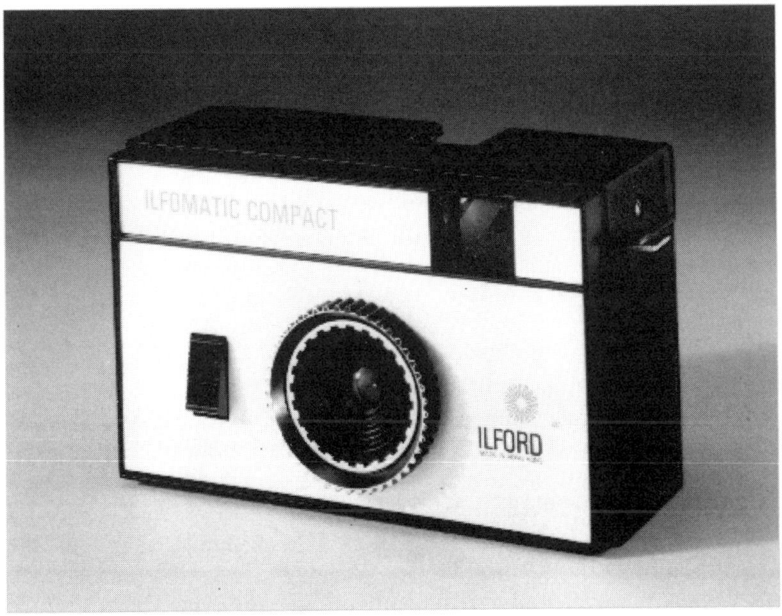

Ilford Instacora - probably 1966

The Instacora range of cameras was my 'last' discovery in the 1980's and the most intriguing. I found some prints and negatives of 3 models (shown on the following pages), within the companies' records held at the Chelmsford record office. At the time I was not aware of Ilford's European marketing activities and as they were un-known to me in the UK I was somewhat mystified.

The name Instacora is presumably based on two parts, INSTA for Instamatic and CORA from Dacora. They all used the Instamatic cartridge system.

Since that time I have come across several variants for sale on Ebay. I believe that they were made around 1966.

Early models used the small AG flash bulbs and a flip-up mirror similar to the Sportsman Rapid III shown on page 189. Later on they were fitted with a Flashcube socket on the top plate.

Some models are 'satin' metal with black leatherette finish. Some have a smooth metal finish instead of the leatherette and finally some have a 'waffle' engineered finish. The latter is an identical finish to the Sportsman Instant range shown on page 164.

Some models have a prominent Ilford logo on the left (facing) side with a light meter on the right whilst others have a weaker logo on the right and no light meter. Some have no makers' logo at all apart from the Dacora lens identification. Dacora did market the same models under their own name using a very similar prominent logo on the left.

The model F (and F2) would appear to be the basic version and are visually very similar to the Sportina Ilfomatic except they have a Dacora Color Subitar lens and do not have a button on the top plate to check the flash battery.

What I find particularly confusing is the Instacora R. You will see on page 208 two Instacora F models, one with a light meter and one without. It is unusual for a camera to progress from one variant to another without a change in identification.

The Instacora - E and R models are similar in that they have a Color-Dignar 40mm lens, flashcube and check button on the top plate and a light meter glass panel on the front face of the camera body to the right of the viewfinder. It is probable that the built-in light meter would have controlled the shutter speed in the same way that the Auto Ilfomatic did. As to the differences between the models I do not know.

From my retrospective and isolated look it would seem that some rationalisation would be required. Confusing to me and presumably the retailers at the time. The Sportsman Instant, Sportsman Rapid, Instacora and Sportina ranges seem to have run concurrently (?) although from a manufacturing and a marketing viewpoint this seems unlikely or at the very least difficult to maintain. The answer may lie in cameras being produced for different countries and a view taken on which name would sell best. The countries that took the Sportsman Instant may have valued the Sportsman name whilst those who took the Instacora maybe preferred direct competition with the Kodak Instamatic. We may never fully understand.

Ilford Instacora E

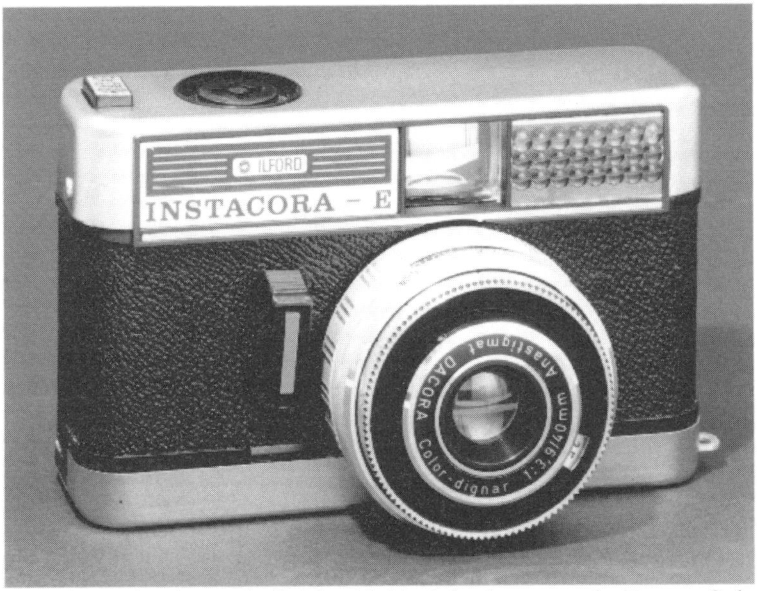

This version has satin finish with black leatherette and a Dacora Color dignar lens. The distance setting can be set with one of the dials and the distance read from the front lower window next to the lens. Next to the Flashcube connection on the top plate is the flashcube eject button. The base of the camera holds a 15 volt battery, which is revealed by a sliding cover.

Ilford Instacora - F

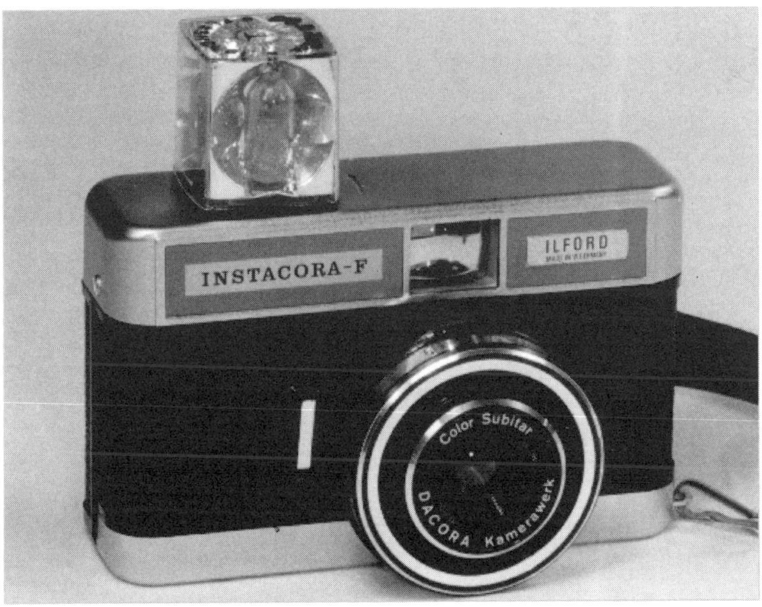

This version has satin finish with black leatherette and a Dacora Color Subitar lens. The Ilford logo is on the right and not so prominent as the E model. The Dacora equivalent used the prominent logo as shown here:

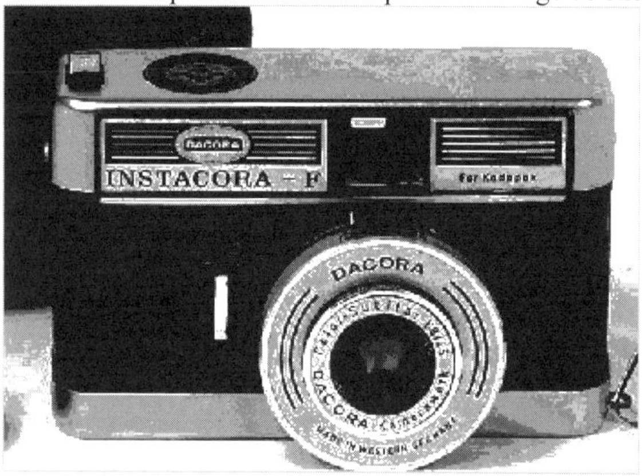

Also, some of the Dacora Instacora F models had the AG flash bulb and flip up mirror as opposed to the Flashcube socket. The example above has black on white lettering on the lens plate as opposed to white on black. It is interesting to wonder why Ilford used the small logo only on their model F and not the same prominent logo on the left as the rest of the Ilford Instacora models.

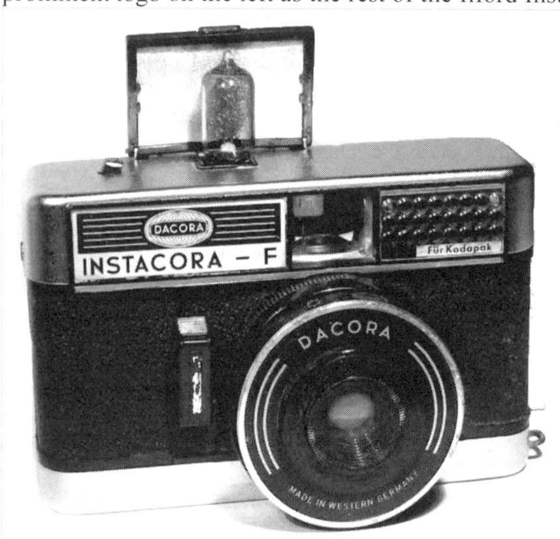

Instacora - F2

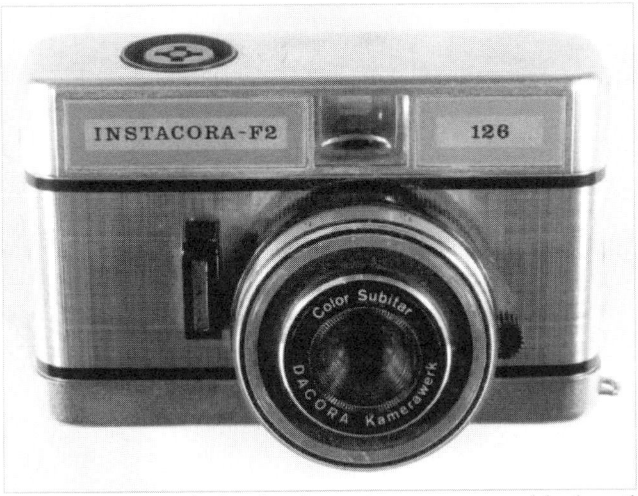

This camera obviously shares its parentage with the other Ilford Instacora models but the example shown does not bear the Ilford logo. It also has a Dacora Color Subitar lens and it does not have the battery test button on the top plate.

Ilford Instacora - R

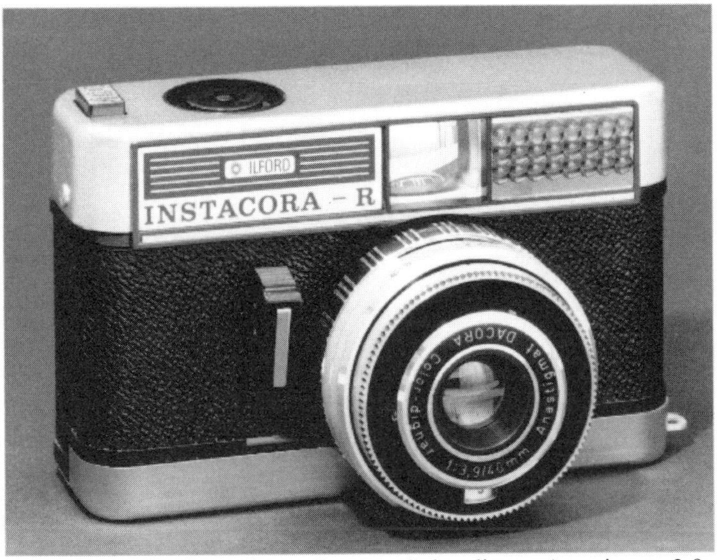

The camera shown has a Dacora Color-dignar Anastigmat 3.9 40mm lens. The distance setting can be set with one of the dials and the distance read from the front lower window next to the lens. Flashcube connection and release button on the top and battery compartment on the base.

Ilford Instacora - R -Version 2

Dacora or Ilford also marketed a version of the Instacora R, which shared the same body finish as the Sportsman R Instant. The two cameras look, from the photos, exactly the same. They both have the Color-dignar-Objectiv lens and neither have a light meter. See page 164.

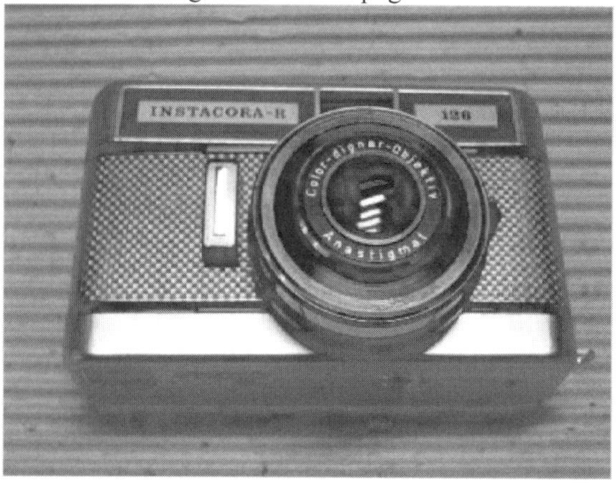

Ilford Ilfoflex

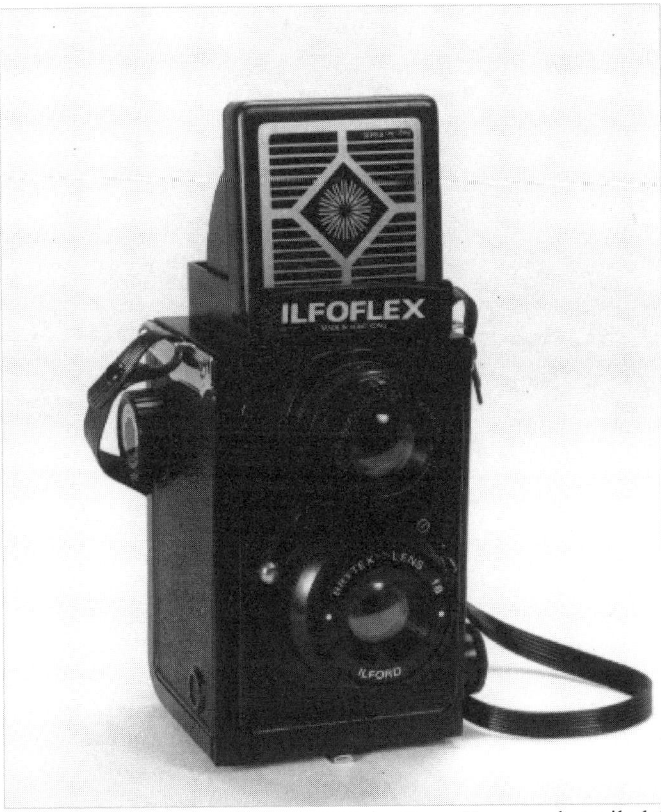

The Ilfoflex was made in 1961 in Hong Kong and retailed for the ridiculous price of 7 shillings and 6 pence. It couldn't possibly be serious could it?

It was made almost entirely of plastic, even the lenses. In appearance it looked like a small twin-lens reflex, though the lenses were of fixed focus and aperture (F/8). It used 127 film with the wind-on numbers shown via the red window at the back. The Everset-type shutter had two settings, "instantaneous" and B. The etched plastic screen gave a good view of the subject.

Results from this camera were much better than would be anticipated.

For a plastic camera of this price it was scrupulously made with much attention to detail. The sides of the body were made with simulated leather grain appearance. As a means of promoting film sales this camera could not be faulted. It was marketed via promotions i.e. send so-many packet tops and we will send you a camera, lens hood, lanyard and a free film!

It was even suggested that the camera could be sold in kit form with a tube of polystyrene glue. Although this idea was tried out within the company it was never sold like this.

This camera must have been the ultimate model for the 'silent salesman'.

Ilford Monarch - 1967

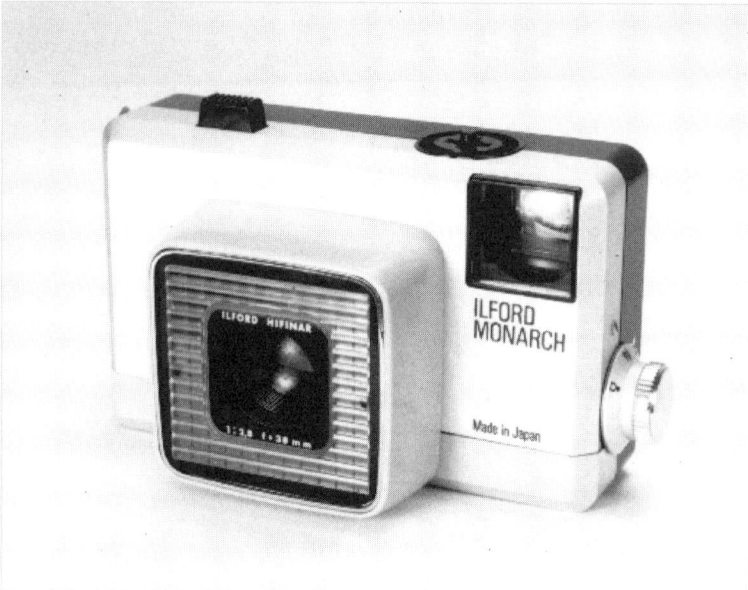

The Monarch was the last camera marketed by Ilford (UK) and with an Ilford logo. It had a Rokkor lens although presented as an Ilford Hifinar f/2.8, 38mm, and took a 126 cartridge pack. It was made by MINOLTA in Japan and would otherwise be known as a Minolta Autopack 500 (although my original notes referred to it as an Autopak 40 which may be either an error or a reference to a camera identification that was never marketed).

It was focused by a knob on the right hand side coupled to a needle, which appeared in the viewfinder window, which was matched against the faces, people and places symbols. It took a flashcube, which would be triggered automatically if natural light conditions were not good enough.

The flash was powered by two AAA batteries, which were loaded in the base of the camera, and the cube would rotate after firing. It had a 'robot controlled' shutter, the electric eye for the built in light meter being around the lens.

This completely automatic camera was attractively styled and sturdily built including case, batteries and strap and sold for £22. 19s. 8d.

It was introduced in 1967 and continued to be produced for just over one year. Like several other Ilford cameras it would not seem out of date in a photographers shop today.

Although there was very little Ilford influence in its design it concluded their (UK) camera marketing in the tradition of providing good quality cameras aimed at specific areas of the amateur market.

CHAPTER 5
Phase 6 -The CIBA Connection (1968 – 1976)

In 1953, Ilford launched a colour print material based on dye bleach technology which continued until 1963.

In 1959, 32 per cent of Ilford's shares were owned by ICI.

In 1962, CIBA acquired the highly respected and long running French company called Lumière based in Lyon, where the Lumière brothers had pioneered cinematography. They also owned Telko, a Swiss photographic company, similar to Lumière, and based at Fribourg. Additionally they acquired Faber at Neu-Isenburg Germany. This company would become CIBA-Ilford GmbH, selling in Germany.

Lumière and Telko already were in business together as Lumière sold the Telcolor range of colour products in France.

Telko was based in Marly, close to Fribourg and was later renamed CIBA Photochemie, then CIBA-GEIGY Photochemie, then Ilford AG and currently, Ilford Imaging Switzerland GmbH.

In 1963, Ilford amalgamated with CIBA-GEIGY Photochemie of Switzerland.

In 1963 Ilford exchanged research ideas with CIBA who were interested in using their dyes for a new silver dye-bleaching process they were developing. Three years later "Cilchrome" was introduced which was later named "Cibachrome". Ilford in conjunction with CIBA-GEIGY, continuously improved the material. By the mid 1970's Cibachrome had become the industry standard for high permanence richly saturated prints from transparencies. (Many of its products had 'CIL' at the beginning of the name being the initials of; Ciba, Ilford and Lumière.)

In 1969 ICI sold their shares in Ilford to CIBA and CIBA became the exclusive owner of Ilford.

Between 1962 and 1972 several product ranges; Ilford, Lumière, Telko and Faber, co-existing and rationalization was required. Additionally, between 1965 and 1970 Ilford colour film was not selling as well as they had hoped and eventually Ilford discontinued selling Ilford branded colour film and paper and eventually all colour film materials, except Cibachrome, were discontinued in 1970. Ilford continued developing its black and white film and papers and Cibachrome products.
In 1976 Ilford left its site in Ilford where it had been for 97 years.

The CIL brand name was used up until 1969 for the new products as obsolete ones disappeared and then Ilford became responsible for the Photographic Group. At this time a single brand name identity "Ilford" was adopted and all packaging was renewed (Ilford Futura logo, white boxes, etc.).
In 1982 CIBA Lumière, was renamed, Ilford France SA.

In the Ilford Professional Catalogue of 1969 which was produced in the U.K. for Ilford retailers there is no mention of any still cameras. Ilford ELMO cine cameras and equipment are listed together with the Weston Master Exposure Meter. Camera marketing in the U.K. had come to an end.

However between 1967 and 1976 additional cameras were made, mostly by Dacora in Germany and at least two from Hong Kong. These cameras were probably commissioned by CIBA in Switzerland or by Ilford-France and sold in Germany, Italy, Holland, France, Belgium and Austria, but not in the U.K.

In 2004 I came across a web site called: www.camera-shopper.com which is published in the USA. It is a small magazine for camera collectors with for sale and wanted adverts along with articles about various cameras and companies. It was there that I noticed an article by F.W. Fokkelman with the title, 'Ilford and Dacora cameras'. I placed an order for a copy of the article and was very glad I did so.

F.W Fokkelman lives in Holland and was a camera retailer from 1958 to 1973. He has written several articles about cameras for camera shopper and other publications based on his long running professional knowledge. In his article about Ilford and Dacora cameras he identified several Ilford cameras that were unknown to me at the time.
His list included:

Camera Model	Year	Made By	See Note
Ilford INSTACORA E	1966	Dacora	
Ilford INSTACORA F	1966	Dacora	
Ilford INSTACORA R	1966	Dacora	
Ilford Sportsman C Instant		Dacora	
Ilford Sportsman E Instant		Dacora	
Ilford Sportsman R Instant		Dacora	
Ilford Sportina Rapid II	1967	Dacora	
Ilford Sportsman F	1967	Dacora	

Camera Model	Year	Made By	See Note
Ilford Sportsman L	1967	Dacora	3
Ilford Sportsman MK2 300	1967	Dacora	1
Ilford Sportsman MK2 300 EB	1967	Dacora	1
Ilford Sportsman MK2 300 L	1967	Dacora	1
Ilford Sportsman MK2 300 LK	1967	Dacora	1
Ilford Sportsman MK2 300 S	1967	Dacora	1
Ilford Sportsman MK2 300 SL	1967	Dacora	1
Ilford Sportsman R	1967	Dacora	3
Ilford Sportsman Rapid III	1967	Dacora	2
Ilford Sportsman Rapid IV	1967	Dacora	2
Ilford Sportsman SL	1967	Dacora	3
CILMATIC Electric 300 S	1968	Dacora	
CILMATIC Ideal	1968	Dacora	
CILMATIC Super	1968	Dacora	
CILMATIC Electric 300	1969	Dacora	
CILMATIC Elite	1969	Dacora	
CILFOMAT 300S	1970	Dacora	
CILFOMAT 300SL	1970	Dacora	
CILMATIC Electronic 126	1971	Dacora	
Ilford 35 CL	1972	Dacora	4
Ilford 35 R	1972	Dacora	
Ilford 35 RL	1972	Dacora	
CILMATIC 300 CC	1973	Dacora	
CILMATIC 300 CR	1973	Dacora	
CIL 1 110	1976	Halina	5
CILMATIC X	1976	Halina	5

Notes:

1. The marketing leaflet for the MK2 Sportsman cameras which was produced in 1967 for the Dutch market details these Mark 2 models (See Page 226)

2. The Sportsman Rapid cameras were identical to the Sportina Rapid cameras that were produced for the UK market.

3. Several existing cameras in the Sportsman range were given new logos during this time – A very small nameplate with black lettering on a sliver background.

4. The Ilford 35 CL is similar to the Cilmatic 300 CC except for the nameplate.

5. Probably made by Haking Wong's Halina company.

Ciba, Lumiere, Ilford - Cilmatic Ideal - 1968

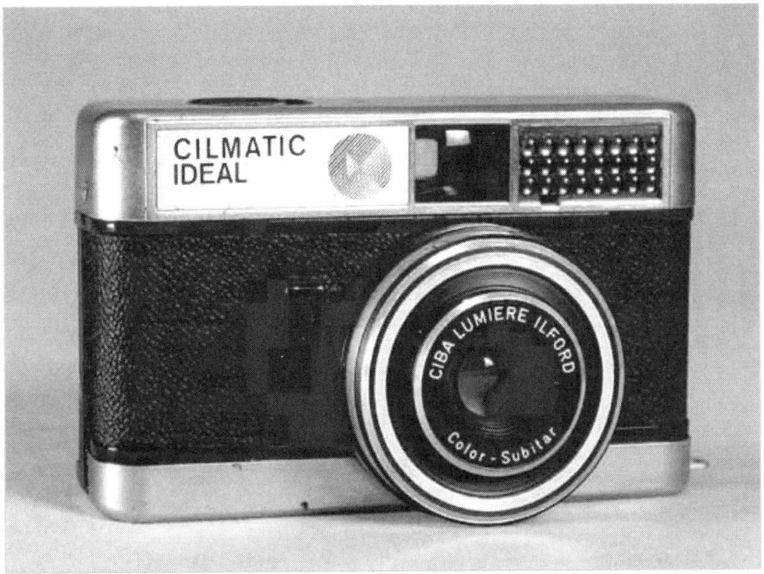

Color Subitar lens, 126 cartridge.

Ciba, Lumiere, Ilford - Cilmatic Super - 1968

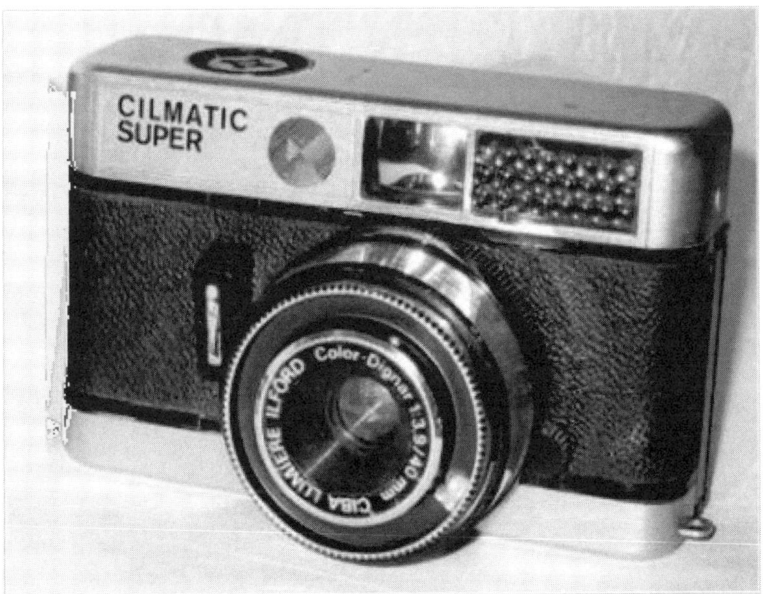

Color Dignar 40mm f/3.9 lens, 126 cartridge.

Ciba, Lumiere, Ilford - Cilmatic Elite - 1969

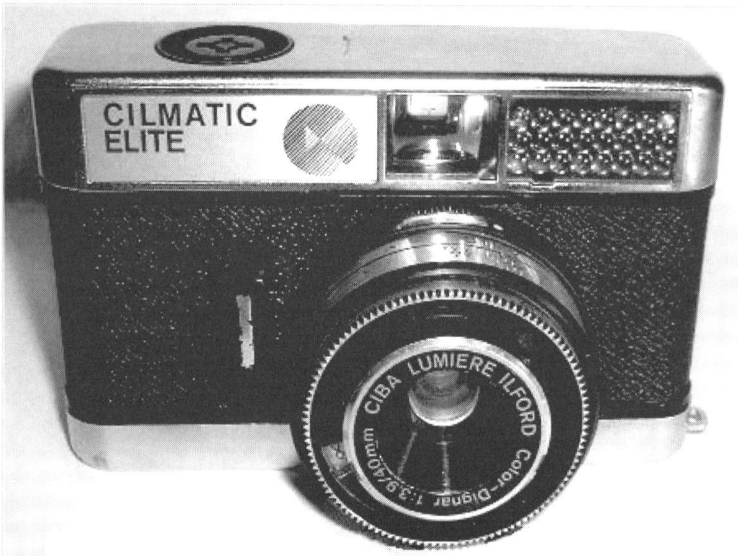

Color Dignar 40mm f/3.9 lens, Prontor 300 Electronic shutter, 126 cartridge, A focussing scale of three symbols or metric values. Automatic exposure also available with an indicator in the viewfinder to indicate if there is enough light.

Ciba, Lumiere, Ilford - Cilmatic Electric 300 - 1969

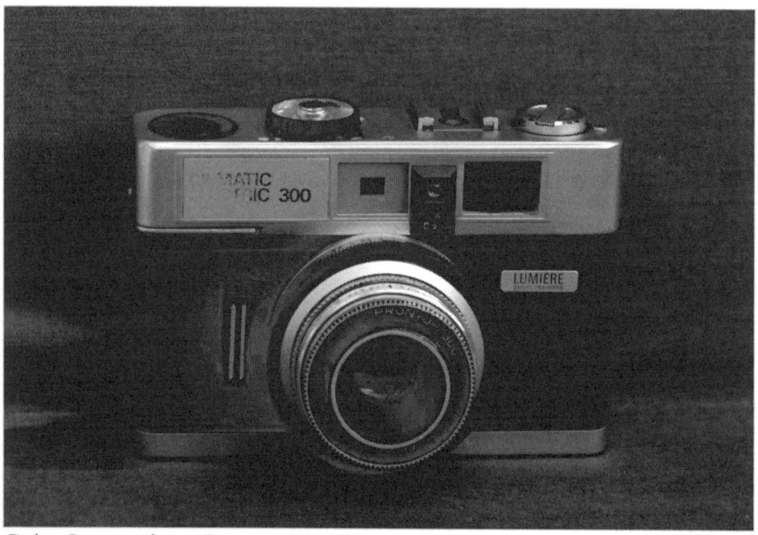

Color Isconar lens, Prontor 300 shutter.

Ciba, Lumiere, Ilford - Cilmatic Electric 300 S (#1) - 1970

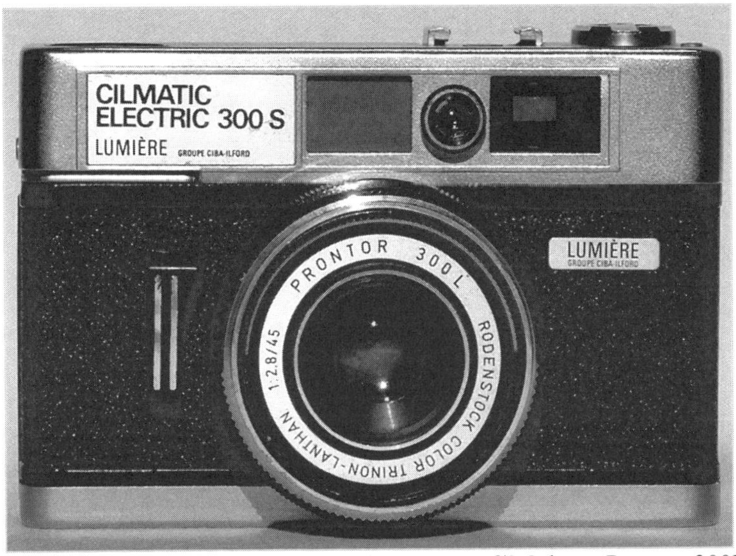

Rodenstock Color Trinon-Lanthan 45mm f/2.8 lens, Prontor 300L Shutter. Fitted with a light meter with an indicator in the viewfinder. Flashcube and flash shoe. Battery compartment and film counter on the base.

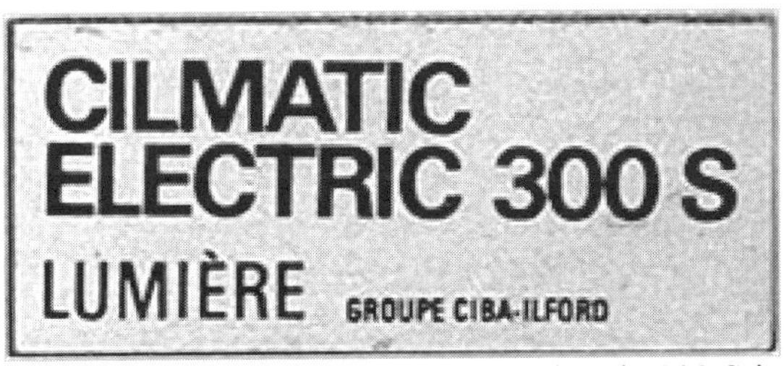

The badge on this CILMATIC Electric 300 S is perhaps the final badge that bore the word Ilford.

Ciba, Lumiere, Ilford - Cilmatic Electric 300 S (#2)

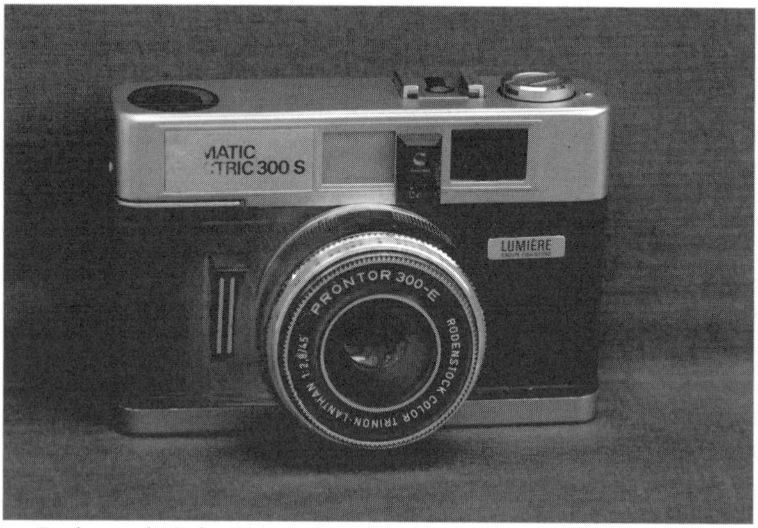

Rodenstock Color Trinon-Lanthan 45mm f/2.8 lens, Prontor 300 E Shutter. Fitted with a light meter with an indicator in the viewfinder. Flashcube and flash shoe. Battery compartment and film counter on the base.

Ciba, Lumiere, Ilford - Cilfomat 300 S - 1970

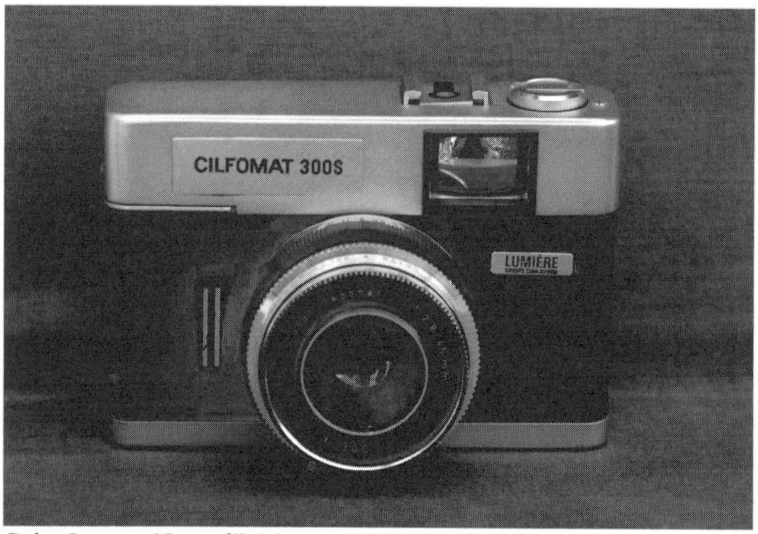

Color Isconar 45mm f/2.8 lens, Prontor X 300 Shutter. No light meter.

Ciba, Lumiere, Ilford - Cilfomat 300 SL - 1970

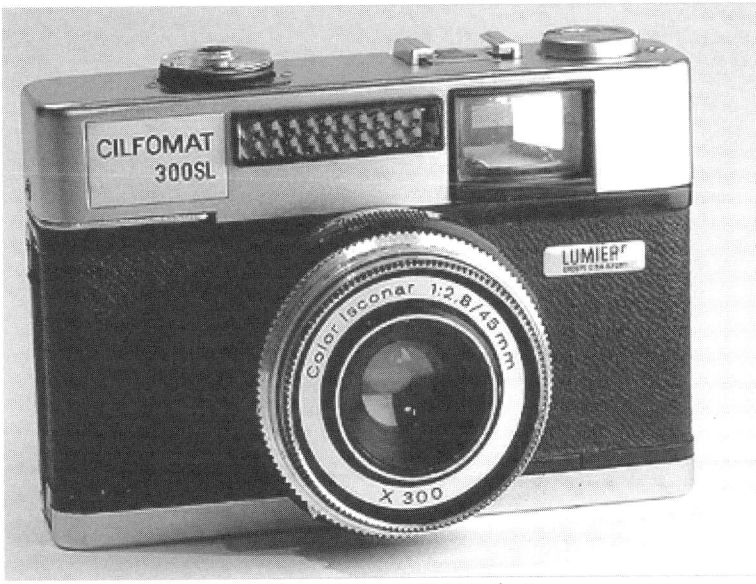

Color Isconar 45mm f/2.8 lens, Prontor X 300 shutter.
The cameras start to look more 'French' from now on.

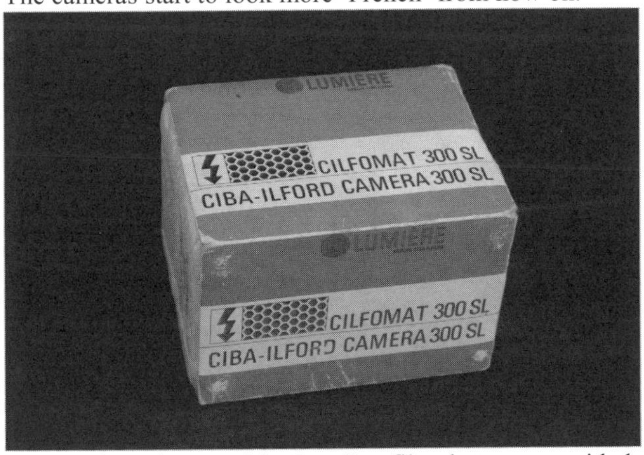

Here is a picture of the Lumière film that was provided with the CIBA-Ilford Camera 300 SL.

Ciba, Lumiere, Ilford - Cilmatic Electronic - 1968

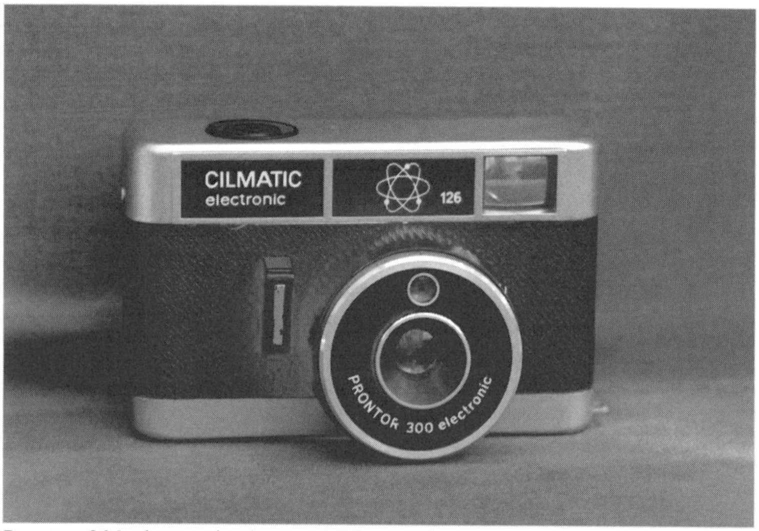

Prontor 300 electronic shutter, 126 cartridge.

Ilford Electronic Instapak (€)

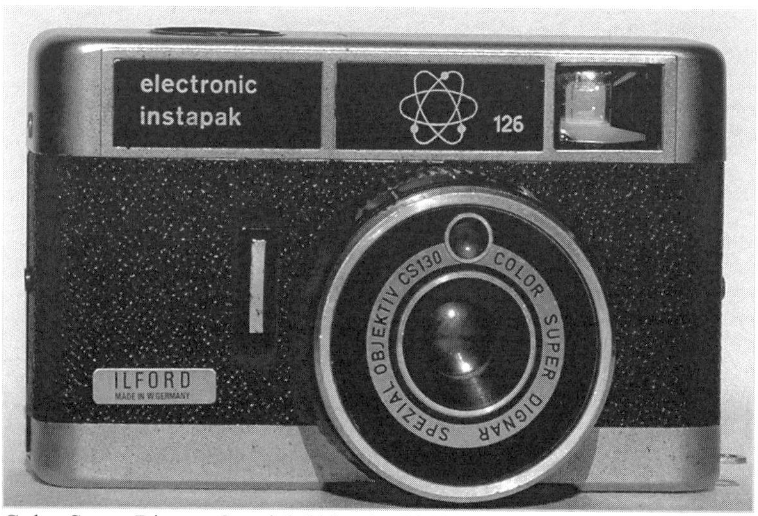

Color Super Dignar, Spezial Objectiv CS130.

Ciba, Lumiere, Ilford - Cilmatic 300 CC - 1973

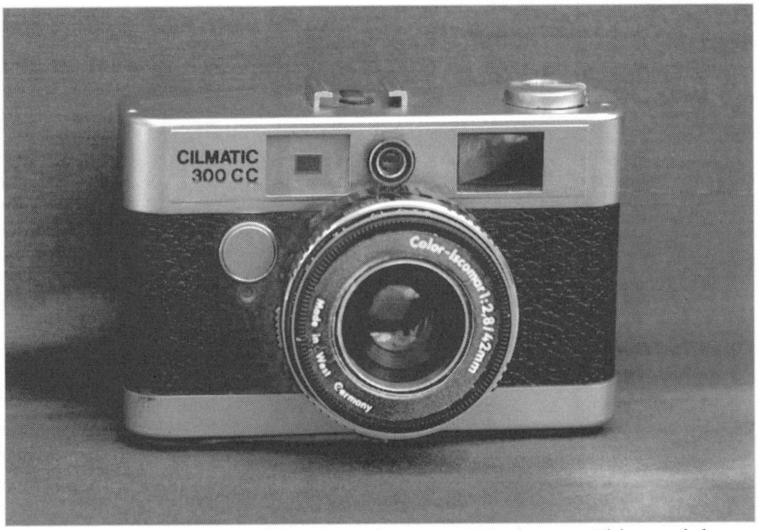

Color-Isconar 42mm f/2.8 lens, Prontor 300 shutter. This model seems to be based on the Ilford 35 CL shown on page 182 and may have been identical to the Ilford 35 CC.

Ciba, Lumiere, Ilford - Cilmatic 300 CR - 1973

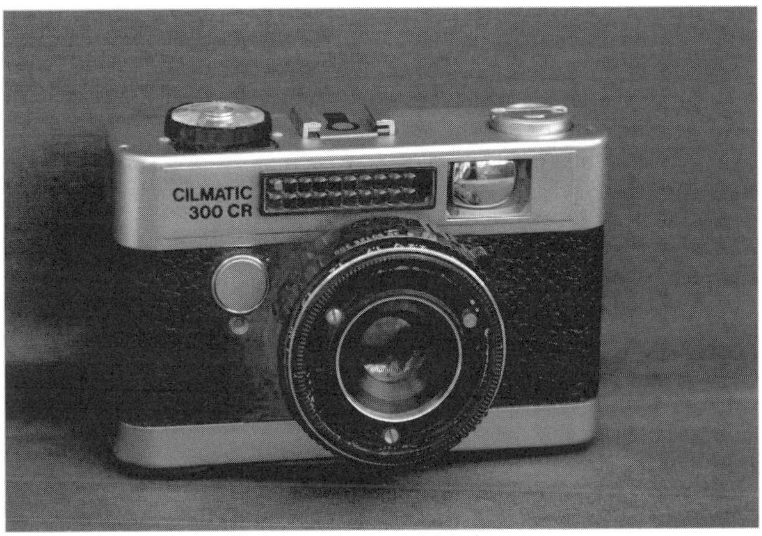

Color-Isconar 42mm f/2.8 lens, Prontor 300 shutter.

Ciba, Lumiere, Ilford - Cilmatic X - 1976

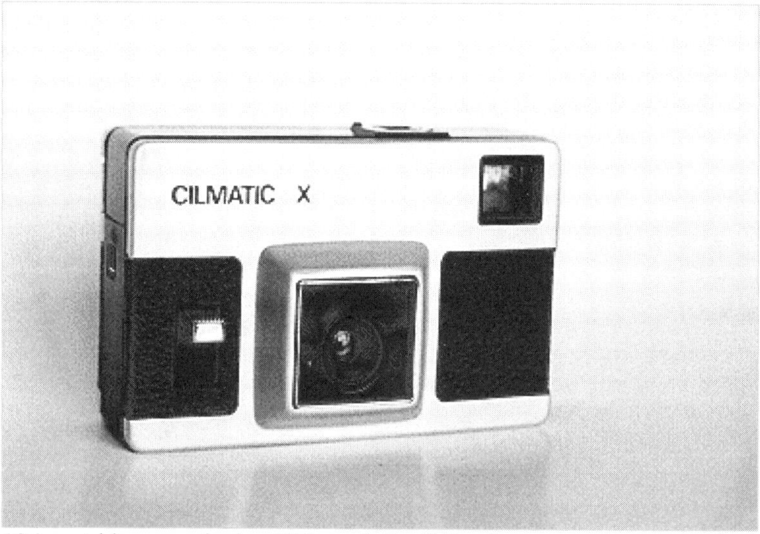

126 cartridge, magicube. This and the following camera were made in Hong Kong.

Ciba, Lumiere, Ilford – CIL 1 110 - 1976

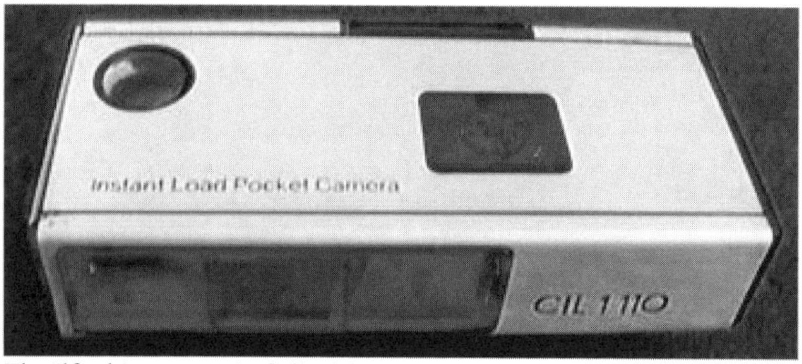

The Ilford 'parentage' of all of the cameras in this book started in 1902.

The Ilford Logo appeared on the cameras from 1948 (Craftsman) up to 1968. (Some of the Falling Plate cameras of 1902 had ILFORD on the shutter plate)

Then the name Ilford only appeared on the lens plate along with the Cilmatic logo (except for a brief time on the Electric 300S)

Finally, with the example shown above, the only reference to Ilford was reduced to the 'I' in the CIL logo.

Ilford Cameras marketed in Holland

In 1967 CIBA-Ilford N.V. Amsterdam issued the following flyer to the Dutch retailers. It is entitled, '**The Sportsman Season has started**'.

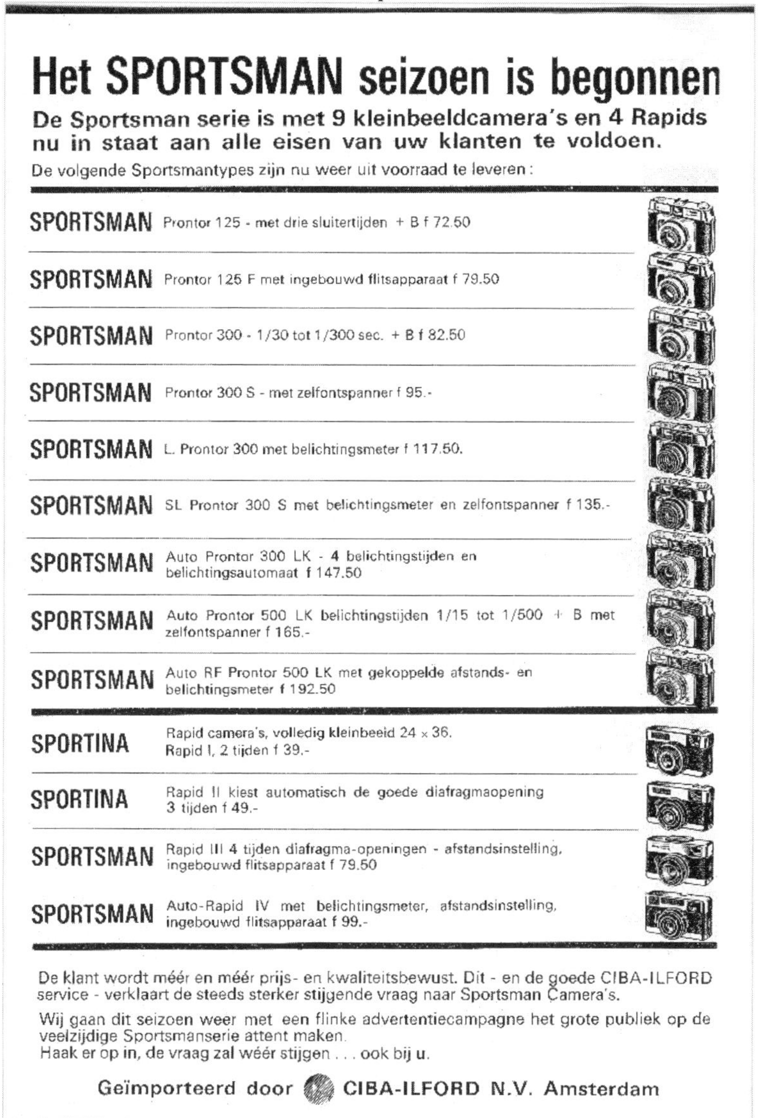

Het SPORTSMAN seizoen is begonnen

De Sportsman serie is met 9 kleinbeeldcamera's en 4 Rapids nu in staat aan alle eisen van uw klanten te voldoen.

De volgende Sportsmantypes zijn nu weer uit voorraad te leveren:

SPORTSMAN	Prontor 125 - met drie sluitertijden + B f 72.50
SPORTSMAN	Prontor 125 F met ingebouwd flitsapparaat f 79.50
SPORTSMAN	Prontor 300 - 1/30 tot 1/300 sec. + B f 82.50
SPORTSMAN	Prontor 300 S - met zelfontspanner f 95.-
SPORTSMAN	L. Prontor 300 met belichtingsmeter f 117.50.
SPORTSMAN	SL Prontor 300 S met belichtingsmeter en zelfontspanner f 135.-
SPORTSMAN	Auto Prontor 300 LK - 4 belichtingstijden en belichtingsautomaat f 147.50
SPORTSMAN	Auto Prontor 500 LK belichtingstijden 1/15 tot 1/500 + B met zelfontspanner f 165.-
SPORTSMAN	Auto RF Prontor 500 LK met gekoppelde afstands- en belichtingsmeter f 192.50
SPORTINA	Rapid camera's, volledig kleinbeeld 24 × 36. Rapid I, 2 tijden f 39.-
SPORTINA	Rapid II kiest automatisch de goede diafragmaopening 3 tijden f 49.-
SPORTSMAN	Rapid III 4 tijden diafragma-openingen - afstandsinstelling, ingebouwd flitsapparaat f 79.50
SPORTSMAN	Auto-Rapid IV met belichtingsmeter, afstandsinstelling, ingebouwd flitsapparaat f 99.-

De klant wordt méér en méér prijs- en kwaliteitsbewust. Dit - en de goede CIBA-ILFORD service - verklaart de steeds sterker stijgende vraag naar Sportsman Camera's.

Wij gaan dit seizoen weer met een flinke advertentiecampagne het grote publiek op de veelzijdige Sportsmanserie attent maken.
Haak er op in, de vraag zal wéér stijgen . . . ook bij u.

Geïmporteerd door CIBA-ILFORD N.V. Amsterdam

At this time the range offered was as follows:

Sportsman Prontor 125	Shutter button slides down
Sportsman Prontor 125 F	Shutter button slides down
Sportsman Prontor 300	
Sportsman Prontor 300 S	
Sportsman L	Prontor 300
Sportsman SL	Prontor 300 S
Sportsman Auto	Prontor 300 LK
Sportsman Auto	Prontor 500 LK
Sportsman Auto RF	Prontor 500 LK
Sportina Rapid I	
Sportina Rapid II	
Sportina Rapid III	
Sportina Auto-Rapid IV	

In 1967 Dutch retailers were issued with a new leaflet, which introduced the Sportsman MK2 series. The MK may refer to Mark as in Mark 2 or may refer to their place of manufacture, which was Munich Kamerawerk when Dacora moved from Reutlingen to Munich.

Most (if not all) of the cameras were badge-engineered version of other models previously available. Perhaps Ilford were trying to consolidate their range under a single Mark and perhaps feedback from the retailers was unfavourable and they were never issued.

The leaflet is shown overleaf. The leaflet is shown overleaf. Note the typo under the L and SL models, which have been crossed over.

The new series Sportsman MK 2 Cameras - 1967

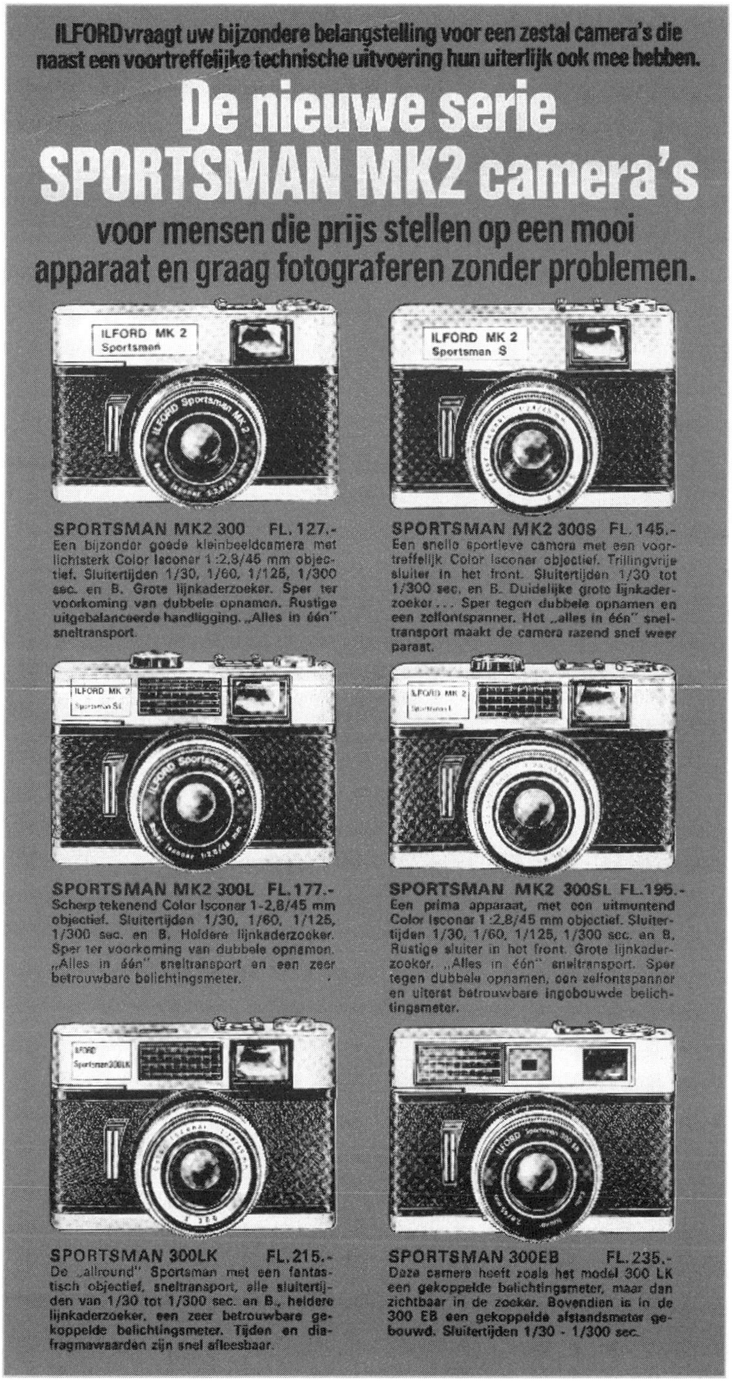

Ilford Sportsman MK 2 300

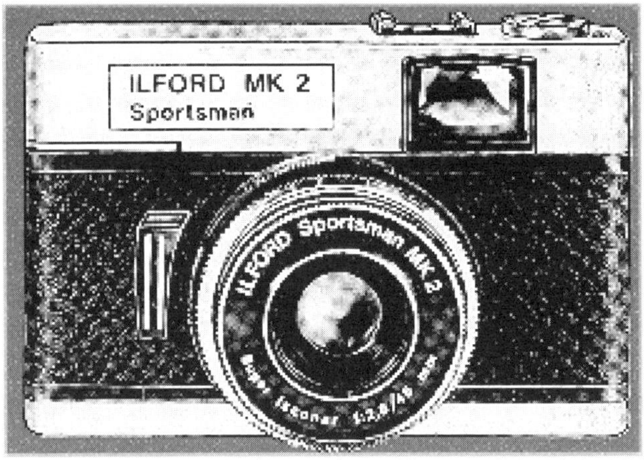

Color Isconar 1:2.8/45mm lens. Shutter 1/30, 1/60, 1/125, 1/300 sec. and B. Price: 127 Florins

Ilford Sportsman MK 2 300S

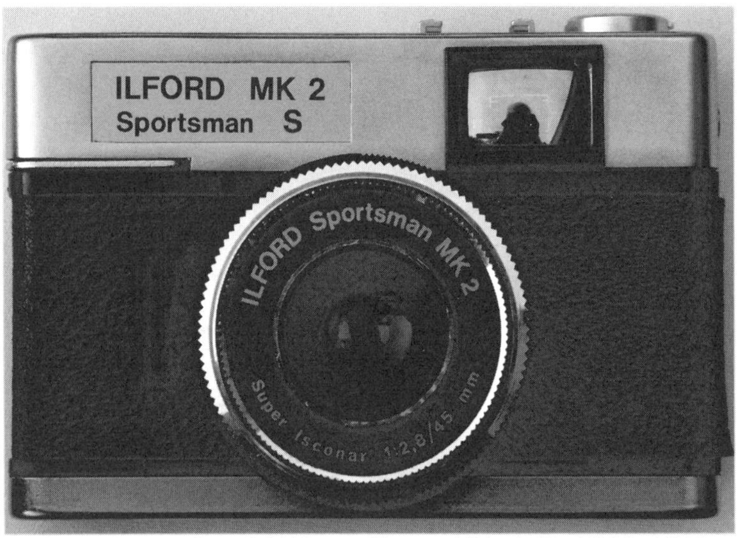

Super Isconar lens 2.8/45mm. Shutter 1/30, 1/60, 1/125, 1/300 sec. and B. Self-timer. Recessed film rewind crank Film counter, tripod bush and rewind release button on the bottom plate.

This specific example differs from the marketing leaflet in that the lens is not a Color Isconar and the shutter is not an X 300. .Price: 145 Florins

Ilford Sportsman MK 2 300L

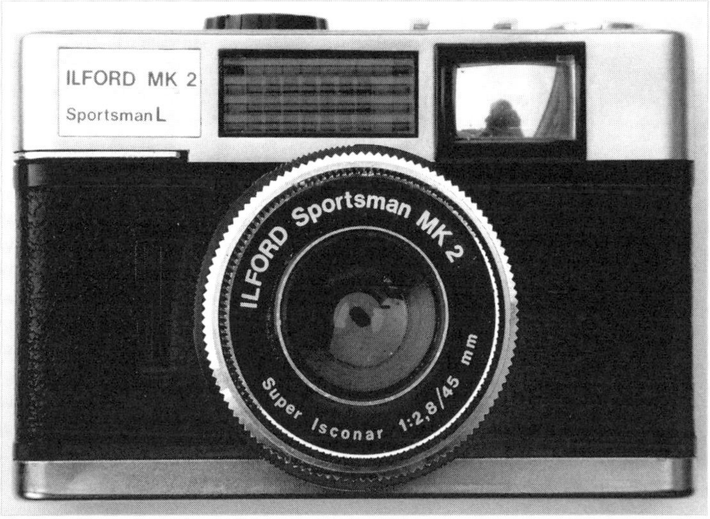

Color Isconar 1:2.8/45mm lens. Shutter 1/30, 1/60, 1/125, 1/300 sec. and B. Price: 177 Florins

Ilford Sportsman MK 2 300SL

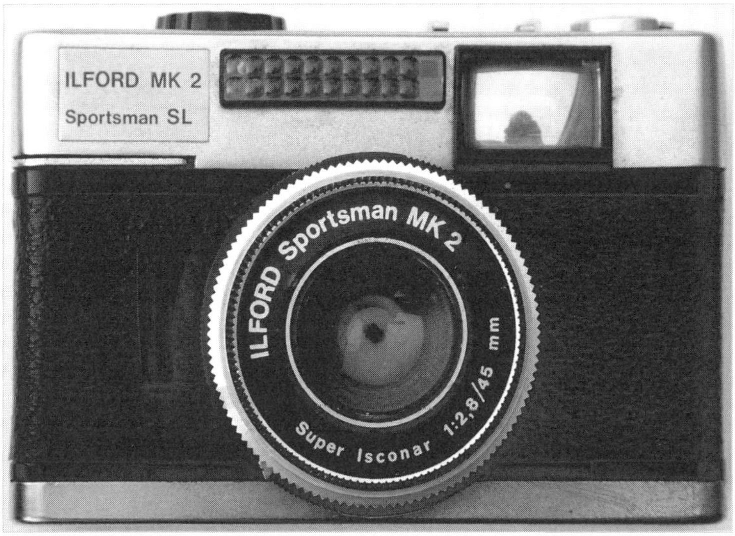

Color Isconar 1:2.8/45mm lens. Shutter 1/30, 1/60, 1/125, 1/300 sec. and B and self-timer. CdS light meter on the top plate. Recessed film rewind crank. Exposure counter on the bottom plate.

It is interesting to note that the camera differs from the marketing leaflet in that the light collector for the CdS meter is narrower that the one shown on the leaflet. The collector is similar to the one fitted to the Sportsman Rapid IV.

Ilford Sportsman MK 2 300LK

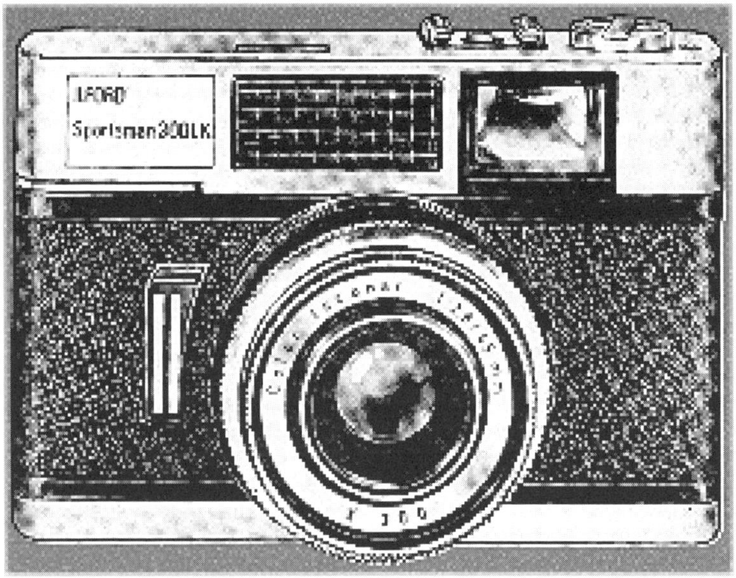

Color Isconar 1:2.8/45mm lens. Shutter 1/30, 1/60, 1/125, 1/300 sec. and B, Coupled light meter. Price: 215 Florins

Ilford Sportsman MK 2 300EB

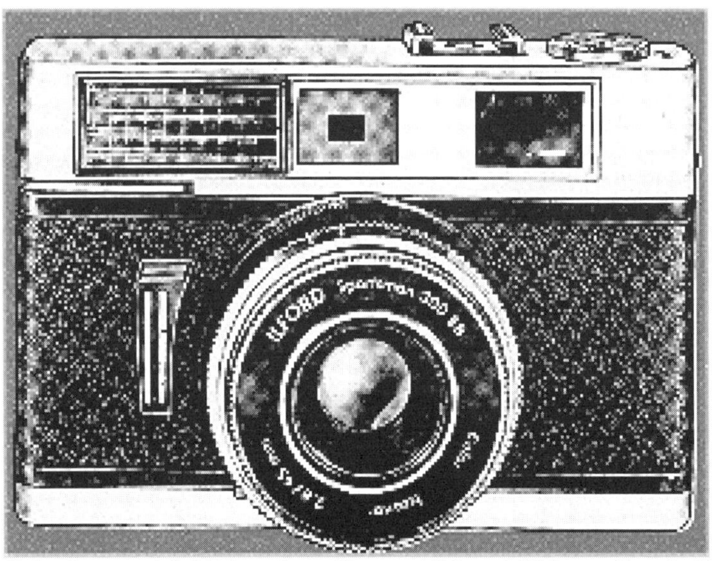

Color Isconar 1:2.8/45mm lens. Shutter 1/30, to 1/300 sec. Coupled light meter. Price: 235 Florins

CHAPTER 6
The Final Camera – 2005

Between 1997 and 2004 Ilford released two new cameras! An XP2 Super Black and White Single use camera and a similar camera fitted with HP5 Plus film.

This is what their marketing leaflet had to say about it:

Black And White - Single Use Camera

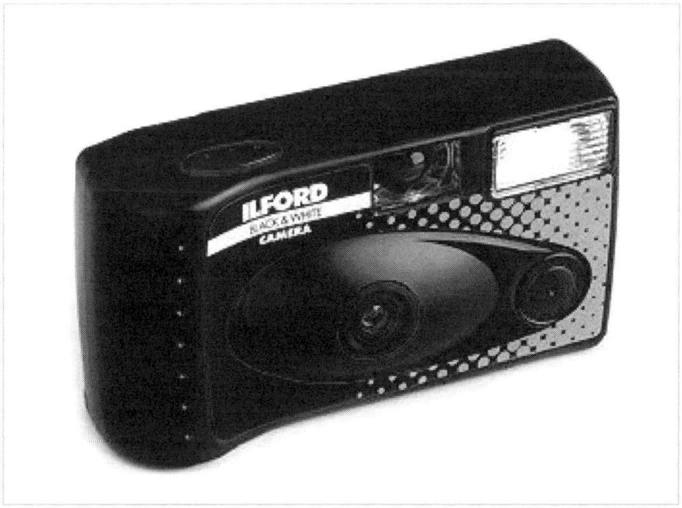

Black and white is back in magazines, music videos, advertising and even major movies. A whole generation has grown up surrounded by colour images and they are excited by the novelty of monochrome images. The easy to use Ilford single use camera offers the opportunity for them to try black and white photography for themselves.

The camera is attractively packaged with strong monochrome images and striking graphics and is ready for counter display. It is loaded with (24+3)

27 exposures of the excellent Ilford HP5 Plus ISO 400/27° film. The price of the camera does not include processing but the film can be processed through any traditional retailer-photofinisher processing route.

WARNING: DUE TO HIGH VOLTAGE PLEASE DO NOT OPEN CAMERA.

The camera has a built-in flash effective up to 3m/10ft, an f 9·5 30mm lens and a shutter speed of 1/100 sec. It is focus free and gives sharp pictures from 1 metre/3ft to infinity. The camera is supplied with the film wound out of the cassette and the film is wound back as each picture is taken. A frame counter shows the number of pictures remaining.
Safety interlocks prevent double exposures or blank frames.

The camera was first available in 1997 and additionally was also available with XP2 Super film. It was discontinued in 2003.

XP2 Super

This camera is loaded with (24+3) 27 exposures of Ilford XP2 SUPER ISO 400/27 chromogenic black and white film.

HP5 Plus – Version 1

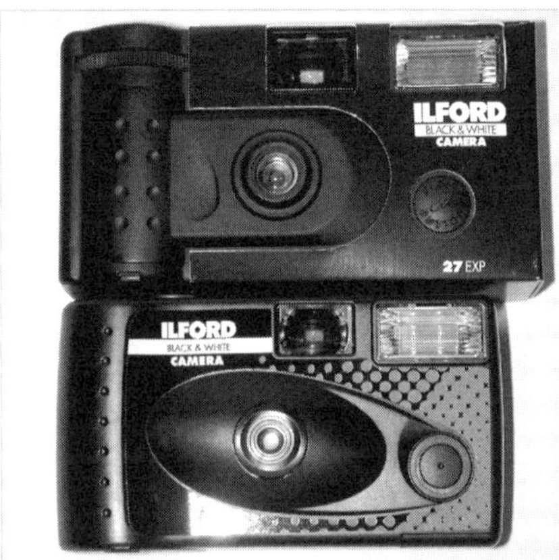

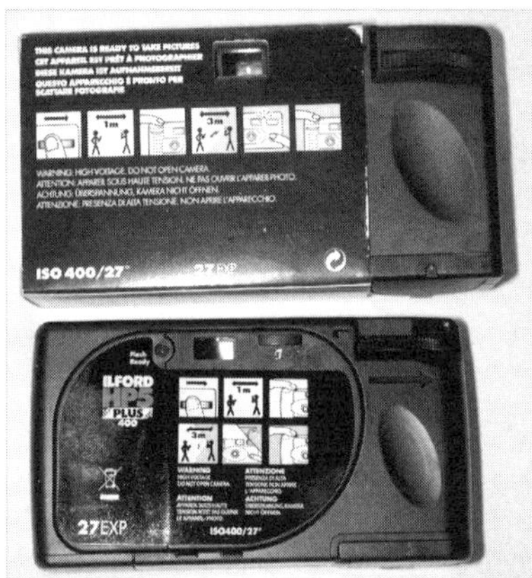

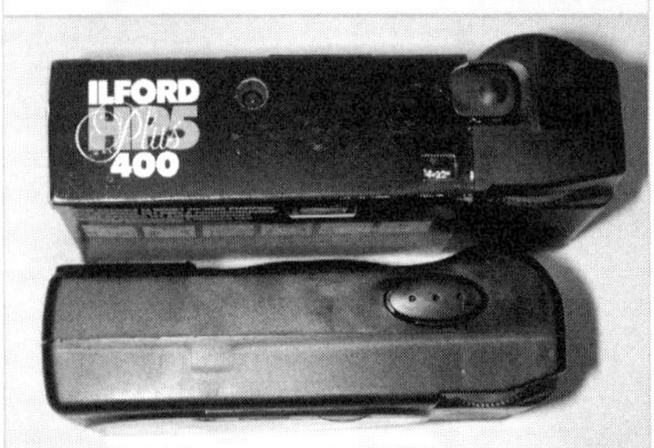

Images courtesy of Doug McGee.

The camera is loaded with (24+3) 27 exposures of Ilford HP5 Plus ISO 400/27° film.

HP5 Plus – Version 2

Both cameras have a built-in flash effective up to 3m/10ft, an f 9·5 30mm lens and a shutter speed of 1/100 sec. They are focus free from 3ft to infinity. The cameras were supplied with the film wound out of the cassette and the film is wound back as each picture is taken. A frame counter shows the number of pictures remaining. Safety interlocks prevent double exposures or blank frames.

Differences

	Version 1	**Version 2**
Flash ready light	Top	Back
Frame counter	Top	Back
Exposure button	Rectangular	Oval

So the story continues.

My father would be very pleased to see this camera especially as it embodies all of Ilford's original design and marketing ideas. A camera which *supports* their film and emulsion business. Most of the original ideas, established in 1946, being retained:

1. Made for Ilford but not by them.
2. Ilford design ideas to be incorporated.
3. A range of cameras in film sizes 127, 126 and 35 mm.
4. To cover the requirements of beginners up to advanced amateurs and professionals.
5. Under the Ilford logo.
6. To carry Ilford film stickers.

As my father once named it, 'The secret salesman', is alive and well.

What goes around comes around.

Ilford (UK) decided to stop marketing cameras in 1969 when the Amateur Products Division was abandoned. The work of disposing of the remaining stocks of cameras took the best part of another year. Most of these cameras went to the premium business. Repair facilities were retained in this period but several of Ilford's repairers had formed groups of small camera repairers and Ilford came to rely on them to effect customer repairs. Repair equipment and some parts were passed to them on favourable terms.

Later still Ilford decided to abandon other activities including X-Ray and Graphic Arts films and to consolidate its manufacturing facilities at Mobberley in Cheshire.

Many of their records were destroyed. Some quantities of paperwork were passed to the Science Museum in 1979 (which have been subsequently moved the National Museum of Photography, Film and Television in Bradford) but there exists no complete record of their camera business.

Hopefully this book goes some way towards rebuilding this lost knowledge.

The End and a New Beginning

In August 2004 Ilford went into receivership. Along with other film manufacturers, Kodak and Agfa included, the predominance of digital photography has caused the film makers to suffer badly. Although many, including myself, thought initially that film would never be replaced and digital cameras were perhaps a fad that would not be able to sustain continuous development, we have been proved wrong. At least wrong for the majority of amateur photographers who have gradually replaced their film cameras for digital cameras, computer image management software and at-home computer printers to print the pictures they actually want printed after viewing them on-screen.

Professional photographers are now rapidly adding high quality digital cameras to their equipment inventory. Wedding photographs are now commonly available on the Internet allowing virtual guests to see and choose those photographs that they would like to order. The transfer of the digital image from camera to an audience anywhere in the world is now an easy and fast process.

The quality of the images that most reasonably priced digital cameras can produce is in my view staggering. All of the photographs in this book were taken quickly, without any fuss or great technical knowledge. The tolerance of the lens and electronic shutter together with brilliant exposure control mean that few pictures are rejected. If however the exposure or framing is incorrect it is a simple matter to delete the image and take it again.

During Ilford's camera marketing period there was always conflict between the film and emulsion side of the business and the camera and accessories side. On several occasions their camera marketing activities were threatened to be closed down. On other occasions the success of their camera marketing business supported the rest of the company during difficult times.

Even in recent years the company, although it saw the onset of digital photography and supported this with Ilford Imaging – digital printers and paper, it still ignored the potential for Ilford digital cameras. Whether this was ever discussed, I do not know.

My own personal and obviously biased view is that they could have invested in designing and marketing digital cameras. Whether this would have helped them to avoid this predicament we will never know.

In 2005 Ilford Imaging UK Ltd. emerged from receivership through a complex and innovative management buy out. The new company will trade under the name of **Ilford Photo** with a new Corporate name of **Harman Technology**.
I wish them and their employees well for the future.

Conclusion

I started my collection and documentation of Ilford's camera marketing business in 1981. By 1997 this book was some 90 pages in length and I considered that it was complete.

It is now 2006. Many of the people who worked for Ilford or their associated companies during the history that I have recorded are now sadly no longer with us.

The book is now some 280 pages long and once again I believe that it is complete. Only time will tell if any more cameras and variants come to light in the future.

If you, the reader, consider that I have omitted anything of significance, made any errors or have seen or acquired a camera that is not documented in these pages then please do contact me and let me know.

I cannot claim that it is a definitive work but I can say that it is a unique and fairly complete documentation of the Ilford cameras. My special thanks goes to my late father for some of the information provided and all of the inspiration.

I have to thank a lot of other people for their information, help and encouragement. Most are listed at the start of the book. Thank you one and all.

APPENDIX A
Patents

This appendix contains details about some of the patents referred to previously in this document. Full details of these patents may be found by going to: http://gb.espacenet.com/ and clicking on the Advanced Search option.

This database holds the text and drawings of many patents filed over a long period of time. The text and the images have been scanned into their system.

For old documents the scanning process occasionally makes transcription errors because the original document was folded, marked or smudged. Where I have reproduced the text I have tried to correct most of the errors that can be seen when you retrieve these old documents.

The Smith's Patent for the Falling Plate Camera

No. 3985 **A.D. 1895**

Date of Application, 25th Feb., 1895
Complete Specification Left, 25th Nov., 1895 – Accepted, 28th Dec. 1895

PROVISIONAL SPECIFICATION.

Improvements in Photographic Cameras.

We, Arthur Charles Smith Patentee and Albert Arthur Smith Assistant, both of 258 Albert Road Peckham in the County of Surrey, do hereby declare the nature of this invention to be as follows:-

This invention relates more especially to hand cameras in which sensitised cut films are used, and has for its object the production of apparatus which shall change such films by the aid of similarly notched backing pieces, but without any special preparation of the films themselves.

Although described as adapted to magazine cameras the principle of changing the films etc., is also applicable to changing boxes and may in that form be used in connection with ordinary cameras.

In a camera made according to this invention the sensitised films are packed in the magazine, together with alternating backing pieces of greater width than the films, and having notches on opposite edges.

The interior of the magazine is fitted on opposite sides with ribs or ridges, extending from back to front. These ridges are of the same shape as the notches in the backing pieces, and when the pack of films and backings is in position the films are between the tops of the opposite series of ridges; while the backing pieces extend into the spaces between the ridges which then enter the notches. The contents of the magazine are acted on by a spring from the back and are pressed against an upper and lower row of projections formed on, or attached to, bars which are caused to advance a short distance towards, and recede from the centre of the magazine in a vertical plane. These bars have not a direct up and down movement, but travel in a transverse direction also. The projections on the bars are so arranged that when most nearly approached they hold the foremost film in position for exposure, after which operation the bars are made to recede and so release the film, and by the oblique movement the projections slip on to the backing piece, at the sides of the notches. The return action of the bars releases the backing piece by taking the projections back to their original position where they retail in position for exposure the next film, the edges of which overhang the tops of the notches.

Motion may be imparted to the bars carrying the projections by any convenient means, but preferably by the aid of inclined clots acting in conjunction with a magazine having a short movement sideways.

After exposure the films and backings fall into the well of the camera and are covered by a flap operated from the exterior of the instrument.

A shutter is provided consisting of a circular disc having a suitable aperture, and arranged so that it may revolve in one direction only. Motion is given by a crank pin attached to the disc traversing a slot made in a driving arm which is pivoted at its lower end and actuated by a spring, bearing at or near its middle.

The shutter is set by giving the disc a half turn and is released by a trigger attachment working in connection with a lever. Provision is made for prolonged exposures by bringing a bent lever into gear, which prevents the aperture passing the lens until the operator removes pressure from the releasing lever.

Dated this 23rd day of February 1895.

ARTHUR C. SMITH
ALBERT A. SMITH

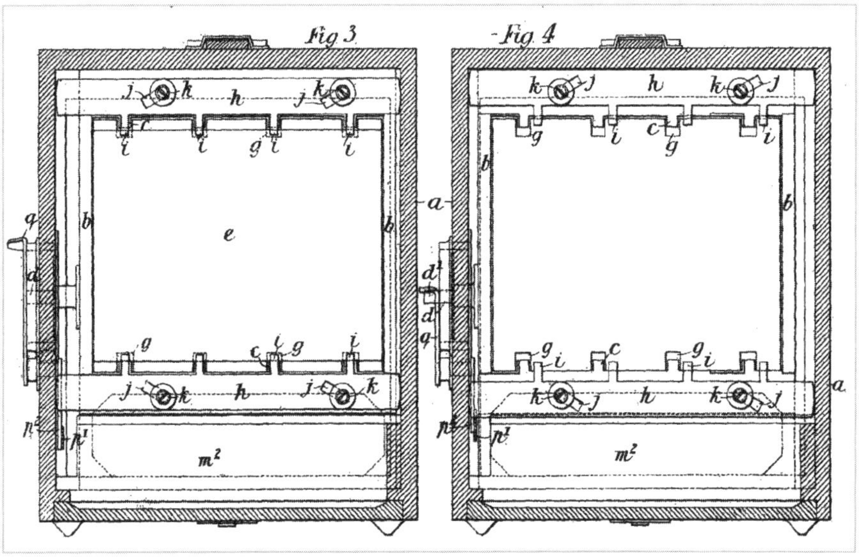

Patents taken out by Werner Julius Rothschild

This first patent would appear to show a fairly traditional coupled rangefinder/viewfinder arrangement, but with a bright-line frame included. Unfortunately it was not incorporated into the Witness.

The Steinheil Casca of 1949 was probably the first production camera to include this feature.

Improvements in or relating to combined viewfinders & rangefinders for photographic cameras

Patent Number:	GB612531
Publication date:	1948-11-15
Applicant(s):	WERNER JULIUS ROTHSCHILD
Requested Patent:	GB612531
Application Number:	GB19460010691 19460406

PROVISIONAL SPECIFICATION

I, WERNER JULIUS ROTHSCHILD, of 40, Mackenzie Street, Astley Bridge, Bolton, County of Lancaster, of German Nationality, do hereby declare the nature of this invention to be as follows:

The invention relates to photographic cameras having a viewfinder of the inverted Galilean telescope type, part of the field of the viewfinder being used for the range finder, which may be of the double image type, and which may be directly coupled to the focussing motion of the camera objective, or may be provided with a separate dial on which the distance of the object under observation can be read off, the same eyepiece being used for the viewfinder and rangefinder.

The object of the invention is to overcome the disadvantage of the Galilean telescope when used as viewfinder, in not giving a sharply defined field of view, and in necessitating a very small eyepiece aperture with consequent loss of illumination in order to avoid errors due to incorrect positioning of the eye.

The combined rangefinder and viewfinder according to the present invention comprises an inverted Galilean telescope with a semi-reflecting mirror between the objective and eyepiece serving to reflect the auxiliary or rangefinder beam of light into the eyepiece after this beam has passed through a lens of the same power as the viewfinder objective suitable means being provided to deflect this beam according to the focussing motion of the camera lens or according to a dial marked in distances, having a frame placed in the auxiliary or rangefinder beam so that its image in the mirror lies at the principal focus of the viewfinder eyepiece, so that its virtual image appears superimposed on the object under observation, the size of the frame being chosen so as to indicate the correct field of view,-and the frame being illuminated through an aperture in the camera wall by light-from the object under observation.

In one form of the invention the rangefinder is coupled to the focussing motion of the lens. The viewfinder consists of the negative lens and the positive eyepiece.

Interposed between these lenses is a partially metallised mirror, which transmits part of the light reaching it from the lens and reflects part of the light reaching it from a prism the axis of which light beam is at right angles to the axis of the negative lens. A lens of the same power as the negative lens but of smaller diameter is interposed between the prism and the reflecting surface. This lens therefore forms with the eyepiece a telescope of the same power as the viewfinder telescope. Thus in the central portion of the field of view two images will be seen, which can be brought into coincidence by tilting the prism about a pivot. This movement may be coupled to the focussing motion of the objective lens, this motion being transmitted to the prism by means of a roller and levers. Coincidence of the two images then indicates that the lens is focussed correctly.

The bringing to coincidence of the two images may also be effected by other well known means, such as two slightly prismatic plates in the beam which can be rotated in opposite directions, of a combination of a negative and positive lens go of equal powers, and with flat outer surfaces, one of which can be rotated about the common centre of curvature of the curved surfaces, so forming a prism of variable angle. A frame is placed in the rangefinder Beam between the prism and the lens so that its image as formed by the mirror is at the principal focus of the eyepiece which therefore forms a virtual image of this frame in the plane of the object as seen through the viewfinder, and therefore gives an accurate indication of the field of view covered by the camera., provided that the size of the frame is properly chosen.

The frame is preferably painted in some light colour, and an aperture is provided in the camera wall, which allows light from the object to fall on the frame.

If the camera is fitted with lenses of different focal lengths, the frame may be mounted in such a way that it can be changed for one of different size to suit the lens in use, or a multiple frame may be fitted, showing simultaneously the fields covered by several lenses, the only limit being that the smallest frame must be larger than the lens between the mirror and the prism.

In a modification of the form of the invention already described a positive lens having its central part removed to accommodate the negative lens is arranged between the mirror and the prism. In this arrangement the frame is placed at the principal focus of the combination of the eyepiece and the positive lens and its virtual image again- appears superimposed on the object as seen in the viewfinder.

The advantage of this arrangement is that owing to the refraction in the positive lens a considerable reduction in the size can be effected, with a consequent reduction in the size of the camera.

In a further modification the positive lens with a negative lens inserted at its centre is replaced by a positive lens at the centre of the convex side of which a concave recess is ground.

In any of the forms of the invention the frame in the rangefinder beams may be replaced by a glass plate on one surface of which a frame is engraved. Light falls on the polished edge of the plate, and is trapped in the plate by total reflection, being only able to escape through the engraved line which therefore appears luminous.

Dated this; 5th day of April, 1946.
T. OWDEN O'BRIEN & SON.
Patent Agents, Manchester, 2.

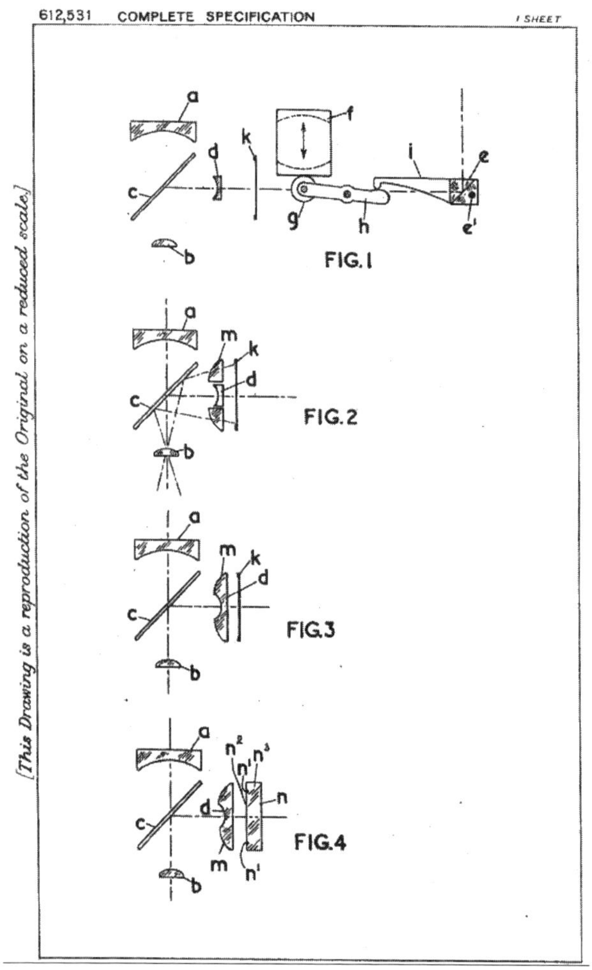

Improvements to shutters of photographic and cinematographic apparatus

Patent Number: GB594276
Publication date: 1947-11-06
Applicant(s): WERNER JULIUS ROTHSCHILD
Requested Patent:GB594276
Application Number: GB19450016693 19460621

PATENT SPECIFICATION

5949276

Application Date: June 21, 1946 No 16693/45.
Complete Specification Accepted: Nov 6, 1947.

COMPLETE SPECIFICATION

Improvements in or relating to Shutters of Photographic and Cinematographic Apparatus

I, Werner Julius Rothschild, of 40, Mackenzie Street, Astley Bridge, Bolton, County of Lancaster, of German Nationality, do hereby declare the nature of this invention and in what manner the same is to be performed, to be particularly described and ascertained in and by the following statement:-

This invention relates to improvements in shutters of photographic or cinematographic apparatus of the type consisting of a moving member such as a rotary disc or a sector forming part of such a disc or a sliding plate arranged to intercept the light falling on to the light sensitive surface, the said moving member having an aperture permitting the light to reach the sensitive surface for a definite length of time, determined by the size of the aperture, and by the speed of the moving member.

The moving member may be located either in front of the camera objective, or behind it, or between two of the components of the objective, the shape of the aperture being usually a circle or an elongated circle.

The object of the present invention is to increase the efficiency of this type of shutter, i.e. to increase the amount of light reaching the sensitive material without increasing the total duration of the exposure and this is achieved by altering the shape of the aperture in the moving member.

The shutter according to the invention comprises a rotating or sliding member having one or more apertures permitting light to pass for a definite time during the motion of the member the characteristic feature being that each aperture is in the form of a curved or straight slot both ends of the slot being of the shape of circular arcs convex or re-entrant towards the centre of the aperture having a radius substantially equal to the radius of the lens aperture and the width of the slot being equal to the diameter of the lens aperture.

With such a shape of aperture in the moving member of the shutter the exposed lens area uncovered is larger at all stages of exposure, other than full opening, than with the usual circular aperture.

In order that the invention may be understood reference will now be made to the accompanying diagrammatic drawings in which;

[This Drawing is a reproduction of the Original on a reduced scale]

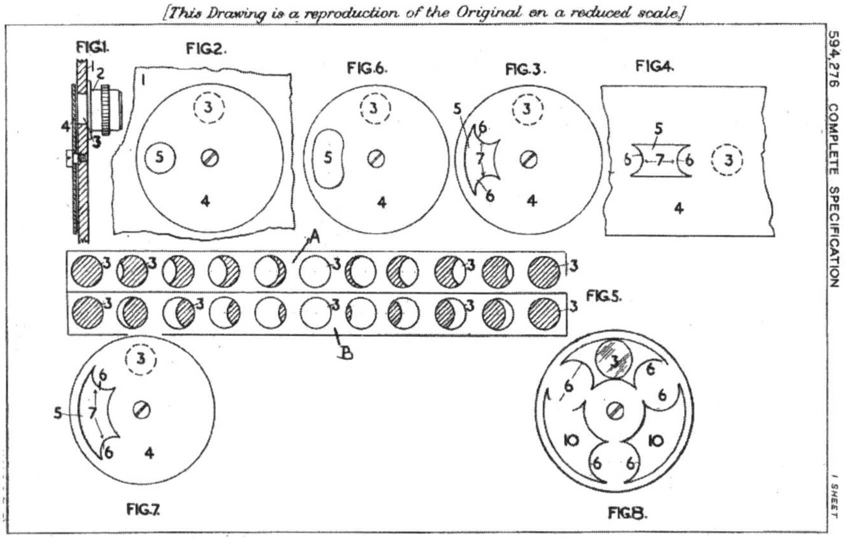

Fig 1 is a transverse section through the wall of a camera showing the objective lens and a rotating disc shutter;

Fig 2 is a front view of the shutter of Fig 1, showing the shutter with a circular aperture of known form of the same diameter as the lens aperture;

Fig 3 is a front view of a rotating disc shutter with an aperture in the form of a slot shaped according to the invention, the width of the slot being equal to the diameter of the lens aperture, and the ends of the slot being formed by circular arcs convex towards the centre of the aperture, the distance between the nearest two points of the two arcs being equal to the diameter of the lens aperture;

Fig 4 is a front view of a sliding shutter with an aperture in the form of a slot shaped according to the invention, the width of the slot being equal to the diameter of the lens aperture, and the ends of-the slot being formed by circular arcs convex towards the centre of the aperture, the distance between the nearest two points of the two arcs being equal to the diameter of the lens aperture;

Fig 5 shows the various stages during the opening and closing of a shutter with the circular aperture of Fig 2 and of a shutter with the aperture of Fig 3 or Fig 4;

Fig 6 is a front view of a rotating disc shutter with an aperture in the form of a slot of known shape, the width of the slot being the same as the diameter of the lens aperture;

Fig 7 is a front view of a shutter with an aperture in the form of a slot but having the ends of the slot re-entrant according to the invention, the width of the slot being equal to the diameter of the lens aperture and the distance between the two nearest points of the re-entrant ends being the same as the distance between the ends of the slot shown in Fig 6;

Fig 8 shows the shutter of a cinematograph projector in which the light is interrupted three times each revolution,

In Fig 1 of the drawings, which illustrates a portion of an ordinary photographic camera, 1 is the wall of the camera, 2 is the objective lens, 3 is the lens aperture and 4 is the shutter. In Figs 2 to 7, 5 is the aperture in the shutter, the shutter being operated in the usual way by trigger controlled spring or other mechanism.

The usual shape of the shutter apertures is that shown in Fig 2 in which the aperture is circular and of-the-same diameter as the lens aperture 3 or that shown in Fig 6 which the aperture is in the form of a slot with circular ends, the slot being of the same width as the diameter of the lens aperture 3.

A shutter having an aperture 5 as shown in Fig 3 or Fig 4 in the form of a slot of the same width as the diameter of the lens aperture 3 and having its ends formed by circular arcs 6 convex or re-entrant towards the centre of the aperture and of substantially the same radius as the radius of the lens aperture 3 with the distance 7 between the two nearest portions of the ends equal to the diameter of the lens aperture 3 will give the same total duration of exposure as the circular aperture shown in Fig 2 but will increase the amount of light reaching the sensitive material during the exposure as will be seen by reference to Fig 5.

In Fig 5 the un-shaded portions of the row A of diagrams show the amount of exposed lens aperture at successive stages during the opening and closing of a shutter having the aperture 5 shown in Fig 2 whilst the un-shaded portions of the other row B of diagrams show the exposed lens aperture at the same stages during the opening and closing of a shutter having the aperture 5 formed as shown in Fig 3 or Fig 4. It will be seen from Fig 5 that at all stages except full aperture, the exposed lens aperture in the row B exceeds that shown in the row A thereof. Mathematical analysis of the diagram shows that the total amount of light transmitted by the aperture of Figs 3 and 4 exceeds that transmitted by the aperture of Fig 2 by approximately $35^{1/2}$ %.

Similar results are obtained by substituting for the ends of an ordinary slotted aperture 5 as shown in Fig 6 ends formed as shown in Fig 7 by circular arcs 6 convex or re-entrant towards the centre of the aperture and having a radius substantially equal to the radius of the lens aperture 3 with the distance 7 between the two nearest portions of the ends equal to the maximum length of the aperture of Fig 6. In this case however the percentage increase in the amount of light transmitted by the aperture 5 of Fig 7 in comparison with that transmitted by the aperture 5 of Fig 6 will be less than the percentage increase between Fig 3 or Fig 4 and Fig 2 owing to the duration of total exposure being longer. The invention is also applicable to cinematographic projection apparatus having a shutter in the form of a rotating disc with two or more apertures, usually three, so that the light is interrupted two or more times in each cycle, one dark period serving for the film movement and the other or others to reduce flicker.

In Fig 8 such a shutter is shown having three apertures 10, the ends of each being shaped according to the invention as circular arcs 6 convex or re-entrant towards the centre of the aperture and having a radius substantially equal to the radius of the lens aperture. Having now particularly described and ascertained the nature of my said invention and in what manner the same is to be performed.

Patents filed by the Kennedy family

The inventiveness and tenacity of the Kennedy family, from the early days through to the current family members is clearly shown by looking at the patents that they have filed. The following table lists just a few of the patents which David and Water Kennedy filed for their various inventions.

Title of Patent	**Patent Number**	**Publication date**	**Kennedy**
Improvements in or relating to Impact Fuses.	GB130395	1919-08-07	David
Improvements in Fuses for Projectiles.	GB130629	1919-08-14	David
Improvements in and relating to flag-posts for golf holes.	GB229114	1925-02-19	David
Improvements in louvre shutters for photographic cameras and other optical apparatus.	GB516451	1940-01-02	David
Improvements in the stop and start mechanism as fitted to power driven photographic cameras.	GB516483	1940-01-03	David
An improved apparatus for making calculations relating to gunnery.	GB579282	1946-07-30	Walter
Improvements in or relating to machine heads for stringed musical instruments.	GB608558	1948-09-16	David and Walter
Photographic contact-printing apparatus.	GB712863	1954-08-04	David
Improvements in or relating to photographic transfer developing apparatus.	GB755881	1956-08-29	David

Patents filed by Albert Holliman

The following is a list of the patents that were filed under my father's name.

Title	Patent Number	Publication Date
Improvements in or relating to the production of mounting corners.	GB623510	1949-05-18
Improvements in or relating to the processing of photographic materials.	GB661392	1951-11-21
Improvements in or relating to photographic contact printing apparatus.	GB781703	1957-08-21
Improvements in or relating to fluorescent screens for use in radiography.	GB796109	1958-06-04

Although the method of creating photographs has changed considerably over the years there is still a need to put photographs into albums. The method of manufacturing the little black adhesive corners was complicated back in 1947, so my father devised a method for manufacturing them as described overleaf.

Improvements in or relating to the production of mounting corners

PATENT SPECIFICATION 623,510 No. 12424/47.

Application Date: May 8, 1947.
Complete Specification Left: May 6, 1948.
Complete Specification Accepted: May 18, 1949.

COMPLETE SPECIFICATION

Improvements in or Relating to the Production of Mounting Corners We, ALBERT RONALD HOLLIMAN, a British Subject, and ILFORD LIMITED, a British Company, both of 23, Roden Street, Ilford, in the County of Essex, do hereby declare the nature of this invention and in what manner the same is to be performed to be particularly described and ascertained in and by the following statement:-

This invention relates to the production of mounting corners for photographs and similar articles.

A common method of mounting rectangular photographs is by the provision of corner elements each of which consists of a triangular pocket which slips over a corner of the photograph, one outer surface of the pocket being gummed so that it may be secured to the mounting surface, e.g. a page in a photographic album.

The advantage of such corners is that the photograph itself is entirely unaffected by the mounting and may be slipped out of the corners if it is desired to remove it from the mounting surface, leaving the corners in position on the mounting surface.

The production of such mounting corners has hitherto required the cutting of material into prepared shapes followed by folding, gumming and other operations.

The present invention is concerned with a method of producing mounting corners from two or more uniform ribbons of paper, i.e. paper tapes, wherein a pre-cutting of the paper to shape is unnecessary.

According to the present invention a process for the production of mounting corners comprises folding a, first tape firstly across its width at an angle of 45° to its length, secondly across its width at an angle of 90° to the first fold, thirdly across its width along a line parallel with the second fold, fourthly across its width along a line parallel with the first fold, the said four folds being symmetrically spaced and repeated along the length of the tape, the folds in each successive pair of folds being in the same direction with respect to the surface of the tape, sticking a second tape to the folded first tape so as to hold the first tape in its folded relation while leaving open the pockets formed by the folds in the first tape, and cutting apart, or separating by tear-off perforations, the individual mounting corners thus formed.

The mounting corners provided by the method just described require to be gummed in order to secure them to the mounting surface; this may be done by the user, but it is preferably arranged that the said second tape is gummed on the surface remote from the pockets so that the mounting corners produced can be stuck directly to a mounting surface.

The invention will now be described with reference to the drawings accompanying the Provisional Specification.

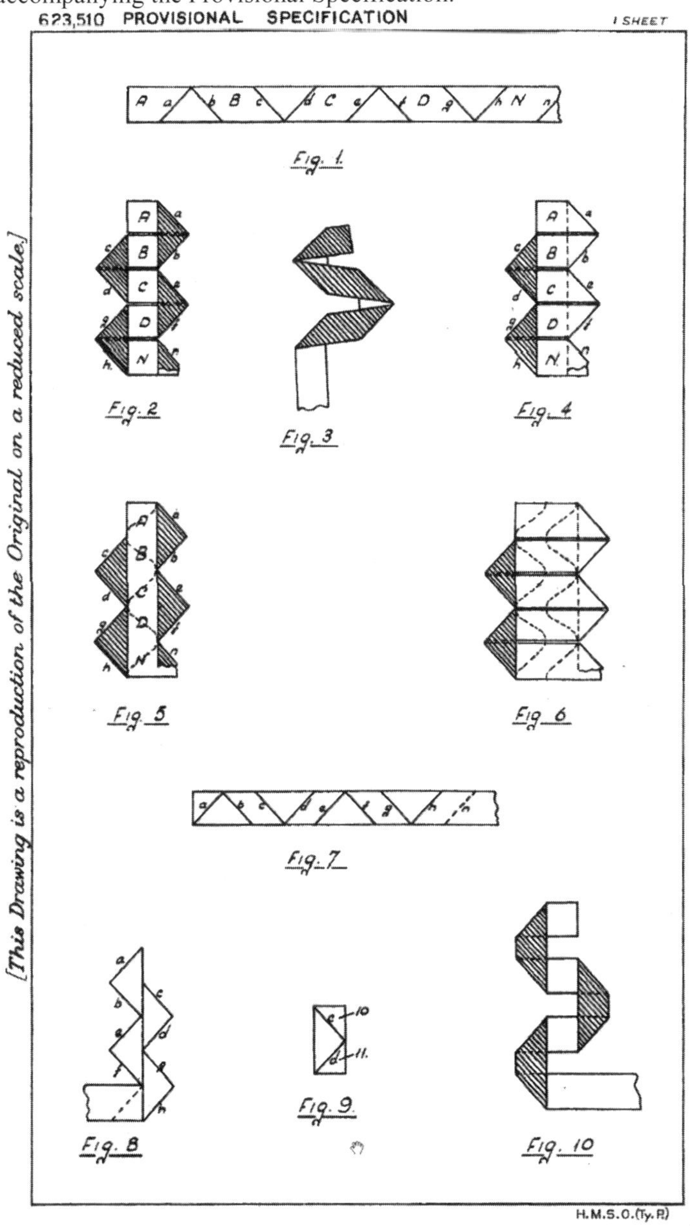

Figure 1 shows a paper tape with fold lines a, b, c, d, c, f, g, h and n. If all these folds are made in the same direction with reference to the surface of the paper strip, the result is that illustrated in Figure 2. The spaces A, B, C, D, N between the pairs of folds appear in succession to form a central strip with pockets ab, cd, ef, gh, etc., formed alternately on either side of this central strip. Figure 3 shows in perspective a rear view of the folded structure of Figure 2 with the strip somewhat pul ed out to show the method of folding with greater clarity. In both Figures 2 and 3 the rear surface of the strip of Figure 1 is shown shaded.

By arranging that the direction of the folds a, b), is opposite to that of the folds c, d, and that this alternation of direction continues for the successive pairs of folds, the result illustrated in Figure 4 is obtained. It will be seen that the pockets on the left of the central strip are formed on one face of the central strip while those on the right-hand side are formed on the other face of the central strip. As in Figures 2 and 3 the reverse side of the strip of Figure i is shown shaded.

By applying a second paper tape (a sealing tape) to lie along the central strip of Figure 2 the product is secured in its folded condition. This second paper tape may be on either face of the central strip, or two paper tapes may be applied, one on each side, if greater strength is required in the product.

By arranging that the second paper tape is gummed on both faces and is stuck on the back of the central strip, a product is produced in which the area of the central strip has an outer gummed surface on the side remote from the pockets.

By cutting the product along the broken lines illustrated in Figure 5, or along similar lines, which may be straight, individual corner mounts are produced each of which consists of a corner pocket with an extension on one face which is gummed on the side remote from the pocket so that the mount may be stuck to a mounting surface leaving the pocket free for insertion of the corner of a photograph.

If instead of cutting the product along the broken lines shown in Figure 5 it is merely perforated, a strip product is produced from which individual corner mounts may be torn off along the perforation lines.

Such a product may be marketed in reel form or in short lengths of strip mounted in book fashion.

Considerable variation may be made in the particular construction within the scope of the present invention. For example, the distance between the pairs of folds ab, cd, etc. may be increased to provide a wider central strip, thus affording a greater gummed area in the final corner mounts.

Figure 6 illustrates such a construction, the folds having been made as in Figure 4. In this case, it is preferable to provide two sealing tapes each gummed on both sides, one to lie along the back of the left hand half of the central strip and the other to lie along the front of the right-hand half of the central strip. Perforation or cutting may be effected along the broken lines shown in Figure 6 or, if the resulting waste of the centre portion of the strip is considered undesirable, the cutting or perforation lines may extend down the whole centre line of the central strip and outwards from that line to the junctions of the corner pockets on each side.

In this case the gummed extension of the pocket will be rectangular in shape and the whole of the area of the central strip will be utilised.

In a further modification of the invention the areas A, B, C, D, N of Figure 1 are reduced to zero whereupon the fold lines will appear as in Figure 7 and the folded product will appear as in Figure 8. In this form of the product there is no central strip and the sealing is effected by applying a sealing tape, gummed on one surface and of a width equal to the width of the folded tape. If now the product is cut or perforated along its centre line and along lines outwardly at the junctions of the successive corners on each side, individual corner mounts are produced in the form illustrated in Figure 9. In Figure 9 the areas of the sealing tape are shown as io and i i. By folding these in the same sense along the lines c and d with the gummed surface outwards, a corner pocket is produced having two gummed flaps by which it may be secured to the mounting surface.

A further modification is illustrated in A; Figure 10 where the folding has been effected as in Figure i, but the fold lines do not quite meet. By following the sealing and cutting or perforation techniques described in connection with Figure 5, a product is obtained in which the corners of the pockets are open. The folding technique of Figure io may, of course, be modified as in Figure 2 and the product sealed and perforated or cut as described in connection with Figures 4 and 6.

It will be apparent that many other variations may be made within the framework of this invention. The invention has the important advantages that paper tapes so of normal structure can be used, no preliminary cutting or "blanking" being necessary, and that the products may be made available in reel or book form so that single corner mounts may be removed, by tearing the perforations, as required, thus avoiding the loss of corner mounts which commonly occurs when corner mounts are sold as loose individual items.

Although in the description of this invention particular reference has been made to tapes made of paper, it is to be understood that the material of which the tapes are formed may be the same or different and may be materials other than paper, e.g. transparent or coloured ribbon formed of a synthetic resin, cellulose or a cellulose derivative, fabric or metal tape.

Dated this 7th day of May, 1947.
V. GALLAFENT,
Chartered Patent Agent.

APPENDIX B
Kennedy Instruments 5 x 4 Monobar Design

The engineering drawing shown overleaf is of a 5 x 4 Monobar camera that was on the Kennedy Instruments drawing board in February 1956, but which was never developed any further. My special thanks goes to the Kennedy family for allowing me to include this drawing.

The original drawing was drawn full size on A0 drawing paper. I had the original document photocopied and made some repairs to the image. I then reduced it and then scanned it. Again I was able to tidy up the image to the level of quality you will see overleaf.

The text written on drawing at this reduced scale is not very legible so I have reproduced it here:

Middle left	SCRAP SECTION CC
Bottom left	SCRAP SECTION THROUGH BB PLATE HOLDER UNIT ONLY
Middle Bottom	4 X 5 MONOBAR CAMERA DRN:- Feb 56 CHD:- SCALE:- 1/1
Middle right	SECTION AA
Bottom right	DK 3559/GA

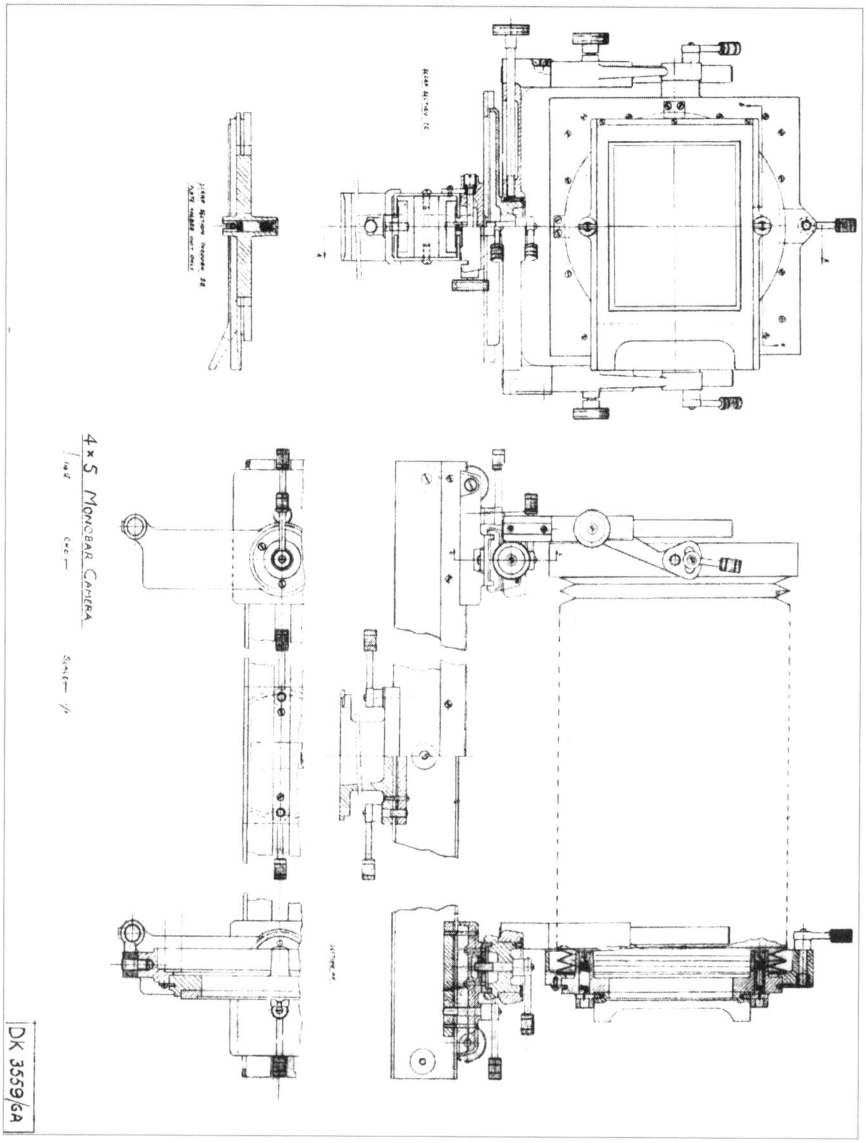
4 x 5 Monobar Camera
DK 3559/GA

APPENDIX C
A Brief History of Dacora and Bernhard Dangelmaier

Because of Ilford's close and long-running history and friendship with Heir Dangelmaier and the Dacora company, it is perhaps worthwhile listing some of the key events in their history as follows. Bernhard Dangelmaier born in 1907. He graduated as an engineer in Bremen. In his early employment he worked in the Stock Exchange and then he worked for Siemens in Berlin.

1946	Created his company, Dangelmaier & Co., Optik and Fein-Mechanik. This company originally made sunglasses and magnifying glasses.
1948	Created Dacora Kamerawerk, Dangelmaier & Co, Reutlingen, Albtorplatz 10. This company gained permission to make cameras. Initially, because of the shortage of metal, these were made in Bakelite. The first camera he made was the DACI box camera. He also made optics and precision mechanical parts. Some time later the factory was moved to Reutlingen, Gustav-Schwab-Straße
	First roll film cameras are made.
1950	His company had made some 600,000 cameras sold in 65 countries.
1953	First 35mm cameras are made.
1953	Ilford Sportsman
1960	Ilford Sporti
	Dacora had sold more than 3 million cameras to 75 countries.
1962	Ilford Sportsmaster
1964	Ilford Sportina Rapid
1966	Ilford Instacora
1968	Cilmatic and Cilfomatic (up to 1973).
	Dacora employed 299 workers, 166 were women.
1969	Ilford Sportina Ilfomatic
	Ilford(UK) / Dacora partnership ends.
1969	Ilford 35
	Dacora Kamerawerk GmbH, Munchen 1 July 1969 Dacora forms a partnership with, "Leach Relays and Electronics"
1972	Company is renamed Dacora Kamerawerk, Nuernberg

On 1st August 1972 the company was bought by Josef Weber KG, and renamed. Weber was a slide- projector manufacturer, manufacturing mainly for the Italian market. They were also a supplier of parts for several different camera manufacturers.

In the same year Weber/Dacora bought the Zeiss-Ikon prototypes of the SL725 camera project along with designs, etc. and had planned to build it and have Carl Zeiss provide the lenses (Contarex mount). The camera was an auto exposure SLR design that was supposed to replace Contaflex/Contrarex models.

The Weber SL-75 remains elusive and I've never seen an example of one apart from an illustration in the book: Contaflex/Contarex by: Hans-Jurgen Kuc. It's pictured on page 191 with a 50 mm f/1.4 Planar lens with what appears to be a dedicated bayonet lens mount. The body shape resembles that of the Contaflex 126 with a big prism finder and short finger grip sides.

It is believed that the Weber/Dacora intention was to convert it to 35mm. format. It turned out to be too costly a camera to manufacture, especially with the Zeiss lenses. Weber showed the prototype SL725 at Photokina. The SL725 was to be the successor to the Contaflex line. It was sold directly by Zeiss-Ikon to Weber. Weber had thought Zeiss-Ikon was to fund production but they chose not to do so, dooming the project. Weber was sometime later was absorbed into Braun.

1972	The Dacora factory in Reutlingen was closed. Ilford / Dacora partnership ends.
1980	End of Dacora between 1972 and 1980 Finally making projectors for Weber.

Bernhard Dangelmaier was not a man to be put down easily. When Japanese camera production caused most European camera companies to close down and Ilford also stopped placing orders with them, his company was finally closed. Following a long period of illness, first he lost one leg and then had his remaining leg amputated. Where most men would have simply have gone into retirement Bernhard Dangelmaier set up a new company, SFR- Formenbau, when he was 64 years old!

1971	Establishment of SFR under the name, Dangelmaier & CO as a private company, making injection mouldings and aluminium forms in rented property.
1980	The unincorporated firm is converted into a GmbH and called Dangelmaier GmbH with a capital stock from DM 300,000. He was managing director.
1981	Entrance into the CNC technology after acquisition of the first CNC steered milling machine in Germany.
1983	At the age of 76 Dangelmaier retires and hands over the company to Horst Reinl a long time friend and associate.
1983	Increase of the capital stock to DM 1.000.000
1985	Appointment of Horst Reinl as the managing director holding sole power of representation
1992	Mr. Bernhard Dangelmaier died on 25th May 1992 aged 85.

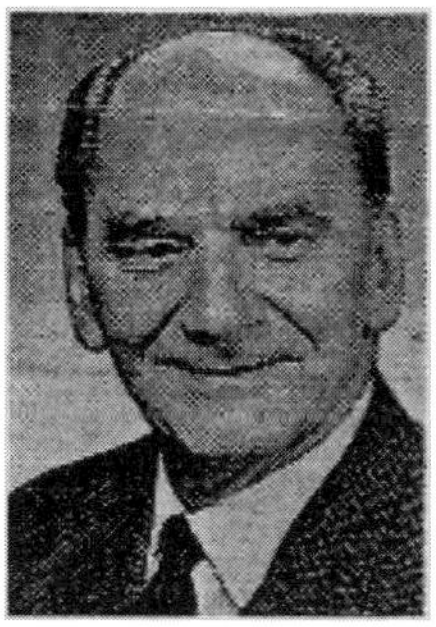

Bernhard Dangelmaier 1907 - 1992

Bernhard Dangelmaier Patents

Dangelmaier filed several patents including film transport mechanisms and multiple flash connectors and the Sportsmaster Automatic 4 button camera mechanism, as listed below:

Title	Patent Number	Publication Date
Film transport mechanism.	DE1002616	1957-02-14
4 button distance and shutter release.	GB901018	1962-07-11
Interlocked shutter release and film wind-on.	GB1082935	1964-05-14
Film transport mechanism.	GB1060176	1967-03-01
Flashcube Adapter.	GB1136797	1968-12-18
Flash mechanism.	DE1497438	1969-07-03

Details can be found from the UK Patents web site at:
http://gb.espacenet.com/espacenet/gb/en/

Dacora Factory

DANGELMAYER & CO. KAMERAWERK

Reutlingen · Gustav-Schwabstraße 6

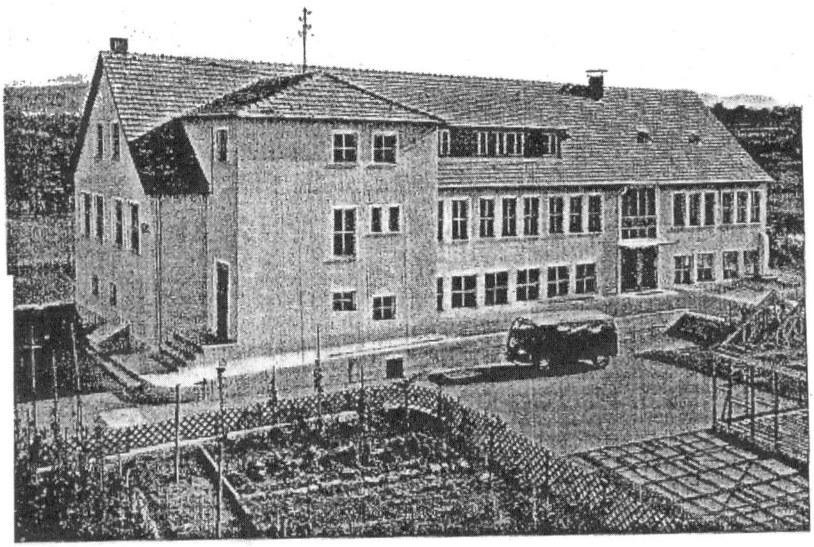

Am 1. Januar 1946 wurde die Firma Dangelmaier & Co., Optik und Feinmechanik, durch den jetzigen Inhaber, Herrn Bernhard Dangelmaier, gegründet.

Die Firma befaßte sich nach Kriegsende mit der Herstellung von Leselupen und Sonnenbrillen verschiedener Ausführungen. Am 20. Juni 1948, nach Genehmigung durch die französischen Dienststellen, wurde mit der Konstruktion photographischer Apparate begonnen.

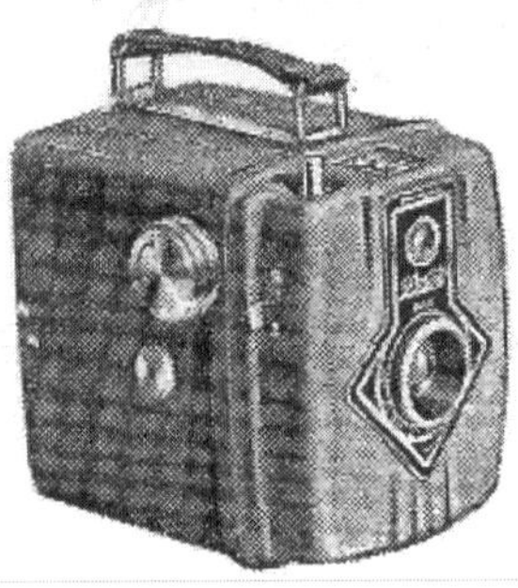

Die erste Box-Camera wurde wegen Mangels an Blechen aus Bakelit hergestellt. Sie kam Ende des Jahres 1948 auf den Markt und hatte gute Absatzmöglichkeiten sowohl im In- wie im Ausland.

Interesting to observe that this article about Dangelmaier & Co. has his name incorrectly spelt, 'Dangelmayer' in the title. In front of the factory are allotments and a greenhouse.

Dacora Assembly Line

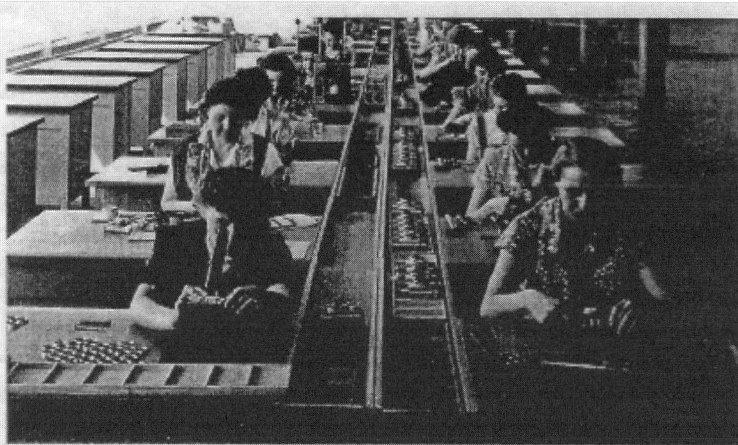

Produktion der »Dacora« -Kameras, Firma Dangelmaier & Co, Gustav-Schwab-Straße 6, 1957.

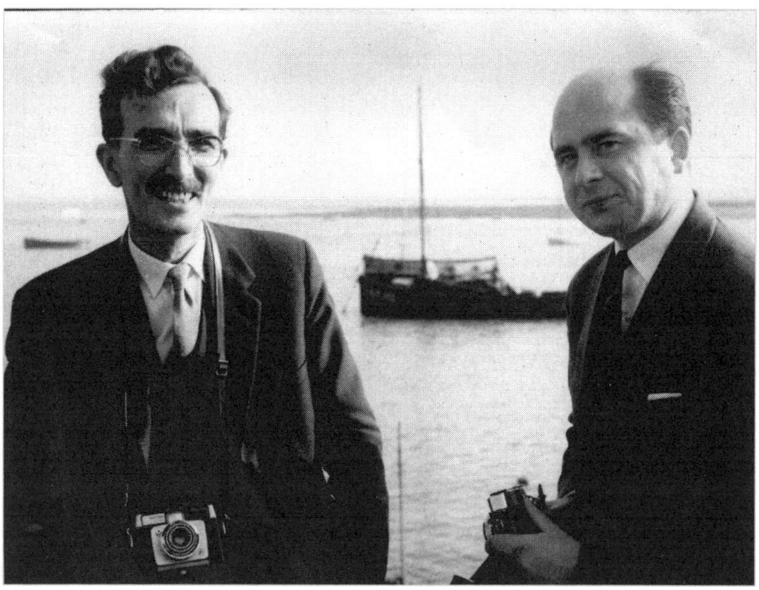

The photo above shows my father Albert (Arthur) Holliman on the left and the Dacora Works Manager (Heir Gottshalk ?) on the right.

Ilford / Dacora Equivalences

This book has predominately researched the Ilford range of cameras using references to the Dacora versions were necessary.
The following table lists the equivalences between the two product lines.

The history of Dacora cameras is as complicated to unravel as the Ilford story not only because they shared the same product lines for a period of time, but also because Dacora independently marketed models similar to but different from the Ilford variants. Dacora also made cameras for other companies. For example the Sportsman Vario (Style 3) was altered to become a Ferrania Lince and the Sportsmaster became a Hannimex Electra II. As Dacora was owned and run by Dangelmaier, he was able to be much more flexible than Ilford as he did not have a board or directors or other interests to compete with. Additionally Dacora were well established and were marketing cameras before Ilford came along. Consequently the following list is by no means complete with respect to the Dacora camera range, as I have omitted all the models made by them prior to their joint venture with Ilford. I have also omitted those cameras that they made completely independently to Ilford of which there were a few. Additionally I have collected the names of the Dacora cameras from a variety of sources and am therefore subject to their accuracy. As has been seen in the previous pages the name of a camera is not always the same as the identification of the camera.

For example, the Ilford Electric SR has; 'Electric SR' on the camera nameplate, 'Sportsman Electric SR' on the manual and is often identified as an, 'Electric Prontor 500 S-E'. Therefore there are various ways in which names are used to identify a camera. Standardisation would only be possible with actual cameras to hand (and possibly another 20 years of research). However despite this, the table is of some use.

35

Ilford	Dacora
Ilford 35 C	35 C
	35 C LK
	35 CB
Ilford 35 CC	35 CC
Ilford 35 CL	35 CL
Ilford 35 L	35 L
	35 LK
	35 N
Ilford 35 R	35 R
Ilford 35 RL	35 RL

Instacora

Ilford	Dacora
Instacora E	Instacora E
Instacora F	Instacora F
	Instacora F 2

Ilford	Dacora
	Instacora K
	Instacora K606
	Instacora K707
Instacora R	Instacora R

Sporti

Ilford	Dacora
Sporti	Digna I
Super Sporti	
Sporti 4	Digna 44
Sporti 6	Digna 66

Rapid

Ilford	Dacora
Sportina A Rapid	
Sportina Ilfomatic	
Sportina Rapid I	D101 Rapid
Sportina Rapid II	D202 Rapid
Sportina Rapid III	D303 Rapid
Sportina Rapid IV	D404 Rapid
Sportsman Rapid III	
Sportsman Rapid IV	

Instant

Ilford	Dacora
Sportsman C Instant	
Sportsman E Instant	
Sportsman R Instant	

Electric

Ilford	Dacora
Sportsman Electric CR	Super Dignette Electric CR
Sportsman Electric L	Super Dignette Electric L
Sportsman Electric S	Super Dignette Electric S
Sportsman Electric SR	Super Dignette Electric SR
	Super Dignette Electric SE

Sportsman

Ilford	Dacora
Sportsman Vario	Dignette
Sportsman Vario Rangefinder	
Sportsman Prontor	Dignette
Sportsman SL	
Sportsman Prontor-SVS	
Sportsman Pronto Automatic	
Sportsman Pronto - Rangefinder	
Sportsman Pronto	
Sportsman Automatic Rangefinder	Super Dignette E-B
Sportsman Automatic	Dacora Matic Prontormat
Sportsmaster Automatic	Dacora Pronto-Matic
Sportsmaster Manumatic	Dacora-Matic 4D
	Dacora-Matic CC
Sportsman 125	Dignette 125
Sportsman 250	Dignette 250
Sportsman 250 S	Dignette 250 S
	Dignette 250 SL
Sportsman 300	Dignette 300
Sportsman 300 S	Dignette 300 S
Sportsman 300 SL	Dignette 300 SL
	Dignette 300 SLK
	Dignette EM
Sportsman 300 EB	Super Dignette E-B
Sportsman F	Dignette F
Sportsman 250 LK	Super Dignette 250 LK
Sportsman 300 L	Super Dignette 300 L
Sportsman 300 LK	Super Dignette 300 LK
Sportsman 500 LK	Super Dignette 500 LK
	Super Dignette 500 S
	Super Dignette Prontor SVS

Sportsman MK2

Ilford	Dacora
Sportsman MK2 300	
Sportsman MK2 300 EB	
Sportsman MK2 300 L	
Sportsman MK2 300 LK	
Sportsman MK2 300 S	
Sportsman MK2 300 SL	

CIL

Ilford	Dacora
CILFOMAT 300S	
CILFOMAT 300SL	
CILMATIC 300 CC	
CILMATIC 300 CR	
CILMATIC Electric 300	
CILMATIC Electric 300 S	
CILMATIC Electronic 126	Electronic 126
CILMATIC Elite	
CILMATIC Ideal	
CILMATIC Super	

Uncertain

Ilford	Dacora
	Dignette L
	Dignette I L
	Dignette I
	Dignette 1F

APPENDIX D
Time Line

The following table attempts to identify when certain cameras and activities started. These dates are based mainly on documents that describe a camera and have a date attached. As previously noted the exact date of the launch of a new camera model can be difficult to ascertain. Most cameras were 'test marketed' in specific U.K. regions before being officially launched. Additionally some reports of the 'new' cameras may have appeared up to 12 months after they were first available to the public. Some cameras were only available to specific markets and may not even have been marketed in the U.K. at all. Finally, it is impossible to indicate when a camera model stopped being produced without any company records. Some models were price cut and distributed to retailers well after their 'end' date in an attempt to remove any surplus items. However the table is still worthwhile and interesting to deduce the concurrent models that were being produced at any one time.

Camera	1946	1947	1948	1949	1950	1951	1952	1953	1954	1955	1956	1957	1958	1959	1960	1961	1962	1963	1964	1965	1966	1967	1968	1969	1970	1971	1972	1973	1974	1975	1976
Falling Plate (1899)																															
Witness																															
Craftsman																															
Advocate				# 1			# 2		# 3																						
Prentice																															
Envoy Wide Angle																															
PIM Monorail																															
Envoy Box																															
Watson Premier Half Plate																															
KI Monobar																															
The Sportsman Range																															
Sportsman Rangefinder																															
Sportsman Automatic																															
Sportsman Auto Rangefinder																															

Camera	1946	1947	1948	1949	1950	1951	1952	1953	1954	1955	1956	1957	1958	1959	1960	1961	1962	1963	1964	1965	1966	1967	1968	1969	1970	1971	1972	1973	1974	1975	1976
Sportsmaster Automatic																■															
Sportsmaster Manumatic																	■														
Sportsman Vario												■	■	■	■	■															
Sportsman Prontor 125																		■													
Sportsman Prontor RF																															
Sportsman Prontor SVS												■	■	■																	
Sportsman Pronto RF																															
Sportsman Pronto Auto RF																															
Sportsman 250 LK Auto																															
Sportsman 250 S																															
Sportsman 250S S-L (€)																															
Sportsman 300																			■												
Sportsman 300 (€)																							■								
Sportsman 300 L (€)																							■								
Sportsman 300 L-K (€)																							■								

Camera	1946	1947	1948	1949	1950	1951	1952	1953	1954	1955	1956	1957	1958	1959	1960	1961	1962	1963	1964	1965	1966	1967	1968	1969	1970	1971	1972	1973	1974	1975	1976
Sportsman 300 LK Auto																															
Sportsman 300 S (€)																															
Sportsman 300 S-L (€)																															
Sportsman 300 EB																															
Sportsman 500 LK Auto																															
Sportsman F																															
Sportsman L (€)																															
Sportsman S-L (€)																															
Electric-S																															
Electric-L																															
Electric-CR																															
Electric-SR																															
Monobar																															
Sporti																															

Camera	1946	1947	1948	1949	1950	1951	1952	1953	1954	1955	1956	1957	1958	1959	1960	1961	1962	1963	1964	1965	1966	1967	1968	1969	1970	1971	1972	1973	1974	1975	1976
Super Sporti																															
Sporti 4																															
Sporti 6																															
Imp																															
Pixie																															
Sprite 35																															
Ilfoflex																															
Sprite 127																															
Sprite Rapid Flash																															
Sportina Rapid																															
Sportina Rapid I																															
Sportina Rapid II																															
Sportina Rapid III																															
Sportsman Rapid III																															
Sportsman Rapid IV																															

Camera	1946	1947	1948	1949	1950	1951	1952	1953	1954	1955	1956	1957	1958	1959	1960	1961	1962	1963	1964	1965	1966	1967	1968	1969	1970	1971	1972	1973	1974	1975	1976
Sportina A Rapid																															
Super 100																															
Sportina Rapid IV																															
Universal 50																															
Universal 50C																															
Super Universal																															
Ilfomatic Universal Flash																															
Ilfomatic Compact																															
Ilfomatic																															
Sportina Ilfomatic																															
Auto Ilfomatic																															
Sportsman C Instant																															
Sportsman E Instant																															
Sportsman R Instant																															

Camera	1946	1947	1948	1949	1950	1951	1952	1953	1954	1955	1956	1957	1958	1959	1960	1961	1962	1963	1964	1965	1966	1967	1968	1969	1970	1971	1972	1973	1974	1975	1976
Instacora E																															
Instacora F																															
Instacora R																															
Monarch																															
Cilmatic Electric 300																															
Cilmatic Electric 300S																															
Cilmatic Ideal																															
Cilmatic Super																															
Cilmatic Elite																															
Cilfomat 300S																															
Cilfomat 300SL																															
Cilmatic Electronic																															
Cilmatic 300 CC																															
Cilmatic 300 CR																															
CIL 110																															

Camera	1946	1947	1948	1949	1950	1951	1952	1953	1954	1955	1956	1957	1958	1959	1960	1961	1962	1963	1964	1965	1966	1967	1968	1969	1970	1971	1972	1973	1974	1975	1976
Cilmatic X																															
Sportsman 35 R																															
Sportsman 35 RL																															
Sportsman 35 CL																															
Sportsman MK 2 300																															
Sportsman MK 2 300 S																															
Sportsman MK 2 300 L																															
Sportsman MK 2 300 SL																															
Sportsman MK 2 300 LK																															
Sportsman MK 2 300 LK																															
Sportsman MK 2 300 EB																															
Ilford UK Camera Marketing																															
Ilford / Dacora																															
CIBA Acquires Ilford																															

Your Notes

Index

A

B

C

D

E

F

G

H

I

J

K

L

M

N

O

P

R

S

T

U

V

W

X

Z